May 17

THE SONG AND
THE SILENCE

THE SONG AND THE SILENCE

A Story about Family, Race, and What Was Revealed in a Small Town in the Mississippi Delta While Searching for Booker Wright

Yvette Johnson

ATRIA BOOKS

New York   London   Toronto   Sydney   New Delhi

ATRIA
BOOKS

An Imprint of Simon & Schuster, Inc.
1230 Avenue of the Americas
New York, NY 10020

First Atria Books hardcover edition May 2017

ATRIA BOOKS and colophon are trademarks of Simon & Schuster, Inc.

For information about special discounts for bulk purchases, please contact Simon & Schuster Special Sales at 1-866-506-1949 or business@simonandschuster.com.

The Simon & Schuster Speakers Bureau can bring authors to your live event. For more information or to book an event, contact the Simon & Schuster Speakers Bureau at 1-866-248-3049 or visit our website at www.simonspeakers.com.

Interior design by Bryden Spevak

Manufactured in the United States of America

10 9 8 7 6 5 4 3 2 1

Library of Congress Cataloging-in-Publication Data has been applied for.

ISBN 978-1-4767-5494-9
ISBN 978-1-4767-5496-3 (ebook)

I dedicate this book to the two sweetest,
most wonderful boys ever to be brought into this world:
You tether me.

You know, they straightened out the Mississippi
River in places, to make room for houses and livable
acreage. Occasionally the river floods these places.
"Floods" is the word they use, but in fact it is not
flooding; it is remembering. Remembering where
it used to be. All water has a perfect memory and
is forever trying to get back to where it was.

Toni Morrison
"The Site of Memory"
in *Inventing the Truth: The Art and Craft of Memoir*
Ed. William Zinsser

Contents

Contents

The meaner the man be, the more you smile. Always learn to smile, although you're crying on the inside or you're wondering, "What else can I do?" . . . I got three children. I want them to get an education. I wasn't fortunate enough to get an education. . . . Night after night I lay down and I dream about what I had to go through with. I don't want my children to have to go through with that. I want them to be able to get the job that they feel qualified for. That's what I'm struggling for . . . I just don't want my children to have to go through what I go through with. . . . "Tell that nigga to hurry up!" . . . But remember, you have to keep that smile.

Booker Wright
Mississippi: A Self-Portrait

Preface

When she returns, her approach is not without sound. She screams, whispers, howls, and roars while they listen. Most don't wait to see her, choosing instead to make a hasty escape. With faces painted in grief and fear, they gather into their arms what they can—children, heirlooms, papers—and flee.

When she returns, some stay behind because they have no place else to go.

Others stay behind for different reasons. They might be clutching desperately to the hope that she'll change her course before reaching them or that by some miracle she'll simply stop. But at least a few refuse to flee out of arrogance. They refuse to submit to her the way she did to them— passively, obediently, like a defeated queen.

When she returns, some watch in awe as she hovers above rooftops, eclipses the sun, and delivers a new sky.

And then she bears down on them.

When she arrives, her waters snatch up weeping cows, screaming pigs, and people as she moves along the ground, suckling her gems, reclaiming the treasure she began collecting long before it ever occurred to them to record time. She pushes against doors and presses into grooves, penetrating the sliver of space where nails meet wood. She swallows houses and farms. The people report hearing what can only be described as the exhaling of *breath and the belch of a monster. The sounds the river makes are almost human, as if she has a soul.*

When she arrives, most of the people are seeing her this way for the first time, but almost all of them have heard the stories. For centuries, the Mississippi River had been running freely through the continent, swelling with the waters she received from multiple tributaries, all the while gathering chunks and heaps of nutrient-dense earth. Her journey always ended with a sweet homecoming as she plunged into the warm waters of the Gulf of Mexico, becoming one with the sea. But just before giving herself away, she would stretch out, widening, spreading her waters over a shallow expanse to the east of her course. That was where she left her treasure—bits and mounds of glorious, abundant earth. Over time, her collection of exquisite gems grew higher and denser until the soil itself was a vast landscape. The people called it the Mississippi Delta.

In journals and letters to loved ones, they recorded their impressions of the land that lay to the east of the Great River. Most described a place that, in spite of its plentiful soil, was almost completely uninhabitable. The Delta quickly developed a reputation as being a deadly place where recently wed brides and young children were often delivered to early deaths by way of harsh conditions and horrific illnesses.

Rumors aside, the Delta truly was a dark place—both figuratively and literally. "Only the trees, some one hundred feet high, burst above the choking vines and cane into the sunshine." One person went so far as to call the Delta a "seething, lush hell."

In the early 1800s, the Mississippi Delta was moist, flat, intensely humid, and nothing if not wild. Filled with bears, alligators, panthers, serpents, stinging gnats, mosquitoes, malaria, cholera, typhoid and yellow fever, dysentery, squirrels, ducks, geese, deer, feral cows, and—in times of flooding—fish of varying sizes and species, the Mississippi Delta was a beautiful, treacherous, untamed expanse of earth. A kingdom belonging only to the water, it was the river's Eden.

It takes a certain type of individual to hear such wretched descrip-

tions of a wild, unwelcoming land and respond by gathering up all they possess—including their spouse and young children—and moving there. Given what they knew, the people who gambled their very lives on the Mississippi Delta must have been recalcitrant, filled with hubris, naïve enough to still believe in wild dreams, yet infused with the strength and discipline necessary to chase them down. If the United States was founded on a spirit of rebellion intertwined with relentless hope, by men and women determined to make a fresh start in an unknown place where they would have autonomy—people who came to define the very word "pioneer"—then surely the first American inhabitants of the Mississippi Delta were among the most pioneering of us all.

Stories about the Delta were quick to spread. However, what people were most interested in were not the dangers, but the opportunities.

"The cotton is about as high as my head," said one. "Nature knows not how to compound a richer soil," said another. Neither was exaggerating. Delta cotton could grow higher than the average man and topsoil there was so deep it had to be measured not in feet but in tens of feet. What so amazed them was a land made of thick, chocolate-colored, near-magical sludge, teeming with life and quick to regenerate. Delta soil had no earthly comparison.

People got drunk on dreams of the extreme riches all but guaranteed to those with the capital and perseverance to endure the land and tame the river.

But they had their work cut out for them because "the complexity of the Mississippi River exceeds that of nearly all other rivers . . . engineering theories and techniques that apply to other rivers, even major rivers . . . simply do not work on the lower Mississippi." But the people were patient, inventive, and stubborn. They built levees to hold back the river's waters and plantations to exploit her treasure. In the end, the intricate system of levees they built was hailed as a true feat of engineering.

Finally, their dreams were coming true, but not without a cost.

Nowhere else did slaves work as hard as in the Mississippi Delta, for not only did Delta slaves tend the fields, they also created them, conquering the land, facing the wild. One planter said, "Everything has to bend . . . Land has to be cultivated wet or dry, negroes to work, hot or cold."

Working in season and out, Delta slaves made cotton king, but because of the intensity of their labor, Delta slaves also had higher-than-average mortality rates.

The solution was simple, one that was being instituted all over the land. Black women became breeders, repeatedly raped so future workers could grow inside their wombs. Of her master, one female slave recalled that he "would have children by a nigger woman and then have them with her daughter."

For White., the Delta was a place of immense profits. For Blacks, it was a place of unspeakable horrors.

Today, the people nod their heads in solemn agreement, but then quickly add that all of these things—the slaves, the rapes, separating the water from the land—happened a long, long time ago.

They're right of course. Those atrocities are in the past.

Yet the river still returns, and when she does, her rampage is indiscriminate and her approach is not without sound.

2013

Booker Wright was a difficult man to know. I'd completed six years of research, including four trips to the Delta, conducted more than fifty interviews—spending hours with people who'd known him for years, shared laughter and tears with him—but in the end, all I'd learned was that none of those people really knew him.

Even though my work kept pointing to that uncomplicated version of Booker, I was certain it was wrong, if only because of the event that sent me to the Delta in the first place.

It all started six years ago when I learned that my grandfather, Booker Wright, appeared in a controversial *NBC News* program that aired in 1966. In the film, he discussed some of the humiliating encounters he regularly faced while serving White people at the restaurant where he waited tables.

But what he did was so much more than that.

My grandfather managed to eloquently convey the pain and degradation he experienced every day living as a Black man in the South. He revealed a kind of pain that transcended racial lines, a picture of longing and suffering that made viewers pay attention. Booker reminded complete strangers of the one thing they all shared with him: a basic sense of humanity. And he did it all in under three minutes.

Four and a half decades later, his story was having a resurgence. People who saw the footage for the first time would tell me how it moved them, broke their hearts, and made them think of what has and hasn't changed, not just for Blacks but for anyone who could be defined as "the other." One university professor burst into tears when he watched the two-and-a-half-minute piece, because Booker reminded him of his lifelong struggle for acceptance as a homosexual male living in the American South. My grandfather had been dead for over thirty years, but once again people all over the country were becoming interested in the Black waiter from an all-but-forgotten Mississippi town.

Amid my joy over the rebirth of his story, a few things kept bugging me: Why would my grandfather reveal fears and humiliating experiences on the national news, ones he hadn't even shared with his own children? What was going through his mind? Were a few minutes on television worth risking his life?

When I traveled to the Delta in the summer of 2011, almost everyone I met agreed that Booker was eloquent and that what he managed to communicate was remarkable. But in addition to being well-spoken, Booker was also either bold or reckless because of where he was living when he spoke out: Greenwood, Mississippi, a place where the local Whites had a reputation for being anything but ashamed of their stance against the civil rights movement. When their US senator, James Eastland, traveled to Alabama to protest the Montgomery bus boycotts, he attended a rally for the White Citizens' Council, where he had thousands of flyers distributed with the following content:

When in the course of human events, it becomes necessary to abolish the Negro race, proper methods should be used. Among these are guns, bows and arrows, slingshots and knives.

We hold these truths to be self-evident that all Whites are created equal with certain rights; among these are life, liberty and the pursuit of dead niggers.

Apparently, White Mississippians didn't have a problem with his views. James Eastland held his post for another twenty-two years, making him one of the longest-serving senators in US history. Ole Miss even named a law library after him.

By the time Booker conducted his interview ten years later in 1965, so much had already been accomplished. The United States Supreme Court ruled school segregation illegal in 1954 and the Civil Rights Act, which barred discrimination in public places, was passed in 1964. The nation was shifting and laws were already changing, so why did Booker go on television and disturb the waters? Why did he risk angering people when the battle was all but won?

As much as I wanted to sit down with my grandfather and ask him all of those questions, I couldn't, because he was murdered the year before I was born, which was also seven years after his appearance in the *NBC News* documentary. For a time, I tried as hard as I could to prove causality between those two events—his moment of truth and his brutal murder—but I couldn't. The pieces to that theory just didn't hold together. When I left the Delta in the summer of 2011, I'd discovered something much more rare and hard to swallow than another story of a Black man losing his life in the segregated South. It took a long time for me to finally digest what I'd found and to accept what it meant for me and for my grandfather, but when I did, it brought me immense peace.

In spite of all I've learned, a few questions still remain.

I spent years collecting memories of my grandfather's life, gathering them from the ones who shared his world—customers, friends, and family. I've cherished and carefully catalogued each and every one of their stories as if they were so many pieces of the man himself.

Maybe because I've spent so much time letting his world seep into mine, there are still moments when I catch myself having a somewhat childish desire. Whenever I learn something new about him—usually some small detail—a sense of longing creeps up on me, a primal craving for the relationship the two of us might have had. I start to wonder what it would have been like to have really known him, not just the image of him I've peered at through the faded and bent fibers of other people's memories, but to have heard his laughter for myself, to have seen him cry with my own eyes, and to have felt the warmth of his hand wrapping around mine.

To curtail this sorrow before it blooms, I spend a little time with the few things I have of my grandfather—four film clips, three of which have no sound, and photographs.

In almost all the photos he's smiling. Early on in my research, people told me over and over again that my grandfather had an amazing smile. It would be years before I got to see what he looked like and when I did, I understood what they meant. In those photos lives a smile that embodies pure, unsullied charisma—warm and generous, shining from the past with bright, enduring vitality.

There's one photograph from my research that I usually have a hard time pulling myself away from. Actually, my grandfather isn't even in it, but for me the photo captures the disquiet spirit that still lingers in Greenwood—a place of infinite beauty, forever maimed by its past. The image is the front of Booker's Place, the restaurant he owned. It was taken the morning after he was shot, so a piece of cardboard is covering the front window, the one that was shattered by the shotgun pellets. On the door handle is a large, puffy, light blue ribbon, tied into a bow.

Sometimes when I look at that bow, I have a feeling that it's being pushed upon. This movement, or pressure, is barely perceptible, as if it's coming from something as subtle as a breath.

Whenever I see it, I'm suddenly back where I was in the beginning, standing in a river of questions. Only this time, one of them rises to the top where it shimmers, as lovely and ruinous as an iridescent, oily film.

Part One
Places in Time

The river is within us.

T. S. Eliot
Four Quartets: "The Dry Salvages"

Where He Was King

On any given Saturday night in the '50s and '60s, the place to be for Blacks in Greenwood, Mississippi, was a little spot called Booker's Place down on McLaurin Street. In those days, McLaurin was lined with darkly lit, poorly maintained one-room bars and juke joints where shootings, stabbings, and robberies were regular weekend occurrences, but Booker's Place was different.

While the owners of the other joints on McLaurin were happy with whatever business stumbled through the door, Booker had expectations of his customers. He knew that no matter how tangy his barbecue sauce was or how juicy his hamburgers were, the type of customers he really wanted to entertain weren't going to tolerate the violence so common on McLaurin. At the first sign of quarreling, Booker would put a stop to it with one of his characteristic lines such as: "Maybe the club you just came from was like the O.K. Corral, but if you gonna come in here, you betta sit down and act right."

Sometimes before a customer with a bad reputation even made it through the entrance Booker would appear at the door and say without apology, "You can't come in here, I don't want you in here." That was usually all it took. That and the butt of the gun protruding from his waistband.

Booker might have considered the gun to be a necessary prop because, without it, he didn't look very intimidating. In the early years, he was tall and thin, but even as he got older and put on weight, he didn't become any more imposing. On the contrary, he had a plump, baby face with copper-colored skin that was smooth and taut. When he smiled his cheeks stretched across the bone and lightened, giving the impression he was backlit by an internal glow. This, combined with his polished smile and manicured mustache, created in Booker not the appearance of a tough nightclub owner but one of a happy-go-lucky kid.

His restaurant developed a reputation throughout the state as a place not to be missed. Its owner was almost as well known, in part because he was so difficult to actually know. Booker had a singular characteristic to him, one that was both elusive and potent. In certain instances, this trait was like a Midas touch, ensuring success and allowing him to evade the financial hardships haunting others like him—Black men living in the Delta. At other times, the quality was alienating, rendering Booker so indecipherable that even those who worked by his side for years could only describe him from a relative distance, as if he weren't a real person but rather a well-crafted representation of one. What most Greenwood Blacks did know about Booker was that they either loved or hated him; few were indifferent.

Even decades after his death, just the mention of his name would cause some of the local Blacks to stop in their tracks, and with looks of indignant defiance, refer to him as an "uppity nigga." More than one Black woman complained that Booker only dated "light-skinned girls," while other people didn't give a reason for why they remembered him as a "scumbag" who was "lowdown" and "mean," even going so far as to say that when he was murdered he got what he deserved.

But there were also Blacks who couldn't wait to tell stories about

Booker's generosity. Like how he let young Black boys eat in his place for free after school just to keep them from running with the gangs, or how he allowed families who were down on their luck to live in his rental properties for free until they were back on their feet. "You'd never meet a nicer person," one man recalled wistfully.

What Greenwood Blacks could all agree on was the popularity of his restaurant, Booker's Place.

Booker understood that when people came to his restaurant they were often in need of something beyond just laughter and good food. Many of his customers were seeking respite from the humid, mosquito-filled air of Greenwood, which, for most of their lives, had been thick with fear and uncertainty.

Greenwood was at the center of a colossal battle of wills. By the mid-1960s, two opposing groups had laid claim to Greenwood and both were acting as though the small town was their "hill to die on." The first was the Council of Federated Organizations (COFO), which included the National Association for the Advancement of Colored People (NAACP), the Student Nonviolent Coordinating Committee (SNCC), and the Southern Christian Leadership Conference (SCLC). COFO was a national grassroots group committed to a variety of civil rights activities, with a primary focus on getting Blacks to the polls. Their volunteers were coming into Greenwood from all over the country to encourage people of color to organize, protest peacefully, and register to vote. Many Greenwood Blacks were grateful for their presence, agreed with their message, and risked their very lives by participating in the cause. At the same time, other Blacks feared that the influx of agitators would make their already difficult lives even more difficult. They weren't entirely wrong.

The other group convinced that Greenwood was a "must-win battleground" was the White Citizens' Council, whose national headquarters were located in the small town. Initially founded to stop the integration of schools, the council evolved into also opposing other civil rights movement initiatives, like the integration of public facilities and equal voting rights for Blacks. Made up of bankers, businessmen, politicians, members of the planter class, and other people of influence, they used the power of their members to oppose integration.

Blacks involved in the civil rights movement, or rumored to be, often had their rents raised, mortgage renewals on their farms refused, and saw their insurance policies cancelled. They were fired from jobs, and if they happened to be doctors or dentists, their patients were warned not to see them. One bank refused to do business with a Black grocer unless he gave them the records for the local NAACP office he ran in his spare time. So long was the arm of the White Citizens' Council that some Black activists were even audited without cause by the IRS.

Many elected officials, both state and local, were members. That may be why in 1962, in a move many felt was a direct punishment for local Blacks involved with the civil rights movement, the county's board of supervisors voted to stop regularly scheduled federal shipments of food, a decision that left twenty-seven thousand residents, of whom most were Black, near starvation.

Word of the unrest in Greenwood became a common topic among the nationwide leaders of the movement. In 1964, Martin Luther King Jr. made plans to visit the small town. The night before he was due to arrive, a woman saw Greenwood police officers throwing bricks through the windows of Booker's Place and two other Black-run businesses in the area. The message was clear: *Do not engage with MLK.*

Given the town's virulent response to the civil rights movement, by simply stepping foot into Greenwood King was putting his life in grave danger. With this in mind, US Attorney General Robert Kennedy contacted the Greenwood Police Force and asked if they would protect King during his visit. They refused.

Kennedy called President Lyndon Johnson to discuss the situation, expressing his concern about how the nation would respond if King were assassinated in Greenwood that summer. President Johnson got the message. He called J. Edgar Hoover, director of the FBI, and gave him instructions to have his agents protect King during his visit, specifying, over and over again, that he wanted King guarded both from the front and the back.

King's visit occurred without incident, but after he left a flyer was distributed throughout Greenwood. It was most likely created either by or with the influence of a man named Byron De La Beckwith, who was a member of the White Citizens' Council, as well as a member of the Ku Klux Klan. The flyer included the following excerpt:

TO THOSE OF YOU NIGGERS WHO GAVE OR GIVE AID AND COMFORT TO THIS CIVIL RIGHTS SCUM, WE ADVISE YOU THAT YOUR IDENTITIES ARE IN THE PROPER HANDS AND YOU WILL BE REMEMBERED. WE KNOW THAT THE NIGGER OWNER OF COLLINS SHOE SHOP ON JOHNSON STREET "ENTERTAINED" MARTIN LUTHER KING WHEN THE "BIG NIGGER" CAME TO GREENWOOD. WE KNOW OF OTHERS AND WE SAY TO YOU—AFTER THE SHOUTING AND THE PLATE-PASSING AND STUPID DEMONSTRATIONS ARE OVER AND THE IMPORTED AGITATORS HAVE ALL GONE, ONE THING IS SURE AND CERTAIN—YOU ARE STILL GOING TO BE NIGGERS AND WE ARE STILL GOING TO BE WHITE MEN.

In this calamitous, murderous, fear-filled world Booker managed—whether through raw ambition, genius, luck, or a combination of all three—to create a space that felt set apart and untouched by terror. The town of Greenwood was politically on fire and just beyond his restaurant door; McLaurin was host to all types of violence between residents and random attacks by local police.

But, unless he was standing by that door to play the role of club bouncer, Booker was almost always a picture of uncomplicated ease. His ability to relax in the midst of all that was going on in his community made him seem controlled, powerful, even peaceful.

When he was in his restaurant, Booker spent most of his time moving between tables and chatting it up with his big spenders while an unlit cigar—his "stump"—hung from the corner of his mouth. But it wasn't just the big spenders who received Booker's attention. No matter what Booker was doing, each time the front door opened, he'd look to see who was entering, a wide smile would spread across his face, and with the sound of that smile in his warm, raspy voice, he'd call out over the hum of laughter and conversation, "Welcome to Booker's, glad to see y'all tonight."

His charm was undeniable, but his food was just as memorable. So popular were the dishes he served that even some Whites made their way not only to the Black side of town but onto the crime-riddled street of McLaurin just to eat at Booker's Place.

During the height of the Jim Crow era and the tensions of the civil rights movement, this young Black man owned one of the hottest establishments in the Delta, paid cash for cars, had Whites who called him friend, and was wealthy, at least by Greenwood standards. He was viewed as a community leader and many Blacks consulted him on their own business matters.

But there was one more thing.

Most days of the week, an hour would come when Booker had to turn the running of his restaurant over to someone else so he could go to his job at Lusco's, where he waited tables, serving local Whites. In the early afternoon, he'd leave Booker's Place and step into the penetrating light of the Delta sun, then climb into his car, which he parked on the curb right out front.

While driving down McLaurin, Booker had to transform himself in a way not unlike a seasoned actor in the precious moments before stepping from behind the curtain. At Lusco's, he would don his costume of crisp black slacks, a sparkling white shirt, a clean towel folded over one arm, and his trademark smile. Then, he would step into the dining room where he displayed his façade, one that enabled his customers to eat, drink, laugh, and forget that just beyond Lusco's storefront, Greenwood's traditions and its shameful inheritance were burning to the ground.

In the handful of minutes it took to travel the eight blocks that separated Booker's Place from Lusco's, his elusive, untranslatable quality shifted, and Booker assumed a different face, one never required of him in the place where he was king.

Scattered

Historian James Cobb once noted that when people announce plans to visit one of the cities in the Mississippi Delta, they rarely say they're going to Greenwood or to Clarksdale; instead they speak of going "down into the Delta," as if it were a place to descend to. He called it "the most Southern place on earth." Famed historian Howard Zinn wrote an entire book on what he referred to as the "Southern Mystique," in which he concluded that the South, far from being "a sport, a freak, [or] an inexplicable variant from the national norm," is a place that actually "crystallizes the defects of the nation . . . It's a mirror in which the nation can see its blemishes magnified, so that it will hurry to correct them."

I went to Mississippi a few times when I was a child, but it was on a trip I took with my older sister that I first began to see the Mississippi that has captivated so many others. I was eleven and my sister, Shundra, was fifteen. We were traveling by ourselves while my parents stayed behind with my three-year-old little brother. Up to that point, my mom had only shared a few details about her father with me. I knew he'd owned a café and that he'd died before I was born, but I didn't even know his name.

The absence of information about her family didn't strike me as odd because my mom rarely spoke about her years in Mississippi. It was as if her life began when she left the Delta. Maybe that's why, when my aunt picked my sister and me up from the airport, I was overwhelmed with a sense of apprehension. Then, as we began to drive out of the city, I noticed that everything—trees, houses, and signs—appeared to be staring at us as if we were going the wrong way and it pained them to watch us do so.

As we got closer to Greenwood, the vast multi-lane interstate turned into four lanes separated by a dividing wall. It continued to narrow until we were traveling down a lonely country road flanked by fields and bushes whose shapes I could scarcely make out in the darkness. Every few minutes, we passed a house with a random light shining out at us and I exhaled, relieved to see evidence of life.

"What do you guys do for fun in Greenwood?" Shundra asked. We were sitting next to each other on the backseat, and she was leaning forward with her hand on the headrest in front of her.

"Well . . ." my aunt said slowly as she watched the road, "I think we may have a bowling alley."

"Is that still open?" the cousin who'd tagged along for the ride asked from the front passenger seat, her voice heavy with doubt.

"What about the mall?" my sister pressed. "Do kids hang out at the mall?"

"Now, we don't have a mall here in Greenwood," my aunt said in a voice that sounded like a warning to lower our expectations and to do it quick. After a few beats of silence, she added with an air of optimism, "We do have a JCPenney, though."

"Do people go to the movies?" Shundra sounded increasingly alarmed.

"Some people go to the movies, but the nearest theater is in Jackson. We don't have any movie theaters in Greenwood. Maybe we'll do that while you're here, maybe we'll go into the city for a movie."

Shundra leaned back in her seat and looked over at me. Our eyes locked and I wondered if she was asking herself the same question I was: "What had we gotten ourselves into?"

I'd lived almost my entire life in San Diego and I didn't even know it was possible for a town to not have at least one shopping mall, let alone a movie theater. Even more perplexing to me was that I couldn't picture my mother—the football player's wife who stood out at every party in her high-heeled shoes, red lipstick, and mink coat—coming from the kind of place my aunt and cousin were describing.

My mom used to say that when she left Greenwood to join my father in California, people told her she'd be back, that she wouldn't make it out west. So determined was my mother to leave Greenwood behind that it often felt as though she came from no place at all. Like a flower that came into being by bursting forth from the ground as if powered by its own will, my mother was a blossom of uncompromising, unflappable beauty. But she wasn't weak. When it seemed that life was determined to assault her, she revealed a stem carved from steel.

"I found lipstick on his shirt," she said one day. I was nine years old and we were in the recreation room, a loft-like space on the first floor of our house that had vaulted ceilings, brown leather couches, and a full-size bar. On one wall hung a larger-than-life wood engraving of my father making a tackle.

I looked up at my mom from where I sat on the carpet. She was standing next to a bunch of laundry piled up on the couch and with her hands she was folding and refolding a faded washcloth. Her face was turned toward the clear glass of the arcadia door, her gaze fixed on something beyond the yard.

She said it again: "I found lipstick on his shirt." I knew she was talking about my father. "Does he think I'm stupid? The clubs close at two and he doesn't come home until the next day. I know where he's at. He's sleeping with hookers, with prostitutes." Even at that young age I understood that certain emotions would fit the moment perfectly. My mother might feel humiliation, shame, fear that he'd leave her, fear that he'd leave our entire family, sadness because of the betrayal, but my mom seemed to feel none of those things. She was angry.

I wasn't surprised by her anger or by what she'd said. A lot of people were enamored with my father because of his job playing professional football for the San Diego Chargers. He'd been a guest on the local morning show, was written about in the paper, and it wasn't uncommon for kids on the playground to ask me for his autograph. Like the crowds that orbited his world, I didn't really know him. I experienced my father from a distance even though we lived under the same roof.

While my mother almost never spoke of the life she lived before her move to California, my father made a habit of launching into stories about his childhood experiences in the Delta at the dinner parties my parents frequently hosted. On those nights, when the meal was done and the adults were sitting around consuming amber-colored liquid from thick, decorative glasses, my father would reminisce about life in the Delta.

There was a showmanship to the way he spoke of his childhood. He was funny and nostalgic but revealed next to nothing about himself in his elaborate tales. Even if he had attempted to unpack his real biography, I was too young to grasp how a person could escape the geography of a place but still be ruled by its unspoken norms, like a former prisoner who can't fall asleep without gripping a piece of metal sharpened to a murderous point. Whether to protect us or himself, my father kept his most precious memories locked away. To me he was like a celebrity in a magazine and I would've believed almost anything about him. That's why, when my mother was folding laundry and telling me she suspected that my father was sleeping with prostitutes, his absences finally made sense to me.

So splintered was our family that, when my dad left, we were rarely told where he was going. I didn't know anything about training camp or how long it took for him to get to his away games. In the years after my mother shared her hypothesis with me, I just assumed that when my father was gone, he was holed up in a motel room with a woman he'd paid to be with.

What did surprise me had nothing to do with what she said, but that she was saying anything at all, because my mother was all but completely defined by turbulent silence. Unless there was another grown-up in the room, she was usually quiet, though rarely at peace.

As a little girl, I made a habit of following her around the house because I craved the sound of her voice. If she was in the kitchen, I'd sit at the table. If she was on the couch, I'd sit on the floor. If she was doing her makeup, I'd perch myself on the side of the tub.

One night, she was walking down the stairs in a long shimmery pale-green nightgown when I accidentally stepped on its hem. In a ruckus of screaming, flailing arms, and lots of bumps, she tumbled down the steps and landed hard on the blue Spanish tile below.

"What was that?" my father called from the other room.

My mother stood up, slowly turned around, and with her hands balled into fists she looked at me and screamed as though in the throes of an uncontrollable fit, "Stop following me!"

But I couldn't. She was magic. My mother had impossibly light brown skin, a perfect smile, a laugh like a song, and she floated through my world just beyond reach. Sometimes when she was doing the dishes I'd walk over to her, reach up, and wrap my arms around her waist. I'd wait for her to return the hug, but she'd remain silent, stiffening her body against my embrace.

I struggled to wrap my mind around the thing that seemed to plague my mother because I loved her, but I also needed to understand her for my own preservation.

When I was in the fifth grade, my best friend, Amy, lived up the street. One afternoon, she was over at my house and I needed to change my clothes. Amy was at the bottom of the stairs and I was at the top. To make her laugh, I started unbuttoning my shirt while swaying my hips. I was performing a mock striptease. Amy couldn't stop laughing, and after a few breathless giggles, she said, "That is so funny, I'm gonna go get your mom."

I stopped dancing and opened my mouth to stop her, but no sound came out. I didn't know what to say. I watched her run off, her blonde hair bouncing on her shoulders. As if I was standing in a forest watching all the birds suddenly fly away, I knew something bad was about to happen.

When the two of them appeared at the bottom of the stairs, Amy's face was red from laughing, but my mother's was stern. She turned to Amy, and in a voice of manufactured sadness, told her that it was time for her to leave. Amy looked from my mother and up to me, her eyes full of confusion. She didn't say anything. Maybe she was sensing it, too. After a moment, Amy put her head down and left.

As soon as the front door closed behind her, my mother called me downstairs. I followed her into the recreation room, where she told me to pull my pants down. When they'd reached my knees she started whipping me with my father's brown leather belt. It was long and its edges were covered in a thin, metallic material that was supposed to look like gold.

"You wanna be a stripper, huh?" she screamed.

"No, Mommy!" I cried.

Most of my spankings occurred against a wall so I couldn't get away, but this time I was in the middle of the room, trying to stay upright even though my pants were below my knees and a world of fury was raining down on my small frame. I was afraid if I fell from the force of her strikes, she'd get even angrier. I stumbled forward but never fell down.

Afterward, the days grew warmer, but I had to wear pants to hide the red, tender welts that crisscrossed the backs of my legs. My mom and I never talked about why I'd received my spanking. I never found out exactly what Amy said to her or what was at the heart of my transgression. Did my mom believe that I really wanted to grow up to be a stripper? Was there something truly wicked about pretending to be one? Or did she think I'd invented a new game in which I would actually begin stripping for all the kids on the street?

Not knowing why I was in trouble was normal. I was rarely able to pinpoint the true offense that warranted the spankings I received. The striptease beating was a bad one, but it wasn't the worst. There were other times when my dad was wearing his belt, so she used hangers, shoes, or telephone cords—anything, really. When she spanked me, I sometimes got the impression that I was incidental. She could've been hitting anything because she was raging not against me but against life itself.

But there was so much more to her.

Almost daily, my mother would succumb to an undercurrent of tenderness, a sort of forced vulnerability. In those moments, her mind would go someplace else while her body was right next to me. She'd be lacing my shoes or cleaning out my ears, when the core of her, the stuff that made her truly alive, would just vanish. As I got older, I grew better at predicting when it was about to happen because I could see it on her face. Deep lines would pop up on her forehead and her lips would begin to move as if she was silently working out a complex equation, or negotiating a deal to gather up the pieces of herself, the ones left scattered across the Delta.

A Yellow Gal

"You ain't no niggra, you's a yellow gal," Rosie heard Old Man Jones say again and again. In Mississippi in the early 1900s, most Blacks ranged from a light caramel to a brown so dark it resembled charcoal, but not Rosie. On a quick glance, she appeared to be neither White nor Black, as though her shade were dreamed up on an imaginary color spectrum. What was obvious about the girl who would become Booker's mother was her beauty. She was so beautiful that it was almost unsettling. Rosie looked as though she belonged to a different time and certainly a different place.

But how she spent her days—what she ate, where she slept, who she played with—and the yellow-brown skin that held the memory of all those beatings, were undeniable proof that Rosie Turner was indeed Black.

Rosie was born in 1913 to a family of sharecroppers on a plantation in Lula, Mississippi, a small town nestled deep in the fields of the Delta. Numerous families worked those fields, most of their houses located at the end of a long road bordered by pecan trees. But the White plantation owner, who everyone referred to as Old Man Jones, forbade the collection of the tasty nut. The pecans fell to the ground where they lay rotting and overlooked by sharecropper children whose bellies were never quite full enough.

Like the other families, Rosie's lived beyond the pecan trees in a shotgun house. The name "shotgun" was derived from the structure's simple design. The houses were built without hallways, with one room leading directly into another, and so on. In theory, if a person stood at the front door and fired a shotgun into one of these houses while all the interiors doors were open, the pellets would move straight through each room and out the back door without touching a single thing.

Rosie's shotgun house, which was really just a worn-out shack, was about twelve feet wide, made of bleached wood, and had one room, a dirt floor, and a tin roof. It didn't have electricity, so meals, as well as heat, came from a potbellied stove in the middle of the room. The shack also lacked indoor plumbing, so an outhouse sat several yards away from it. When night came and the light had surrendered itself to darkness, Rosie and her brothers and sisters were too afraid of the dark to make the trek from the shack to the outhouse, so a bucket for bodily waste stood in the corner.

The shack they lived in rested on pillars, leaving a space beneath it big enough for the children to play when they weren't working. And there were plenty of them to play. Rosie's mother gave birth twenty-two times. Only eleven of those babies lived to see adulthood, so before even reaching her teens, Rosie had experienced the stifling odor and wrenching ceremony of death over and over again.

Maybe she was too young to process so much pain. Maybe her youthful mind wasn't sophisticated enough to grasp the layered complexities of loss. Either way, when Rosie was still just a girl, one of her younger sisters lay in bed for weeks marching toward death, quickened by a combination of measles and pneumonia. When she finally slipped away, the only thing that came to Rosie, all she managed to say to her mother, was, "Now who's gonna help me with these dishes?"

But Rosie wasn't heartless. In her world, death was a traveling cousin stopping by whenever he saw fit. The only gift he bore was a reminder that the future was guaranteed to no one. Amid all of those uncertain tomorrows, Rosie did make one promise to herself about her own future. Come what may, she was determined not to end up like the other Black girls living on the plantation, many of whom—whether by choice or not—slept with the White men who worked among them.

Rosie kept herself busy by picking cotton, even though she hated the fields. Cotton picking was difficult, hard on the body, and because of the often sweltering heat, it was exhausting. All of this, though, Rosie could tolerate, because, in many respects, she was a strong and fearless girl. If she saw a snake, she had the bravery to kill it, to stomp it dead. There was something besides snakes, though, living in the fields, something that caused Rosie to panic and lose control.

Whenever she encountered a worm, moving slowly along a cotton bush, Rosie would snap. Consumed with fear and unable to control herself, she would cry out, stop her work, and run away. Luck was rarely on her side, because many times when she fled from a worm, the plantation manager just happened to be watching and wasted no time in executing her punishment—a whipping.

Old Man Jones was the one who rescued her. He began calling Rosie from the fields to help him with his favorite pastime, training racehorses. He took her under his wing and worked closely with her. It turned out she was a natural. Rosie came alive when she was with the horses. Old Man Jones even gave her one of his daughter's old riding suits—a true treat for a sharecropper's kid. Finally, life on the Jones Plantation was more than just bearable, it was wonderful. For a season, it appeared that Rosie's life had turned a corner.

Then, the season was over.

Years later, Rosie would be fairly tight-lipped about why she left the Jones Plantation. All she'd say was that someone tried to have sex with her and so she fled because she refused to be "a piece of meat."

The year Rosie left, whether or not she was on her own or what she did for money are details lost to time. Her story picks up again in 1926, the same year that unseasonably heavy rains began to fall from the sky. While the Mississippi River was steadily rising, growing thick with sludge and portent, Rosie Turner was living in the small town of Grenada, about 80 miles south of the Jones Plantation, and preparing to give birth to a little boy named Mack. Later, everyone would call him Booker. When her son was born, Rosie was thirteen years old.

Part Two
Family

How can we live without our lives? How will we know it's us without our past?

John Steinbeck
The Grapes of Wrath

Black Is Beautiful

"You're a nigger because you come from Nigeria."

When I heard those words, I was standing next to a wall-size map of Africa that my third grade teacher had instructed our class to observe. That particular observation was made by a brown-haired boy with a bowl-shaped haircut who was staring at me quizzically, as though he'd just ripped the wings from a fly and wanted to watch it squirm.

"What?" I asked.

"You're a nigger because you come from Nigeria," he said, a crooked smile fighting with his lips.

I looked down at the cracking skin that poked through the straps in my sandals and waited. After a few moments, I took a chance—hoping that maybe he'd moved on to observe something else—and I lifted my eyes up to him. He was still staring at me. They were all staring at me with their creamy white faces. I quickly looked away again and ran my fingers down the length of my chestnut arms. I didn't know what a nigger was, but I suspected it had something to do with the color of my skin.

In those days, Black women with glowing skin, wide hips, tight waists, plump breasts, and eyes swimming with desire looked boldly out at me from billboards and the back covers of my mother's Black magazines—a modern day version of the sirens from Greek mythology. The phrase "Black Is Beautiful"—the only lyric in their siren song—was usually stamped in bold letters next to them. I was eight years old and I was just beginning to realize that the phrase "Black Is Beautiful" was a calculated campaign to reshape how the world saw people who looked like me.

At the time, I had fat, unruly pigtails, brown lips, ashy skin, a wide flat nose, and legs covered with curly brown-black hair, and I was desperate to believe I could be made beautiful by the force of good advertising. The sirens told me to simply embrace my blackness, as if my own love of self would solve everything. But their message didn't stand a chance.

In the sweet afternoon hours between getting home from school and sitting down for dinner, my sister and I made up a game. We fastened long skirts around our heads to cover our real hair, and then we turned our heads really fast so that our pretend hair flew from left to right. We clumsily walked around in my mom's high-heeled shoes, strutting back and forth with our heads held high and our chests sticking out.

We pretended to drink martinis while we sat around and talked about playing golf at the country club, sending our kids to boarding school, and falling in love with men named "Spencer" or "Chuck." Like Mary Tyler Moore, we had jobs in the city; we rode horses like the women on *Dallas*, and we said "kiss my grits" to each other like Flo from *Alice*. We didn't care if the people we pretended to be were rich or poor, as long as they were White.

When the game was over and I'd pulled my fake hair off, I slowly returned to reality. Not only was I Black in what seemed to be an all-White world, I was ugly and Black.

From where I stood, White people had a thousand paths spread out for them, while my dreams were held captive beneath a dark, thin layer of skin. Being White meant having a story, or at least the hope of one. In books, on television, and in music they were falling in love, getting rich, traveling to foreign lands and finding themselves. They had so many stories, while Blacks only had one.

"A woman was sexually assaulted while she was alone in her home last night." "The bank on Tierrasanta Boulevard was robbed." "A car was stolen." "The sky is falling." It didn't matter. "We have a description of the suspect. He is Black and about who cares how tall and who cares what he weighs. Here is a sketch." A man's face, with extra shading to represent Black skin, would come up on the screen. With a wide, firm jaw and clenched teeth, he'd stare back at me, unafraid—eyes void of humanity.

The only other place I ever saw eyes like that were in the heads of evil villains in comic books. Those eyes seemed absent to me, as if they belonged to people whose souls had been chased away, leaving behind only red-hot hate. Then the sketch was gone and the ivory-colored newscaster was moving on to another White story.

I lived with my parents, my sister, and my little brother in a big house on a long, curvy road in an upper-middle class community. My neighborhood, which was full of canyons and green rolling hills, was also home to a senator, a television news anchor, advertising executives, and the like. During the thirteen years I lived in that neighborhood, I'd often meet people who would tell me, with a spark of excitement, that another Black family was living close by. I never bumped into them. In time, I figured the rumor about a Black family living in our neighborhood was probably just a rumor about us. I think they were trying to make me feel as though I wasn't all that different, but I was. The difference wasn't only about the color of my skin, either. Somehow traces of my family's Southern heritage fell off my family like a trail of dust.

Even though we never discussed where these traditions came from, whenever the kids in my house got really sick my mom would smear a towel with a sticky mixture of olive oil and Vicks VapoRub, heat it in the oven to an ungodly temperature, and place it on our chests. When my sister's tonsils bothered her, my mother "mopped" them with iodine.

She also made dishes that none of my classmates had ever heard of, like collard greens for dinner and warm grits. One day, I got into a conversation with some kids in my neighborhood about what we'd eaten for breakfast that morning. None of them had ever heard of grits before, but one of them had at least seen them. He explained to everyone that grits were like mashed potatoes for Black people.

With eating something like mashed potatoes for breakfast, greens for dinner, calling a sink a "face bowl," and straw-like hair that couldn't be washed more than once a week, I was an anomaly to the kids in my community, as they were to me—with their roast beef sandwiches, petite butts, love of volleyball, skin that changed color in the sun (and then peeled off!), Vans, and station wagons with wood paneling. And that hair. It was as soft as feathers and always seemed to fall right into place like magic petals floating from the sky, coming together to make a perfect rose every time. Their hair was nothing like the coarse locks that stood up—like licks of fire moving in all directions—from the top of my head.

There was a girl in my class who reminded me of the Doublemint twins because her hair was the color of honey, touched with varying shades of brown and blonde. It was the kind of color grown women spent hundreds of dollars to achieve. Hers was long, past her bottom, and it cascaded behind her when she moved. She'd twist it in her hands, wrap it around her arms, or spin, spin, spin, making her long tendrils fly like the thin legs of a thousand showgirls. I coveted that hair.

It was one day after school when it happened. Almost all the kids were gone from the vast playground that was used by both lower and upper elementary grades. Somehow, we were talking—me, the girl with the magic hair, and one of her friends. I smiled at whatever she was saying and almost immediately I started to daydream about the future of lifelong friendship that lay before us. I saw us riding bikes, going to dances, and sharing clothes. She would share more than clothes with me, though—she would share her story, one of the dream-fulfilling life paths that lay before her. Her beauty would rub off on me and in her friendship I would find meaning and escape.

Just as the clouds were moving across the sky, I heard something strange in her voice. It took a moment for me to wrap my mind around it, the thing she'd left dangling between us, hanging in mid-air. But there it was—a punch line. The girl with the magic hair had pulled me into conversation to mock me.

A bright burst of sunshine blinded me like a flashlight in the eyes. I tried to look at her but I could only see parts—freckles carefully placed on the tip of her nose, an eternally rosy cheek, and a smile on her pink lips from which escaped a taunting giggle. In slow motion, I saw her turn to her friend, who was also laughing at me. I lowered my eyes and noticed they were both standing with their hands on their hips, waiting for me to respond.

A jealousy aneurysm must have exploded deep in my brain. That's the only possible reason I can come up with for why what happened next happened at all. What I know for sure is that it seemed right, like the natural order of things, for me to raise a hand, grab that lovely hair, twist it so that my grip would not be compromised, and pull the beautiful girl to the ground. With another large chunk of her silky soft hair in the other hand, I started to walk backward, dragging her across the playground while her friend took off running. The girl with the magic hair was kicking her tan legs, screaming desperately, and frantically batting at my hands with hers, but her hair was so long that I was able to pull her while staying over a foot away. She couldn't reach me.

I knew eventually this would end, my backward walk of redemption, but while it lasted I felt as though I was lifting the heavy weight of my lot in life, of all my girlhood grievances, and tossing them aside. I was judge and jury and I was making things fair in my world. For a moment, I wasn't invisible, because I mattered to this White girl. I mattered to her a lot.

I must have dragged the girl with the magic hair for a long time, because when the clouds once again hid the sun, we were on the other side of the playground. Her screams had turned into breathless sobs and her kicks had slowed, reminding me of what happened to people in movies when they were being choked and the fight was sliding out of them.

As I woke from my waking dream, I knew I was in trouble. I stopped walking and looked around; surely there were witnesses. What would my mother say? How would I explain this? There was no explanation for this. I clumsily tried to untangle my dark, ashy fingers from her soft blonde hair, accidentally taking strands of it with me as I worked faster and faster to free myself. Finally, she fell to the ground with a lifeless thud and lay there, whimpering pitifully like a wounded fawn.

Then I ran. And when I did, she began to howl.

The sounds of her screaming and crying followed me like an accusatory soundtrack that pulsated in my head as I ran to the edges of the playground, past other kids, through the opening in the fence, and into the packed parking lot where I found my babysitter's dusty white car parked in a row with several others. Miraculously, it was unlocked and empty. I climbed into the backseat and crouched on the dark floor. I shut my eyes and an image floated up behind their closed lids—a sketch of my face on the evening news. "A sweet, innocent, angelic White child was brutally attacked by a wild Black girl. Tune in at seven for the horrifying details."

Through the cacophony of laughing kids, mothers calling for their children, horns honking, engines starting up, and the distinguished voice of the newscaster in my head, I heard her—choking, crying. Her sound was getting closer, getting louder. I tried to hunch down even lower, willing myself to be smaller, mashing my brown limbs into the floorboard. I knew if I peeked they'd see me, but I couldn't help myself. I lifted my head for less than a second, not even enough time to locate her, but that was all it took for the girl with the magic hair to find me. "There she is! I see her! I see her!" I crouched down and shook wildly, my knees banging against the floor, my head knocking the seat.

I forced myself to take a deep breath. Something in me said that cowering on the backseat of a car was unbecoming of even the vilest bully. Plus, hiding was a sure admission of guilt. Bewildered denial was my best defense.

I decided to get up and sit on the seat. When I slowly began to rise, I saw something that let me know there was a God in heaven who understood my anguish—the unrelenting pain of being differ-ent that could turn from sorrow to rage just by the sound of a taunt-ing laugh from one of the most beautiful girls in the world.

I hardly recognized the girl with the magic hair. Most of it looked like a cloud of swarming bees on top of her head; the locks that usu-ally framed her delicate face were now stuck to it with goo from her snot and tears. She was being dragged again, but this time it was by a teacher who probably just wanted to go home. All I could see were the back of his white shirt and the shiny, over-starched beige slacks pulled up high on his waist. His hand held her elbow as he pulled her back toward the playground. She was facing the other direc-tion, facing me, eyes desperately locked onto mine. In those eyes, I could see her burning with pain and confusion at the unfairness of what had just happened. As I studied her expression, I realized she hadn't yet discerned, might never discern, that her looks—her magic hair and the creamy, soft skin that covered her long, slender limbs— afforded her a level of privilege in life.

The more he pulled her away, the more she flailed against him, kicking her knees high. The magic hair that had been stuck to her cheeks lifted into the air in snotty clumps while she stomped and screamed, aggrieved eyes penetrating mine, face dark and twisted like a pounded beet, "There she is! I see her! I see her! I see her!" I turned away, covered my ears, and lowered my head just as my bones liquefied and my body slid back down to the floor. Her cry became more and more faint.

After several minutes, I opened my eyes and looked up at the sky. It was usually a deep shade of ocean blue, with a brilliantly orange sun. Floating above me that day were dingy clouds locked in a slow, reluctant dance. My chest heaved, searching for air, as shame and shock threatened to suffocate me. There, in that artificial silence, I was overcome because I'd never felt so afraid, so very afraid of myself.

Coming to Terms

A few years after my mother's revelation about my father's night-time activities, a knee injury ended his football career. He'd spent his life in the limelight, honing the skills of tackling and sprinting. When he played ball, the crowds were always cheering, the parties never ended, and a hum of adoration and awe followed him around like a repeating sound track. When his body gave way, the silence that followed came so quickly and was so consuming that it sucked up everything—dinner party invites, autograph requests, and, of course, the money.

To make ends meet, my dad hired some guys and started a janitorial service. So many people had loved being with the football star that my parents spoke frequently and confidently about how his business would certainly thrive. They talked and talked about how well it would go, each time seeming to fall just short of convincing themselves.

One afternoon, I was sitting on the carpet in our family room reading a book, when the phone rang and my father rushed from the kitchen to answer it. He was six feet eight inches tall and was covered in muscle, so whenever he moved quickly or spoke with anger, he reminded me of the coming of thunder.

I listened to his deep, faltering voice. "What do you mean they didn't do it?" Distant rumble. "They shoulda done it—I tol' 'em to." Thunder crackling.

I pretended to keep reading, but I listened. I knew he was talking about work. Whoever he was talking to must have been cutting him off because my father kept starting sentences and then abruptly stopping. Then the storm erupted. He shouted, cursed, and slammed the phone down so hard that I glanced up to see if it had shattered. Our eyes met.

He looked down at me from his great height, and I felt as though I was seeing him for the first time, or at least the first time in years.

A messy beard swallowed up his cheeks, his upper lip was hidden behind an uneven mustache, his brows were unruly, and his medium length, ill-kept afro sprouted in varying directions. From behind the thick, curly vegetation that hid his face, he peered at me with eyes black as night, filled with fury. He knew I'd been eavesdropping.

I looked away from his gaze, down at his neck. I feared that if I completely looked away it would seem disrespectful, but staring into those eyes felt like a challenge to something in him that had turned primal.

I heard air rush out of his nose and he seemed to want to shake his head, but instead a tremor moved through his body, making his chest swell. He curled his long, thick fingers not into a fist but into a kind of claw, the way he had so many times before when holding a regulation-size football. Finally, he turned and stomped out of the room. I realized I'd been holding my breath.

A few years later, when I was fourteen, right before I was supposed to start high school, my mother decided it was time to leave my dad. His janitorial business had never taken off, and neither had the job selling Simple Green, or anything else he tried after football. She'd secured a position answering phones at the local university and was finally making enough money to move out. My sister wanted to stay with my dad, so my mom, my brother, and I made plans to move from our spacious house in the hills to an apartment behind a strip mall.

For weeks, boxes piled up in our formal dining and living rooms while my father spent most of his days in the small world he'd created, which consisted of the family room and the kitchen. If he wasn't staring at the TV from his recliner, he was in front of the refrigerator searching for sandwich fixings, and he always wore the same thing: a loosely tied, navy blue bathrobe. It was too short for his large frame, so the hem of it knocked against his knees as he paraded around the house like he was the stuff of greatness, the orb around which our lives floated. He seemed to think by simply being, by breathing, he could keep us from going, that the very sight of him would knock sense into us.

Whenever one of us was in the same room with him he'd mutter, "She ain't goin' nowhere," followed by a chuckle.

Then one day, the moving truck came. People arrived to help my mom load it while my father sat in his recliner, flipping through channels. Several times throughout the day I heard him say, with that same chuckle, "You ain't really leavin'."

Finally, we were all packed up and making our way through the house to confirm we hadn't missed anything, when the doorbell rang. My mother answered it to find a man with pale skin, salt-and-pepper hair, a matching mustache, and an easy smile. He told her he was a substance abuse counselor and that my father was addicted to alcohol and cocaine, but was getting help. With a soothing voice and passionless logic he encouraged her to stay.

Without a sound, my mother headed out the door. I hurried to follow so she wouldn't leave me behind. I don't think she even looked back, but I did. My father was no longer in his recliner. He was in the rec room, sitting on the brown leather couch, staring at his hands where they hung between his knees while a stranger tried to save his family. I turned away and followed my mother out the door. Ten years would pass before I'd spend more than a few minutes with my father again.

Everyone in our family was struggling. I watched as other members of my extended family—aunts, an uncle, and favorite cousins—struggled with alcoholism, went to jail, skipped college, had cars repossessed, and got evicted from cheap apartments. What the hell was wrong with my family?

Before I graduated from high school, I developed a desperate, irrational fear that soon became a conviction. What plagued us must have something to do with the one thing that set us apart from everyone else. We were failing because we were Black, doomed because we couldn't escape the pitfalls of our racial heritage. Were we marked by something that set us on a direct path for failure? I couldn't share these concerns with my mom. She was strong. She never seemed to entertain the idea that there was anything she couldn't do. And somehow, even though she didn't say it out loud, I sensed that my mother felt something akin to resentment or bitterness—but not exactly either of those emotions—toward White people.

She was guarded with our neighbors and suspicious of my teachers. It was like there was a part of her, just below her surface, that would dramatically shift each time we entered into a space where White people were present.

If she ever had even the slightest reason to believe someone was mistreating her or her children because of race, she was instantly whipped up into a frenzy. Like someone performing an exorcism, she'd storm through the house declaring our intrinsic value with moving, passion-filled words. She'd rage at the powers that be and explain out loud, to no one at all, of her plans to write letters, call someone's boss, hire attorneys and on and on.

Bringing up questions about race with my mom meant taking the chance that I might set her off, igniting that thing in her that I knew would burn and burn until somehow it cooled off on its own, in its own time.

Left to my own limited understanding of the history of relations between Whites and Blacks, I spiraled deeper and deeper into despair.

I began to see myself and the members of my family as beings in a postapocalyptic world, surrounded by people whose own worlds were flourishing, whose lands still produced the seeds for happy tomorrows. Filled with a certainty that something buried in my genetic code would cause my every endeavor to fail, I stumbled through life, waiting for the curtain to fall.

WHEN I WAS SEVENTEEN years old I moved out but still tried to keep in close contact with my mom. The truth was that I both clung to her and pushed her away. She was all I had. My father was gone, I hadn't stayed in touch with my aunts or cousins, and I didn't have any close friends. I wanted her affection, but I didn't want to be like her. I tacitly communicated my disapproval of her explosive responses toward Whites. She wanted to stand up for something; what I didn't know. I just wanted to belong.

Even though we were no longer living together, we held on to some traditions. We'd always loved a movie called *Terms of Endearment*. She'd taken me to see it when I was eight. The story follows a mother and her daughter through their lives and examines the myriad complexities that exist between them. If *Terms of Endearment* was on television, we'd call to let the other one know and then we'd both watch it, calling again to reconnect while the final credits were rolling. Over the phone I'd laugh through tears as she made jokes about Shirley MacLaine's wigs and commented on how good Jack Nicholson still looked. I always cried because no matter how many times I watched it, I couldn't stop hoping that somehow the ending would change and Emma would pull through. But my mother would laugh her lovely songbird laugh and I'd remember that it was just a movie.

Then when I was nineteen—no longer a child but still pretending at adulthood—I woke up early to start a new job at a call center. I got into my car just before 5:00 a.m. and headed to the grocery store to pick up something for lunch. It was still pitch black outside when I parked, went into the store, made a purchase, and then returned to my car to find that it wouldn't start.

This had never happened to me before, and I wasn't sure what to do. Did I need to call a tow truck? Where would they tow it? I was anxious. I'd be late to work on my first day. I needed a solution. Across a small stretch of grass, I saw a pay phone. I checked to make sure I had change, and went to call my mom.

I told her what had happened. Toward the end of my explanation my voice cracked and I said, "I just don't know what to do."

In a whisper that sounded like a wire about to snap she said, "If you start crying, I'm gonna hang up on you." I knew she meant it. A lot of our phone calls ended with my mom hanging up on me.

I covered my mouth as, silently, I began to cry. I didn't take in what else she said because I was worried about what I'd do when it was my turn to speak. She'd be able to tell I was crying, and then she really would hang up. There was no one else to call and I only had a few hundred dollars to my name.

She asked me a question, but I didn't hear it because I was drowning. Did she know I was drowning?

I heard myself yell, "Fine, fine, hang up! I don't care anymore!" I slammed the phone down onto the receiver and stared at it.

I'd never spoken to her that way before. Without panic, I began to wonder what had just happened, but I already knew. I'd flung her—and the hope of help—far, far away. There was no one else. Only one of my roommates owned a car. I could call her or someone

from church, but everyone I knew would find a way to tactfully communicate just how much I was putting them out. That was something I couldn't face, not then, not when I was drowning.

It was January, cool but not too cold. The San Diego morning
was still dark, barely beginning to stir. Out of its silence emerged
a knowing, a truth that wrapped itself like a fist around my throat:
Everyone needs family; it's the thing that keeps people tethered
to the world, keeps them from drifting away into an irrelevant
oblivion.

I could feel my heart pounding, but the sense of alarm hadn't yet
reached my mind, which was steady and calm. I looked around. In
the parking lot, my car sat in what struck me as a kind of slouch, as
if it had already given up. The cracks in the sidewalk were growing
dark with moisture as the morning fog descended. Drops of dew
shimmered in the grass.

I pushed my hands into my pockets and inhaled deeply. The air
that filled my lungs was so salty it felt artificial. I turned away from
the pay phone and headed back to grocery store for one final purchase. Then I walked home, where I used my forefinger to push as
many sleeping pills down my throat as I could.

ONE OF MY ROOMMATES, the only one besides me who owned a car,
returned home from work early and rushed me to the hospital, where
I was informed that I'd have to stay for a few days before they'd release me. The people working at the hospital seemed very concerned
for my welfare and kept a close watch on me. One nurse noticed, in
the middle of the night, that I was having trouble sleeping. She came
in and offered to give me a massage. I felt so cared for, but I knew
they'd all forget my name within a week. They weren't family.

The hospital I was taken to was on the campus of the university
where my mom worked. The front door to her office was about half

a mile from the entrance. When she came to visit me, she rushed in wearing a flowing outfit and carrying a large handbag. For a moment, I flashed back to my favorite scene in *Terms of Endearment*, when Emma's best friend, Patsy, visits and finally explains what their relationship means to her.

Naively believing that life could be just like the movies, in the few seconds it took for her to walk to the chair next to the window, I managed to convince myself that this was the time when my mom and I would figure out how to say all the things we needed to say.

She fell into the chair as her oversize Louis Vuitton bag flopped onto her lap and she said, "Don't you ever do this to me again!" She crossed her arms and looked away from me. She only stayed for a few minutes before rushing out, her long skirt barely clearing the door before it closed.

I waited for her to visit me again, but she didn't.

Each morning, I imagined her driving by the hospital entrance on her way to work and then passing it again at the end of the day on her way back home. I couldn't help but wonder if, when she drove past, she looked up toward my window or stared at the road ahead. In my mind it occurred the same way every time. Behind a sheath of thick mascara, her dark brown eyes were fixed on the road ahead, and beneath a perfectly plump, rouged cheek were a clenched jaw and unsmiling red lips.

I sat in the hospital as hours ticked by without anyone from my family visiting or calling to see how I was doing or to offer me a place to stay while I recovered emotionally. I began to wonder how I'd managed to miss out on an essential aspect of human life. *Connection* and its offspring, the feeling of being wanted, of being enjoyed.

I looked out my window and searched the silent sky. I could feel my emotional self going over a waterfall, sliding along a wet rock face, my eyes searching for something to grab hold of, for a way to gain a purchase in an impossible predicament. I didn't feel sad. This was heavier than that. I didn't feel alone. This was darker than that. What welled up in me was a burning, raging sense of shame. I was so lonely it was embarrassing, so disregarded it felt like a joke, a comical exaggeration.

The doctors, nurses, and psychiatrist they assigned to me would often strike up conversations about mundane things, but it felt more like they were trying to remind me about beauty and all of life's possibilities or maybe it was my own mind going to those topics no matter what was being discussed.

Either way, I found myself thinking more and more about how everyone needs something to tether them, something with roots planted deep underground, so they don't just drift through life. For most people, the thing that tethers them is family. Even if they don't speak for decades, many people will stand by their family when it counts. Family is a place to land when we fall, a touchstone. Family explains our place in history, in geography, connecting us to all that came before and all that comes after. Even if the relationships are fraught with tension and bickering when families do gather together, there's still a sense of home, something familiar in this unsympathetic world.

I spent the next several months pondering this idea before coming up with my own solution. I realized that I'd spent my entire life wishing for a different story, so in the end I just made one up. In my new story, I didn't care about my race or my family. I tamed my hair, learned how to apply makeup, and got a corporate job. I willed myself to stop thinking about my sadness and to just be. When the smothering fog of loneliness did roll in, I told anyone who might ask that I was busy with work and then I holed up alone someplace until I had the strength to put my façade back on. In time, I even began to believe my fake story. I threw my past off like it was a worn-out coat. I began to live as if I'd come from no place at all.

Get Off This Place

Rosie gave birth to Mack "Booker" Wright on October 17, 1926. The two of them lived in Grenada, a farming town whose western edge meets up with the Delta's eastern border. She was able to raise her child while working as a maid for a young, White couple named the Russells. When Booker was still fairly young, possibly two or three years of age, the Russells decided they needed to move over 250 miles south to a town called Gulfport so Mr. Russell could pursue a new career. Fortunately, the Russells invited Rosie to join them, so she wasn't in danger of losing her job.

Aside from working in the homes of White folks, Black women living in the South in the 1920s and '30s had only a few ways to support themselves. Most farms only allowed a woman to work as a sharecropper if she had a man living with her. A single mother in the Delta was like an endangered species. Women like Rosie lived on the edge of life with no one to catch them if they fell.

It's unclear whether or not the Russells asked Rosie to leave Booker behind for the initial move so she could help them get settled, or if Rosie herself felt that she needed to move first, find housing, and then return for Booker. What is clear is that Rosie shared her concerns with a Black, older, married couple who lived near her: Willie and Annie Wright. The Wrights didn't have any children of their own and, after considering Rosie's predicament, offered to keep Booker for her while she moved to Gulfport.

Taking the Wrights up on their offer, Rosie went ahead and made the move with her employers. While she was still in the process of getting settled she received alarming news from someone back in Grenada. The Wrights had moved away. Rosie found out that Willie and Annie had moved to a plantation in Baird, Mississippi, sixty miles west of Grenada, and they'd taken Booker with them. She wrote a letter to the Wrights and sent it to the Baird Plantation. In it, she explained that she was coming to pick up Booker. Rosie waited for a reply from the Wrights but never received one. The young mother decided to make the trip anyway.

Rosie took a train from Gulfport to a station in Moorhead, Mississippi. Moorhead's train station was made famous in a 1914 blues song, "The Yellow Dog Rag," by W.C. Handy, as the place where the "Southern crosses the Dog." "Southern" referred to the Southern Railroad and "Dog" referred to the Yazoo Delta Railroad, which many called the "Yellow Dog." It was at this station where Blacks— fleeing the poverty, violence, and degradation they regularly faced while living in the South—caught the train that would take them to Chicago and the hope of better living.

When Rosie arrived in Moorhead, the train station was likely packed with hopeful travelers who were all leaving behind the only way of life they'd ever known, but possibly also by angry Whites determined not see their workers flee. "Greenwood whites had an especially bad reputation for mistreating blacks at the train station . . . They were roughed up and threatened by law enforcement officials [and] train porters were harassed as well."

After disembarking from the train, Rosie stood in the station looking around. She had no idea how to get to Baird. In the hubbub of people, she began approaching strangers to ask them if they knew how she could reach her destination. What happened next felt lucky, but in the years to come it would seem like part of a deceptive plan.

Rosie ended up in a conversation with a Black man who lived and worked as a runner, or a driver, on the Baird Plantation. He ran various errands, including carting White men back and forth between the train station and Baird. Rosie explained her predicament to him and he offered to give her a ride.

When they got to Baird, the runner introduced Rosie to someone who could help her, one of the White men who worked on the plantation. Rosie explained the situation. She'd left her son with the Wrights for a brief time while she got settled in Gulfport. The Wrights were never supposed to move away with Rosie's child. She'd always intended to get him back.

He listened to her story, but apparently he was unmoved by it, because instead of helping Rosie, he placed her in an even more dire predicament. He explained that if she wanted to remove her son from the plantation she would have to pay for him.

It was the late 1920s. Rosie was a young, single Black woman talking to a White man who, simply because of the color of his skin, had more power and influence than she could ever dream of having. She did not argue with him, nor did Rosie reiterate that her arrangement with the Wrights never included money. Instead, the young mother assumed defeat and complied passively, obediently. The only thing she said was, "Alright," and then she let the runner take her back to the station.

Rosie returned home empty-handed. Whether it was from utter shock at the immensity of her despair or just basic human compassion, when Rosie told the Russells what had transpired, they offered to give her the money she needed to buy back her son. There were just two problems: Rosie didn't know how much she needed, and she also didn't know how she'd ever pay the Russells back.

Her employers were undeterred. They gave Rosie a sizable

amount of cash and told her they'd just start withholding a little here and there from her regular pay. The Russells seemed to grasp that Rosie simply would not be able to make it without her beloved child.

With renewed hope, Rosie wrote another letter to Willie and Annie Wright. Again she waited for a response. Again, none came.

Rosie went back to the train station and traveled to Moorhead. When she arrived, something interesting happened. The same runner just happened to be there. She explained to him that she'd brought money with her because this time she didn't want to leave without her son. The runner heard her out and took her back to the plantation.

Just like before, the runner took her to one of the White employees. She explained the situation, but this time she made sure they understood that she'd brought money with her. The man climbed into the vehicle with Rosie and instructed the runner to drop him off at the main house on the plantation. When they pulled up in front of the house, the White man got out, explaining that he was going to find out the price Rosie would have to pay for her son. He left Rosie with the runner, who drove her to his own home on the plantation.

The runner took her inside and, without offering an explanation, he left. She wasn't alone for long, though. After several minutes the runner returned in a state of urgency. He told Rosie that she'd been lied to. The White man had actually gone into the main house not to find out how much Rosie needed to pay to get Mack back but to look for someone who would come out and whip her. They had no intention of giving Rosie back her son. The only thing they'd give her was a reason to never come back.

"Get off this place!" the runner implored her. "Come on, let's go, 'cause he's gone to get that White man to come 'round here and whip you."

Rosie quickly gathered her things, rushed out of the little house, and climbed back into the truck with the runner. He dropped her off at the station at Moorhead without an explanation or advice about what Rosie could try next. Somehow it was all settled. The young mother boarded a train that took her home.

Years later, Rosie married a man named Erby Butler and moved to Chicago, where she had five more children. One died as a young girl, but the rest would live into adulthood. For years, she wrote to the Wrights to find out if there was any way she could be reconciled with her firstborn son. They never wrote back.

Rosie was living a parent's worst nightmare. Many young mothers have laid in bed at night wondering what they would do if someone ever tried to take their child. It's probably safe to assume that few envisioned themselves reacting the way Rosie did. Her response was a nonresponse. When threatened with violence if she continued to ask for her son's return, she seemed to believe there was no hope and she simply left. Yes, she wrote more letters, but she did not storm the plantation to get back her firstborn son. She did not, as far as anyone can tell, go to the authorities.

For Rosie, the odds were slim that anyone would have believed her version of the story over a White man's anyway. Blacks throughout the Southern states had been lynched for far less than accusing a White person of kidnapping. And Rosie wasn't living in just any Southern state; she was in Mississippi, where tensions between Whites and Blacks had grown exponentially more combustible after what transpired during the Great Mississippi River Flood of 1927.

What would come to be known as one of the worst natural disasters in US history was also a catastrophic disaster between the races. When the Mississippi River flooded the Delta, she left twenty-three thousand square miles of land underwater, more than half a million homeless, and at least 250 people dead.

But the flood itself was a culminating event in a region that was already pulsating with fear and tension.

It began quite simply. Heavier-than-expected rains fell from the sky in the summer of 1926 when Rosie was still pregnant with Mack. The rains caused the Mississippi River to rise, and whenever she rose, a sense of foreboding in the surrounding communities rose along with her. Historian John Barry once noted:

"There is no sight like the rising Mississippi. One cannot look at it without awe, or watch it rise and press against the levees without fear. It grows darker angrier, dirtier; eddies and whirlpools erupt on its surface; it thickens with trees, rooftops, the occasional body of a mule. . . . When a section of riverbank caves into the river, acres of land at a time collapse, snapping trees with the great cracking sounds of heavy artillery. On the water the sound carries for miles."

As the waters rose, so did the fear of local residents.

Small river systems throughout the Midwest and the South were failing. The Yazoo in Greenwood overflowed, causing hundreds to lose their homes. At the time, the smaller floods seemed unfortunate but unlikely to have an effect on the Delta. In retrospect, it's clear they were an omen of what was to come. "It was as if the Mississippi was . . . sending out small floods as skirmishes to test man's strength. Those who knew the river always felt that it seemed a thing alive, with a will and a personality. In 1927, its will seemed intent on sweeping its valley clean of man."

The residents were assured the levees would hold. But, as a precaution, the Army Corps of Engineers gave instructions for them to be inspected for weak spots and to be raised at certain points.

The work of raising and inspecting the levees was dangerous because, if they did fail, anyone standing on top of them or nearby would surely be swept away. "In towns on both sides of the river, every morning the police ran patrols through the Black neighborhoods and grabbed men off the streets and sent them to the levee. If a Black man refused, he was beaten or jailed or both; more than one was shot." Many Blacks were forced to relocate, to live in the makeshift tents that were set up along the river and on barges on top of the water.

The work Blacks were required to perform was brutal and exhausting. They had to fill sandbags with wet dirt. Once filled, these bags often weighed more than a thousand pounds. All day and into the night, they had to fill, cart, and pass the sandbags, which were then stacked higher and higher. Someone standing on top of one of the levees to lay sandbags in place noticed that "a black man beside him slipped and fell; he fell the wrong way, into the river, and disappeared, his body never recovered, never even looked for. Work went on without interruption."

Accidents weren't the only way Blacks lost their lives while rebuilding the levee.

Finally, on April 21, in a violent show of her power, the river pushed the levees, literally moving them along the ground, before rolling over the tops of them. When she breached the levees, the Mississippi River was a wall of water thirty feet high, almost a mile wide, and for three weeks she moved across the land, stopping just before reaching Greenwood.

As the waters came rushing in, "One planter put his black sharecroppers in his cotton gin and nailed it shut . . . They broke out." The planter may have figured that if some died, the ones who lived could stay and work, but if he let them all go they might never return.

He was not alone in his concern. While their lands were being swallowed by waters, many Whites expressed fears about what would happen if too many Blacks fled the Delta. There wouldn't be enough people in the labor class to clean up the mess left from the flood. Furthermore, there wouldn't be enough people left to tend the fields once life returned to normal.

These fears were so prevalent that in Greenville, about an hour from Greenwood, a law was passed forcing all Blacks to work at the levees or be arrested as vagrants, but most towns didn't need a law to force Blacks to work. The National Guard was employed to patrol "the perimeter of the levee camp with rifles and fixed bayonets. To enter or leave, one needed a pass. They were imprisoned, and fed barely enough to stay alive. Blacks were kicked or hit with guns for not moving fast enough, talking back, or trying to leave."

It wasn't until late July 1927—almost a full year after the rains that started the flood began to fall—that the Mississippi collected herself and eased her waters into the Gulf of Mexico.

It's not surprising that it was in the aftermath of the flood that the manager of the farm where Mack was living felt entitled to keep him. It was becoming clear that, at least where Blacks were concerned, freedom and equality were ever-changing equations in which the value they were assigned depended upon who was doing the assigning. At a time when Blacks in other parts of the United States were getting college degrees and having their votes courted by political candidates, Delta Blacks were being forced to live and work in demoralizing and dangerous conditions.

Historian James C. Cobb wrote that "by the end of the 1920s, most Delta blacks lived in severe economic deprivation, politically and legally powerless to improve their material circumstances or even protect themselves from violence, coercion, or unlawful incarceration bordering on slavery."

Cobb also details the story of a man named Dave Ross, an elderly sharecropper whose furniture was confiscated by a local planter who'd advanced Ross money. Since Ross was unable to pay the money back with cash or labor because of his "broken health," his family slept on the floor while Ross went to jail. He was imprisoned even though all of his furniture had already been confiscated.

A Black Coast Guardsman named Sam Edwards didn't fare much better. While visiting his mother in the Delta he was arrested for

"trespassing without money," and hauled into a grocery store "courtroom" where, when it was discovered that he did indeed have money, the charge was changed to vagrancy. For this offense he was sentenced to thirty days at hard labor and a twenty-dollar fine. The judge, incredulous that a Mississippi black actually did not know how to pick cotton, promised to send Edwards to a place where he "could learn."

It may have been a Black man determined to flee the Delta who explained conditions the most accurately and succinctly when he spoke of "this cursed South land down here a Negro man is not good as a white man's dog."

What Blacks experienced in the Delta was something words could never capture. Their daily reality was one of such pain and humiliation that it could smother a human soul. That season gave birth to a raw, mournful, contemplative sound that moved and unnerved anyone who heard it.

It was called "The Blues."

Part Three
Surface of the Deep

There are victims of the Holocaust
who haven't been born yet.

Reed Farrel Coleman
Empty Ever After

Colorless

After leaving the hospital, I entered a very strange season of life, one in which I felt completely untethered from the world. While I was pretending what mattered most to me really didn't matter at all, a series of events transpired that managed to completely reshape how I viewed my mother and the way I felt about being Black.

I was about twenty years old, working at a design firm, when I realized I had a problem I didn't know how to solve. The phone system was set up so that if someone called a person's direct line and got voice mail, the caller had the option of dialing "0" for the receptionist, who would then page the employee. I had lots of meetings with outside vendors and also with other employees, so I needed to be paged multiple times a day. Each time the receptionist had to call my name her voice grew more and more shrill, irritated. She sounded as though she thought they were personal calls, but I never heard her do this when she paged anyone else. There were employees in other departments who were paged much more often than I was.

One day, while I was in a planning meeting, I heard my name over the paging system, "Yvette!" It was the receptionist, and she sounded ticked off. She continued, "Another call for you." My co-worker looked at me and raised her eyebrows as if she was wondering what I'd done to piss off the receptionist. I knew I had to do something about the way she was paging me. If I was in a meeting with a potential vendor, a page like that could hurt my credibility. The problem was that I hardly knew her. There wasn't any tension between us as far as I could tell.

By this time, my mom had been promoted to a managerial position at her university job. She was responsible for a budget in the hundreds of thousands. Since she'd been successfully navigating the work world for years, I went to her for advice. At first, it sounded as though she was going to provide me with insight that was both logical and tactful. But then she started raising her voice in indignation, ". . . and you tell them that you're the only one she does this to, and you're also the only Black person who works there!" She went on, but I'd stopped listening.

She was right about one thing: I was the only Black employee, but I had not even noticed it until my mom pointed it out. She was always like that, blaming every problem on race. It drove me nuts. As part of the story I was creating for myself, I'd chosen to evolve into a person who didn't notice color. Actually, the fact that I hadn't realized I was the only Black employee until she mentioned it made me realize just how far I'd come, how far I was moving away from my family, from the people who didn't seem interested in loving me.

The truth was that I never thought about race anymore, but my mom certainly did. For months her neighborhood was abuzz about a new fast food chain being built there. The company sent mailers to the residents, and like everyone else, my mom was really excited to try them out because apparently they sold burgers that were somehow healthier and fresher than the competition's.

I was with her the first night she went to eat there. She was pretty upset to find that they'd only hired White kids. "Now, they know they could've hired at least one little Black girl," she said. I didn't respond, but I felt disbelief. Checking to see how many employees were Black vs. how many were White would've never occurred to me. I felt confident that it hadn't occurred to the hiring managers, either. It was the 1990s, after all.

It seemed to me that there was a force alive within the nation—like a powerful living, beating heart representing our collective conscience, our sense of right and wrong—that had come to realize the magnitude of what it had done, of how it was complicit in the systematic oppression of an entire group of people. The weight of this was so strong that the core of the nation, the intangible sense of community meant to bind and unify us, was racing like the wind to just move on.

These things weren't really said out loud, but someone like me, someone desperate to find her place in the world, someone who was paying incredibly close attention, could see there was a new set of rules at play. Questioning whether or not an incident, situation, or social problem had anything to do with race relations was simply anathema to who we were as a nation. It was an idea spread by the uninformed, the radical, or by angry Blacks who coddled some sort of "reverse racism," or, God forbid, were themselves "crack babies." The only other people still talking about race relations were the entitled, like the "welfare queens" who hoped that by playing the "race card" they'd get just a little bit more.

I was definitely not going to take my mother's suggestion. I was confident that if I said to anyone at work that the receptionist was calling my name in a voice that made it clear that I didn't deserve her time, but even worse, that with her tone she seemed to be communicating that I was somehow less than her because I was Black, they would've thought I was crazy. Instead I went to the receptionist and asked if there was anything I could do differently in our work relationship. She had a few suggestions, and in time, it smoothed itself out.

That was one of the last times I went to my mom for advice. I was determined not to segment the world into camps of Black and White, even when race was obviously the issue.

There was a mall in downtown San Diego that I enjoyed visiting. It was an outdoor mall with several floors. It felt like a little village, separate from the outside world. They had an upscale department store, and whenever I entered, the sales ladies would approach the women walking in—always the ones before me and the ones behind me—to ask them if they needed help. The saleswomen were tall, attractive, and always approached with a smile and outstretched hand as they walked right past me.

I knew what would happen if my mom were in my shoes. She would just assume she was being passed over because of her race, then she'd storm into the manager's office screaming and making a scene—a perfect embodiment of "the angry Black woman." The manager would glance at the saleswomen, who would shrug their shoulders, look bewildered, and say they must have just missed her, but they'd be happy to help her find whatever she needed. Score: 1 for the Department Store and 0 for Progress.

I was not my mother. If I wasn't being helped, it was because there was something wrong with the way I was dressed or an odd coincidence. I refused, absolutely refused, to believe that not being helped had anything to do with my race. To test my theory, one day I went to the department store dressed in one of my finest outfits. Back then, I was blowing most of my paychecks by purchasing a new suit almost every week; some cost more than a thousand dollars.

When I entered that day, dressed up and feeling good, there was a woman standing next to the makeup counter. It was instantly clear that she was good at sales. She looked confident as she made eye contact with everyone who passed by her. She was dressed in all black, her hair was colored a deep, dark red, and she managed to convey charisma without a shred of desperation when she called out to the women walking by, "Do you want a free makeover?" With her high heels and perfectly made-up face, it felt like she'd be doing them a favor.

At the time, I was still struggling to find eye shadow and lipstick shades that worked best with my dark skin. I wanted that makeover. I moved closer to the woman at the counter so I'd be ready to accept her offer when she made it. But she didn't offer me anything. Instead, she awkwardly adjusted her body so she could look past me and then motioned to another woman, "Free makeover." I wanted to believe the best. This was not about race. Somehow she just wasn't noticing that I was interested.

I stood in front of her, smiled, and said, "Hi, I'd like a makeover."

Her persona of crisp excellence and warmth fell away in an instant. She let her shoulders sag, rolled her eyes, and said, "If I give you a makeover, you're gonna have to buy something."

Quickly, I said, "Of course I intend to buy something." She sat me down, began my makeup, and allowed her mood to lighten. As I sat there listening to her share stories about this and that, I kept wondering what it was about me that made her think I was a waste of her time. We finished and I bought a bunch of makeup.

Nevertheless, I left feeling proud. My mom would've made that interaction about race. I refused to do so. This place of disagreement became the location where I put all of my hurt and confused feelings about my mom and my race. I didn't say these things out loud to myself. I wasn't quite self-aware enough to put together just how and why I was letting things with my mom fall apart. I would need time to myself and time in the Delta before I'd even have the ability to consider how I'd let our differences on race define the fault line between us.

In my new way of thinking, the reason my mother and I had such a troubled relationship was because I saw the world as being beyond race, while she was obsessed with it. At the time, I remembered that when I was in my early elementary school years, my mom had instructed me not to trust White people, but she knew she was sending me to a school that was almost completely White. How was I supposed to manage? Who would I play with?

Coming into my own as a woman, I began to dump the fears of my youth, the fears that something was wrong not just with me but also with my entire family. I thought there was nothing wrong with *us*, there was something wrong with *her*, something wrong with the way she saw the world. I could be free from whatever ailed my mother and the rest of my family because I wasn't going to wear my race like a martyr's cloak. I was beyond race. It didn't matter to me or to anyone else what color I was. I would never be accused of playing the race card.

When I was twenty-four, I met a man who fell in love with the self I'd created, and I chased that love to Phoenix, Arizona, and got married. I married someone who was half-White and half-Black, allowing me to continue in my ambivalence.

My future seemed so bright. My husband was college educated, and we paid our bills early, saved money, bought cars with cash, and abstained from drinking alcohol. We began to dream of having children who would thrive in our loving, stable environment. So, we made our dream come true. We had two boys: Bishop and Dexter.

To friends and my husband's family, I was a picture of peace. But inside, something was always moving and shifting, as if I was carrying a heavy load. There were moments when I was filled with rage, others when I was consumed with fear. I didn't explore the origins of those emotions. I just moved past them and turned back to writing my story, making revisions as necessary.

"Are you okay, Mommy?" Bishop, my two-year-old, asked one day while I was sorting through papers.

I looked down at him and smiled what I hoped was a radiant, sunny smile. "I'm okay, sweetheart."

He put a tiny little hand on my thigh and shook his head. "Mommy, not okay," he whispered, then turned and sauntered off.

Something was beginning to break. My lovely story was nothing more than the surface of something deeper. Beneath that surface was an unplumbed sea of shame and fear that pressed against me, threatening to burst free.

About a year later, I was home alone with my two boys when my story, my protective surface, ebbed away. I was standing in front of the kitchen sink, looking out the window, lost in the green of the leaves that sprouted from the palm trees in my yard. Warm water was running over my fingers as they moved a sponge in and out of a water glass. I felt a tug on the left side of my shirt. I glanced down to see Bishop. He had wide, vulnerable eyes, insanely long eyelashes that curled up at the ends, and smooth, caramel-colored skin.

He was staring up at me with a concerned look on his face, his little brow bent with worry. He stuck his arm out and rubbed his tiny little fingers along its smooth skin. "Mommy, why am I this color? Why do I look like this?"

My mouth opened, but no sound came out. I felt as though I'd been playing "White" with my sister and someone had come in and pulled off my wig, just ripped the skirt from the top of my head.

He touched the skin on my chestnut-colored arm and said, "Why are you that color and Daddy is a different color?"

I smiled a smile that felt plastic even as it was spreading across my face. This wasn't part of the story. The mother of happy kids who defied racial stereotypes—that was my story. The mother of boys who felt colorless, who were blind to their difference—that was my story, his story. I tried to smile wider, dried my hands off, and lifted him into my arms. He wrapped his legs around my waist and let his bottom rest on my hip.

"There are lots of people who look like you, just not here in Arizona," I said, and then fumbled through an explanation of colonization. He looked at me as if I'd responded in a foreign language, wiggled down, and ran off.

But that was just the beginning. Over the next several weeks, he kept asking questions about his color and talking about being brown as if it was the worst thing on earth. I put on a strong front and offered him answers that sounded like things he might hear on *Sesame Street*. The truth was that I didn't have any answers for him, just like I hadn't had any answers for myself. I pulled out the script of my made-up story and repeated the lines I'd memorized to get through life: *Nothing in my life has to be influenced by my race unless I allow it to be. I don't think of myself as Black or White, and no one else does, either.*

I continued my routine. I went to book club and church, met friends to exercise, read to my children, cleaned my house, applied my makeup, and kept going.

One night a few months later, I was sitting on the patio of a restaurant with some girlfriends. We were telling funny stories about our husbands and sharing silly things our kids had done. In response to a joke, I tossed my head back as if I had magic hair of my own. In the middle of that simple motion, I caught a glimpse of myself in the reflection of the darkened restaurant window. My breathing quickened and I was struck with a feeling of alarm.

I was the only dark image in a sea of white. I was suddenly aware of how loud I was, how my clothes were too bright, and my lipstick too red. With hair sticking up in a way that White hair never does, I felt as though I'd been caught pretending I belonged. As I smoothed my hair down and dabbed my lipstick, I shut my eyes and, for a moment, I could almost make out the sound of someone screaming—"I see her, I see her, I see her!"

Surrounded by laughter, the smell of warm cobbler, and wine, I looked at the hands on my lap and rubbed the skin that covered them the same way Bishop had.

I'd been willing to settle for a made-up story as the only answer for myself, but the mother in me desperately wanted something better for my sons. I wanted an honest story, one they could hold on to with pride, but I didn't have one to give them. I longed for a tale I could wrap up like a gift, one they could return to every time they doubted themselves or wondered about their color.

I wanted to find a way to tell my sons what it meant to be Black that would leave them feeling proud and excited about the future. I imagined a place for them to stand in the massive narrative of the Black story, a spot that would enable my boys to see themselves the way I did. In my eyes, they were glorious.

But part of me feared that a story wouldn't be enough. The truth was that something was wrong with my family. Even the word "wrong" felt inept. There was something there that managed to trip us up. I'd let myself believe I was so different from my parents, but maybe I wasn't. Had they once dreamed a dream for me? When they left the Deep South, they must've had some hope of giving their children a better life with more opportunities. Was there something they had tried to escape?

I pictured my parents gathering up the strength of all their hope and thrusting the old story away before turning and running toward a western sea, away from the land of their ancestors—only to have the story find them again. But not just them. Somehow this thing, this crippling, suffocating thing, had dislodged itself from where it lay in the Deep South and traveled across a thousand lands until, once again, it struck my parents, and then their children, and now their children's children—efficient, void of mercy, like a malevolently enchanted boomerang.

A Catalyst

I didn't know how to start. When Bishop began expressing concerns about being Black while everyone else in his world seemed to be White, I'd looked a lifelong anxiety in the eye and decided to face it. I promised myself that this was it; this was where it was going to end. Like stopping a cycle of abuse, we were no longer going to feel confused or ambivalent about our race. Days later, when I began taking apart what it was I actually hoped to accomplish, my audacity quickly began to fade.

It was 2007, and I was a stay-at-home mom living in Arizona and finishing up my college degree while the kids napped. I was already overwhelmed by my responsibilities. And I had another problem. My knowledge of Black history was dismal at best. When my elementary school teacher taught us about the Underground Railroad, Harriet Tubman's accomplishments sounded more like an extended road trip than a series of courageous, death-defying journeys.

I figured the best place to look for stories that would help my kids see Blacks as heroic overcomers was the civil rights movement. Unfortunately, aside from a few names and approximate dates, the story of those fiery speeches and impassioned marchers was little more than a pile of embers to me. Even the ongoing stories in the media about the link between socioeconomics and race, debates over affirmative action, and questions regarding the high prison rates for Black males were little more than occasional crackling sounds from already wasted wood. I was pretty convinced that the raging fire described every February during Black History Month had definitely lost its roar.

I decided that, instead of trying to make sense of a time period so massive, I would focus on my own family first. I started by pulling together the data I already had, which was basically a pile of disconnected stories.

As a child, I'd seen very few photographs of my grandparents, their siblings, or their cousins, but I knew just enough about several of them to imagine what they might look like. I made a family tree in my mind, filled with faces I'd constructed based upon the roles each person played within the stories I'd heard. My father and his brothers wore sheepish grins because they were always getting into scuffles with other kids from the neighborhood. My mother's maternal grandmother had a set jaw and stubborn eyes because in one of her stories she'd held her own against a group of White men who tried to enter her home late one night.

As I continued to sift through the stack of memories they'd shared with me, I kept coming across a blank face, one person who I knew so little about that I couldn't even begin to imagine what he might have looked like: my mother's father. I remembered that over the years there were a few times when she'd mention something about him having a café, but I couldn't seem to conjure up any other details. I'd never seen any photos of him, didn't know his name, or even how he died. I felt curious about him, but I wasn't quite sure where to start. I even wondered if he was to blame for whatever seemed to be plaguing my family. Maybe that was the reason my mother hardly spoke of him.

At the time, I was looking for a summer class I could take to fill a requirement and I noticed that Arizona State University offered a course called Family History Writing. I enrolled. I figured that if I was going to be spending time on this research, I may as well get college credit for it, plus I was hoping to get some help with how to find out more about my grandfather. The first assignment was to do an interview with someone over the age of sixty who was not a parent. I was irritated, because I really wanted to focus on Booker. Then I realized that I did know someone who fit the parameters of the assignment.

When I was a little girl, my aunt Vera had lived with us for a while. Over the course of several weeks, during a particularly hot summer, she'd spent countless afternoon hours sitting on our brown leather couch in the rec room reading novels out loud to me and my sister. No one had ever done that for me before. I always credited her with my love for reading, but what I remembered the most about her, what came through clearly from the past, was that at Vera's core was pure kindness. She was one of the most genuine and thoughtful people I'd ever met, and I knew she'd help me. After living in California for several years, Vera moved back to Mississippi, to a town called Greenville, a one-hour drive from Greenwood.

I called her on the phone, explained the assignment, and she agreed to tell me about her life. We made plans to chat in detail the following week. When we spoke, Vera talked about the work she and her siblings had to do every day to keep the family going. They had an extensive garden that provided the majority of their food. "We took care of that garden and it took care of us," she said.

During the majority of our conversation she was the Vera of my memories—sweet, thoughtful, and generous in her recollections of others. All that changed when we began to talk about Greenwood. When I asked her what it was like to grow up there, Vera paused, took in a deep breath, and then, in a voice filled with such disgust it sounded as if she was on the verge of spitting on the floor, she said slowly, "Greenwood was a *racist, racist* town."

"What do you mean?" I asked, wondering more about the sudden change in her tone than about what she'd actually said.

"It was a *racist* town. One night, Vette," she continued in a tense whisper, "I was driving my car and I pulled up to a red light. Some White men pulled up next to me. They started saying, 'Do you smell something? I smell something. It smells like nigger.' I was too afraid to even turn my head. I just sat there waiting for the light to change. It was only me and them on the road, and I was so afraid. I can still remember how I felt sitting there in my car. I just knew they were going to kill me. I really believed I was going to die that night."

When she finished talking, I sat there trying to work out in my head how I should respond. I wanted to say something to comfort her, but I couldn't think of anything to say besides, "That's awful." I felt inept. I'd initiated this conversation, and it was clear I was un-prepared for what I was hearing. I didn't know what to do with the answers to my own questions.

The silence between us was making me feel uncomfortable. I quickly scanned my list of questions and decided to ask Vera about some of the major assassinations that took place in the '60s. Every time I'd hear people talk about the day John F. Kennedy died they'd begin by explaining where they were when they heard the news, how they waited to hear what would happen next, and so on. That's not how Vera responded.

"When they killed JFK and then Martin Luther King Jr., we thought they'd kill anyone who tried to help Black people. We thought it was all over. If they could kill the president, then no one was safe." Nothing Vera was saying was all that different from the types of things I'd heard about the civil rights movement when I was a kid in school. What was different was that it was my aunt Vera—not Rosa Parks, not a legend or an icon—it was my sweet-hearted aunt Vera who'd believed her life was about to meet a terrifying end simply because she'd been Black and driving her car one night in Greenwood. It was my aunt Vera who believed, for a time at least, that all hope was lost for Blacks and that anyone, from the most powerful man in the free world on down, would pay with their very life if they tried to help someone who shared her skin color.

Whether or not she sensed my discomfort I didn't know. But I was thankful when she began talking again. This time, she recalled her college years and her start in teaching. At one point she explained, "All my life I had been told never to look a White person in the eye, because then they'd say I was an *insolent* nigga. But then when I got a job, I had to work right next to them. That was one of the strangest and hardest things I've ever been through, learning how to look a White person in the face."

Each time she made a comment like that, racially centered, infused with hurt, not anger, I found myself wanting to say something meaningful, but nothing came to mind. Discomfort swelled in me as I tried to think of a way to move out of the emotionally charged territory we'd veered into. "Wait a minute," I said, surprising myself with how excited I sounded. There was at least one date I knew from school about civil rights. I did some quick math in my head. "The schools were integrated in the mid-1950s when you were in first or second grade. Didn't you go to school with any White kids?"

In a voice that sounded like she was explaining to a grown man the truth about Santa Claus, Vera said, "Vette, they didn't really integrate the schools. Just because they passed a law doesn't mean thangs changed. I graduated high school without ever being in a class with a White person. When they passed the law to integrate the public schools, the White people just put their kids in private schools."

I felt my insides begin to shrink. I'd assumed that when legislation changed, people changed, customs changed. The moment Vera said the schools didn't really integrate, I knew without a doubt that my belief had not only been false but grossly naïve.

As she spoke, I was not confronted with how little I knew about Black history, because I was already aware of that. Rather, listening to Vera made me realize how little I knew about what living that history actually felt like. It seemed that, just a handful of decades ago, living as a Black person in the South was to live in terror.

There was something in her voice that made me sense it was time to wrap up the call. I was preparing to express my thanks when I realized I hadn't even asked her about her father, the main reason I'd chosen to interview her in the first place. I felt reluctant. Just speaking to Vera had made it quite clear to me that there was no way I could understand anyone's life without understanding the world they'd lived in. But I was also resistant because she was already worked up from talking about the movement and I didn't want to upset her any further. I figured her father must be the source of some shame, otherwise she probably would have mentioned him.

I couldn't have been more wrong. When Vera began to talk about her father, something in her shifted. She became calm and certain, focused, self-possessed. I sensed that, instead of avoiding the story, she'd been waiting to take me there until she was confident I was ready to make the journey.

When Vera presented me with her father's story, she did it with care, unwrapping it for me as if it were a delicate treasure wrapped in fine, century-old paper.

Willie and Annie Wright never told Booker about his mother, Rosie. Instead, they said they'd found him one day on their doorstep when he was just a toddler. Whoever placed him there hadn't even left a note. According to the Wrights, no one ever came back for him or checked to make sure he was okay. Since they didn't know what to do with him, Willie and Annie let Booker stay and raised him more out of pity than out of love.

Booker played that story over and over again in his head. There was one aspect about it that stuck with him, one he just couldn't resolve. How could someone have abandoned him? Why didn't his parents ever return to make sure he was okay? When he spoke about how he'd been left on a doorstep, Booker would always tell his children, "That's why I'm going to see after you all, I'm not giving you to nobody, nobody's going to take you, you're mine, you're mine."

The Wrights raised Booker with a sterilized, arms-length-away style of parenting. They never had any kids of their own and made little effort to make the boy they'd "found" feel like family. Booker wasn't allowed to go to school, so he reached adulthood without ever learning to read and write. He worked for years as a waiter at a restaurant called Lusco's, where he served White folks. Vera explained that since it was difficult for Blacks to get home loans at the time, Booker saved up his tips for more than twenty years until he had enough to open his own restaurant.

I could hear the smile in her voice as Vera said, "When he opened Booker's Place, he felt like he was his own man." Almost sixty years later, and her father's joy was vivid to her.

She also cleared up questions I had about the family tree. When Booker was still in his twenties, he fell in love with my grandmother, Doris Cooley. Doris came from a desperately poor family that lived in Baptist Town, a Greenwood neighborhood known for its poverty and violence.

Her parents ruled their house with a heavy dose of religious fervor. Since Booker wasn't the churchgoing type, they had deep reservations about his involvement with their daughter. They believed she could do better if she'd only wait. In spite of their reservations, Doris and Booker got married. They had two children in under two years—my aunt Vera and my mother, Katherine.

Not long after my mother was born, Doris crumbled under her parents' criticisms and filed for divorce. She went on to have more children, five in all. She married again, but her second husband was murdered one night when he was on his way home. He was robbed and set on fire while he was still alive.

Doris and her children continued to live in her parents' house, but during the summers, Vera and Katherine went to stay with Booker, who worked hard to be an intricate part of their lives. He could always make Vera laugh, taught her valuable lessons, and never seemed to feel sorry for himself even though he'd grown up in a home where he knew he was unwanted.

In time, Booker fell in love with a woman named Mildred, who everyone called Honey. With skin that matched her name and soft curly hair, Honey was one of the most beautiful girls in town.

I didn't know how to feel. My grandfather was responsible, joyful, funny, attentive, determined, and accomplished. I could hear in Vera's voice that she was swelling with pride for him, but there was something else there as well. Saddled with her affection for her father was an unmistakable sense of loss that was so deep it humbled and silenced me.

Vera told me that her father's death was somewhat random. Booker was shot by a Black kid everyone knew from the neighborhood who went by the nickname "Blackie." After the shooting, Booker survived for three days in the hospital before passing away.

Vera and I stayed on the phone for a few more minutes, expressing gratitude for one another before saying good-bye. After our conversation, I couldn't stop thinking about Booker, mainly because of how Vera had come to life when she spoke about him. The more she talked about her father, the more her voice changed—hope, love, and immense loss were all bound together and riding on her words. I wanted to bottle up her sound, her emotional resonance, and share her Booker Wright with the world.

I had one more question that I doubted Vera would be able to answer: Why hadn't my mother shared this beautiful man's story with me?

IN THE DAYS THAT followed, I wanted to know more about my grandfather, but in some corner of my consciousness, I decided not to act on my curiosity, opting instead to settle for the glow rising up inside of me. So much of my life and my parents' lives were lived on the surface—the football star who couldn't read, the beautiful mother who rarely spoke, and me, so hopeless with my feelings about race and family that I'd resorted to pretending they didn't exist at all. I wondered if Booker's story was the same way, ideal on the surface but less so underneath. My knowledge of him probably would've remained shallow if it hadn't been for what happened next.

The second assignment for my Family History Writing class was to reconstruct a place from the past. Each student had to have their place approved before completing the assignment. During a telephone conversation with my instructor about the locations I was considering, she recommended that I write about Booker's Place. I chuckled and explained that since Greenwood was such a small town, there probably wasn't any information available about his restaurant.

She responded by telling me to check my inbox.

I found an email from her with a link to an article written by an oral historian named Amy Evans. Evans was at the University of Mississippi at Oxford, and she'd conducted an interview with the owners of a restaurant called Lusco's. I remembered Vera saying that Lusco's was where Booker had worked for more than two decades.

The interview was from the 1990s when a woman named Karen Pinkston was running the restaurant with her husband, Andy, the great-grandson of the people who'd first opened Lusco's. It was seventy pages long. I quickly scanned the document for my grandfather's name. Booker wasn't mentioned much, but Karen did say that he'd been the restaurant's most famous waiter.

Then I searched online for information about the woman who'd written the piece, Amy Evans. I was curious to find out whether or not she knew more about Booker. I found her on the university website, where a phone number was listed for her department. Without really thinking about what I was going to say, I picked up my telephone and dialed the number.

"Hi, my name is Yvette Johnson, and my grandfather was a man named Booker Wright. I was just looking through an article you wrote about—"

"Booker Wright? Did you say your grandfather's name was Booker Wright?"

"Yes. I was reading an interview you did with Karen Pinkston. I just wanted to know if you knew anything more about him," I asked, climbing out of the chair and pacing back and forth through my office, living room, and kitchen.

"Well, yes, of course—well, wait, wait; you should talk to John T. He knows more about your grandfather than I do; he's been studying Greenwood and Lusco's and, well, let me just get him for you." Then she was gone, and I was on hold.

As I waited for her to come back, I walked over to my kitchen table and moved my fingers along the lines in its black wood. I was going over her tone of voice in my mind. Was it just in my head, or did Amy Evans sound excited?

"This is John T. Edge," a voice said. "Now, Amy said that you're Booker Wright's *granddaughter*, is that right?" He sounded quintessentially Southern. His voice was nasal, unhurried, and he overstated his vowels, slowly drawing them out as if there was no such thing as time.

"Yes," I said, as I now considered both he and Amy might be

referring to a different Booker Wright. "My grandfather was from a small town called Greenwood, he owned a little café—"

"Booker's Place. It was called Booker's Place. I had no idea that he even had any children," John T. said, sounding as though he was talking more to himself than to me. Then, "Wow, where do I start? Well, your grandfather was really just an amazing man. When he was on the news back in, oh, what year was it . . ."

"What do you mean he was in the news?" I asked.

"You don't know about him being on the news?" He sounded incredulous, as if getting oneself on the news was a monumental feat.

"No," I said.

"Okay, have you heard of Lusco's?"

"Yes, yes, that's where he worked."

"Yeah, well, Lusco's was one of the most, if not *the* most, popular restaurant in Greenwood, and your grandfather was the favorite waiter there. Everyone knew him. One day, some news people went down to Greenwood—this was back in the sixties—and they were interviewing people to find out about the civil rights movement there. Well, they asked your grandfather what it was like to be black in Greenwood, and everyone thought he'd say things were fine, but he didn't. I haven't seen the footage, but he told them how bad it was. He let 'em have it. He didn't hold back. What he said shook up that whole town. He lost his job after it aired. It was a big deal what your grandfather did. I tried years ago to find the footage but never had any luck." He paused for a moment and then said slowly, "Hey, well, you're the family. You have a right to that footage. You have a right to see it for yourself."

I put the phone down. I felt like a gust of wind had just rushed into my house and inside my body. As silly as it sounded, I felt like Booker's spirit was seeking me out. Through the quagmire of time and death, he was reaching out for me, and, like a deft surgeon, his story was going to heal the wounds of my shame-filled existence, leaving only the most minute scar.

I couldn't believe this was happening

As great as my excitement was, as alive as I felt in that moment, my joy was tempered by a small amount of fear. How had I never heard this story before? Was there a chance it wasn't true? Was this really my grandfather? Next to the strong, intricate hold Booker's story had on me, there lay a tiny seed of doubt.

Did my aunt Vera know about this? If she did, I was certain she didn't know how important other people thought it was, because she surely would've mentioned it to me. I pulled out her number and dialed it. I stumbled over my words and asked her if she knew about Booker appearing on the news. She didn't. I told her about my call with John T. Edge and his excitement about finding a descendant of Booker's.

After a long pause she said slowly and carefully, "Vette, did you tell them it was Booker *Wright*?"

"Yes, Vera, yes. They say that what he said on the news changed Greenwood." I realized I was shouting into the phone. I paused to give her a chance to process it all. She was quiet for an agonizingly long time.

Then she said, "Okay, Vette, well, let me know how it goes. Alright." She was using her good-bye voice. We exchanged I love yous and ended our call.

In spite of her lackluster response, I was determined to cling to my joy. In the days that followed, I sat in front of my computer each night while my young sons slept upstairs, trying to find something, anything more about Booker. I searched civil rights archives, books about Greenwood, but I couldn't find anything else about his accomplishments, if there were any.

One night, it occurred to me to search through the online archives of SNCC, SCLC, and the NAACP to see if there was any mention of my grandfather. Excitement pulsed through me as I dug through the Internet, looking at their lists of veterans of the movement. After several hours, I still couldn't find my grandfather's name mentioned in association with these historic civil rights organizations. It seemed that if Booker Wright had been an activist at all, he'd been an accidental one.

I did find one thing. In those disappointing midnight hours of searching, I stumbled upon a reference to someone in my family. It was in a book about the movement called *Weary Feet, Rested Souls*. "The first black sheriff's deputy in Leflore County, Charles Cooley, was hired in 1971, and he went on to a twenty-five-year career in law enforcement."

Charles Cooley was my mother's uncle. He'd helped take care of my grandma Doris and her children. During my childhood, I'd always assumed my mother's father had died when she was young because, while she almost never spoke of Booker, she did mention Uncle Charlie more than a few times. My grandmother passed away in 2002, and a few weeks after her funeral, Uncle Charlie was sitting in his house watching television with his wife and children when he got up, walked into the bathroom, and shot himself in the head.

That night, when I saw my uncle's name in that book, I felt almost duped. I'd been searching for evidence of my grandfather's involvement in the movement, but all I found was more evidence about how my family was broken.

I began to fear that if I looked any deeper into my grandfather's story, I'd disturb the towering legend I was determined to build in my mind. I was beginning to contemplate giving up when I stumbled upon a description of a roundtable discussion that had taken place at a conference on Southern cuisine, in which a Mississippi State senator had led a discussion about Booker Wright, who he described as being a "catalyst for the movement."

A catalyst for the movement.

I read that line over and over again, fireworks going off inside of me. By "movement" he had to mean the civil rights movement. Was this really happening?

I felt as though I was standing on the precipice of a brand-new tomorrow for myself and for my children. I called a friend to share my joy with her. I was talking too fast, stuttering, and trying not to cry. Finally, a flood of tears overtook me, and in a rush of emotion I blurted out, "I always thought I came from nothing, but maybe not. Maybe, maybe I come from something."

Part Four
Some Sort of Charm

There had been a kind of innocence in everything about the old years that gave some sort of charm even to the worst of it. In a way, of course, the innocence had survived everything too. But it seemed a kind of innocence, now, that has no business being so innocent.

James Agee
"1928 Story"

A Place for the
Planter Class

Not long after John T. Edge moved to Oxford, Mississippi, in the 1990s to attend graduate school at Ole Miss, he began taking a particular weekend trip over and over again. He would drive first west and then south, leaving behind the lights and hustle of his college town. The farther south he drove, the deeper he went into the flat, damp, ever-blooming Mississippi Delta, where jade-colored trees and grasslands consumed the landscape. After about ninety minutes, he would pass a wide-open field where a brown, weather-worn sign proclaimed, "Welcome to Greenwood, Cotton Capital of the World." The welcome message was embraced on either side by two just-ripe cotton bolls, painted in feminine curves.

After another fifteen minutes of driving, John T. would reach his destination. On Carrollton Avenue, nestled between a Black Baptist church and the offices for a local cemetery, was Lusco's, a restaurant with an unassuming exterior of aging redbrick walls and large windows that revealed little beyond its foyer.

When John T. parked his car and passed through the double doors leading into the restaurant, he was rarely alone. Oftentimes, he had sweet-talked dates and friends into accompanying him on these dining excursions by describing the restaurant's tantalizing tempura-battered onion rings or the deceptively escalating heat of the buttery Lusco's shrimp sauce. He used these sensual descriptions to lure his companions to the restaurant, but in reality, it wasn't the shrimp sauce that drew John T. there. It wasn't the oysters on the half-shell, the mouthwatering crabmeat, or even the restaurant's reputation as one of the oldest and most well-known establishments in the Mississippi Delta. It was something else altogether that compelled John T. to make that drive again and again.

Lusco's seduced him. It gently pulled him into its "anything goes" atmosphere, where one could create secrets, then leave them behind. Lusco's was a place where the drinking of illegal whiskey was once commonplace and questionable behavior still passed without question.

Most nights, John T. didn't eat in Lusco's main dining room or at its bar. John T. and his companions were usually led down a central hallway, off of which were Lusco's curtained booths. These were small, numbered rooms, or cubicles, each separated from the main hallway by colorfully patterned curtains. The cubicles or booths, as they were called, each had a freestanding table, chairs, and a button that would ring in the kitchen as an indicator to the waitstaff that service was needed. The curtained booths provided a sense of seclusion, while the Lusco's staff delivered an unspoken promise of silence. More than once, John T. explored the boundaries of that promise, like the time when he ate dinner at Lusco's with his pants down.

On that particular night, he and his three companions—two male and one female—were seated in a booth. The men consumed their food, leaning over plates to filet pompano and slice into a T-bone, while their trousers rested around their ankles. John T.'s lady friend kept her skirt on, but removed her black bra and placed it on a lamp in the center of the table. At one point, John T. pressed the button to call for the waiter, who brought them ice and asked if they were enjoying their meal. In regards to their attire, the waiter didn't even raise an eyebrow.

On another occasion, John T. was with a friend who had way

too much to drink and ended up falling over in his chair. The staff was so swift and quiet when they came and swept him away that John T. didn't even notice his friend's departure. John T.'s experience at Lusco's wasn't unique. For decades, the Lusco's brand was greatly influenced by two things: the quality of its food and the experiences created by its waitstaff.

John T. was fascinated with the restaurant. In spite of Lusco's upscale clientele and amazing food, it was located south of the river in a neighborhood that was becoming more and more depressed economically. Decades before, the land south of the river but north of the train tracks was where many White Greenwood residents made their homes and managed their fortunes in business offices throughout the area. During those years, the train tracks served as a dividing line between the races, and Lusco's was just north of them.

In the 1970s, Blacks began buying houses in the neighborhoods north of the tracks but south of the river. As they moved in, more and more White residents sold their homes and moved into North Greenwood, on the other side of the river. Lusco's never moved from Carrollton Avenue, even though crime and abandoned buildings were becoming the norm for the historic street.

Many Whites maintained business offices in South Greenwood, but by nightfall, the streets, stores, and neighborhoods on that side of town were almost completely void of White faces. Nevertheless, Andy and Karen Pinkston could still count on their regular customers—the Greenwood gentry, remnants of the planter class—to keep the restaurant going. Night after night, Greenwood Whites would leave the north side of town, with its towering oak trees, perfectly trimmed lawns, and private schools, to travel down into Baptist Town to eat at Lusco's.

It seemed to John T. that for some people Lusco's was more than a restaurant; it was "a kind of redoubt, a last bastion for the planter class." He decided to make Lusco's the research topic for a graduate seminar class. His trips to Greenwood continued, but now he began conducting interviews with people who'd been regulars at Lusco's for years, some for close to half a century.

Once his research began, it wasn't long before John T. began to notice something familiar. Again and again, he encountered people who wanted to reminisce about one person in particular. Almost as if on cue, his interviews would begin to veer into a land of sweet remembrances, and John T. would be entertained with stories about Lusco's most famous and dearly loved waiter.

Even though almost thirty years had passed since Booker Wright had waited on his last customer at Lusco's Restaurant, the regulars remembered him with both joy and an irritation about something they couldn't seem to reconcile. In a town where stories of the olden days were told again and again, each one treated like a cherished strand in a never-ending tapestry, there was one strand that stood out, twisted, unyielding. Booker's importance in, and then apparent dismissal of, the Greenwood planter class was still as vexing for Lusco's regulars in the '90s as it was on that infamous night when Booker appeared on national TV.

When he started working at Lusco's around 1940, the restaurant didn't have printed menus. If they had provided customers with printed menus, then Booker may have never even met the man who interviewed him. The night when Frank De Felitta met Booker, he'd been dragged to Lusco's by a friend who wanted him to hear Booker sing the menu.

There are a variety of theories about why Lusco's didn't offer printed menus. Some believe it was to ensure that the only people who came in were those who could afford the food regardless of how much the restaurant charged. Others think it was a way to maintain segregation. Without having to say that only Whites were welcome, the restaurant could send the same message by charging a Black person twenty dollars for a cup of coffee.

A few members of the Lusco's clan have floated the idea that since the restaurant started out as a place that just served a few dishes to locals, there wasn't a need for menus. But some people who worked there believe there just wasn't any sense in printing menus, since no one on their all-Black waitstaff could read or write anyway.

This last theory may be the closest to the truth. When Booker started working at Lusco's in the early 1940s, illiteracy in the Black community was common. Most Blacks working in Greenwood at the time were the children of sharecroppers, and in the Delta, "the school calendar was built around the cotton season, which meant that most black youngsters were in school only when they weren't needed in the fields." Some estimates indicate this applied to children as young as five years of age.

Sharecropping families who refused to keep their children out of school could be fired, which would mean, in addition to being unemployed, they would become homeless. With this double threat hanging over their heads, most sharecropping families complied when farm managers insisted their children stay on the farm to work instead of attending school.

It's also true that in the early days, the menu at Lusco's was just a few signature dishes. However, the menu eventually grew into an extensive list of offerings. Some of the waitstaff developed their own style of note taking to help them remember their customers' orders, but not Booker. The customers were amazed by his ability to recall every order, including special changes, regardless of how large the party was.

Over time, Booker transitioned from simply telling his customers the menu to singing it for them. He developed a jovial-sounding, lighthearted, rhyming song that he'd perform whenever someone needed to know what dishes the restaurant served. Even the regulars, who knew what they were going to order before they even entered the restaurant, would often ask Booker to perform the menu. His song became an added value for Lusco's, part of the experience enjoyed by only the wealthiest members of Greenwood's planter class. Booker Wright was woven into the very fabric of their way of life. He was a familiar comfort. They came to expect and look forward to the waiter's humor and his song. It wasn't so much that Booker was one of them. Really it seemed that, in a way, he belonged to them.

A Magical Town

When Booker began working at Lusco's, he was about fourteen years old and had already lived a long life. When he was eight years old, Annie decided she'd had enough of Willie Wright, Booker's father, an angry drunk and a gambler. She took Booker and the two of them left Willie and the tense, unstable, and violent household he'd created. They moved away to a small town near Greenwood. The only problem was that Annie was ill. She may have thought she'd recover when she and Booker moved away from Willie. Later, Booker speculated among friends that Annie was likely suffering from cancer.

Since Annie was so sick, securing food for the two of them was left to Booker. He never mentioned all that he had to do to survive, though years later on the national news, he'd describe how "Night after night I lay down and I dream about what I had to go through with. I don't want my children to have to go through with that." Booker was fourteen when Annie died.

He ended up in Greenwood. In some ways, Greenwood was the perfect place for someone like Booker, and in other ways it was the worst.

The idea of a mid-twentieth-century, mostly White, all-American suburban small town where problems are simple, communities are inviting, and a solid moral fiber is valued above all else is considered by most to be just an overdone cliché popularized by television shows like *Leave It to Beaver* and then later mocked by the *The Stepford Wives*. But if there was ever a town like that—not the comical, stifled, repressed version portrayed in Hollywood—but a real town in a real place where a collection of strangers came together to build a community in which almost everything was centered around family—that town was Greenwood in the early 1900s.

One of the town's most memorable citizens was a woman named Sara Criss, who was fond of saying that her life began in Greenwood, Mississippi, on April Fool's Day. Born in 1921, Criss would go on to work for thirty years as the Greenwood Bureau Chief for the Memphis-based *Commercial Appeal* newspaper. In the 1990s, she penned her memoir, leaving explicit instructions that it was intended for family and no one else. Having not only lived through the tumultuous civil rights years but having covered them for her newspaper as well, Sara understood more than most the potential for her writing to open old but still festering wounds.

It wasn't until after Sara passed away in 2009 that her daughter, Mary Carol Miller, began to read through her mother's written memories. Realizing their historical significance, Mary Carol made the difficult decision to go against her mother's request and to post Sara's writings online on a website called *Daughter of the Delta*.

In the introduction, Mary Carol describes her mother's love for Greenwood by explaining, "Had you asked her if there was ever a more enchanting town in which to be born or a more comforting and adventurous street on which to grow up . . . she would have given you that 'Why in the world would you ask me that?' gaze and shaken her head, 'No, of course not.' It was the best of times in her mind, with the best people."

Sara wasn't alone in her sweet sentiment for Greenwood. A good number of people who called Greenwood home developed a covetous love and a feeling of belonging to their town that ran so deep they became defined by it. They knew Greenwood when it was little more than damp earth, and it was on that earth where they'd constructed a city out of hope and dreams. There is nothing clichéd about the devotion those early residents felt for their town; their commitment to Greenwood was authentic and lasting.

The residents weren't only committed to Greenwood, they were committed to one another as well. It's almost impossible to overstate just how much they loved being together. After her mother died, Mary Carol and a few of her friends decided to make a series of picture books about Greenwood. The three volumes they published are packed with images of the town when it was still in its infancy. About the photographs taken at the turn of the century, Mary Carol writes that they "generally illustrate an almost exhausting vitality in Greenwood. Parades with lavishly decorated cars and marching children winding through town, pageants with elaborate tableaux and commemorative trinkets, football teams and festivals and church socials and patriotic fervor."

The exhausting vitality Mary Carol describes didn't dissipate with time. Decades later, during her own childhood, the townsfolk would gather for almost anything, including "the apex, the ultimate: Friday afternoons when Greenwood High School's band took over Howard Street, complete with cheerleaders, floats, and pep rallies."

The infatuation Greenwood residents felt for their town was directly proportional to how hard they'd worked to build it.

Initially, the town wasn't a destination in and of itself.

Even though Greenwood is in the eastern section of the Delta, almost an hour from the Great Mississippi, it's still a town of waters because it is surrounded by rivers. Greenwood's northernmost border is the Tallahatchie River, which meets with the Yalobusha on the northeast corner of town to create the Yazoo, which flows south and then makes a sharp turn west, cutting through the heart of the city to separate the communities of North and South Greenwood. North Greenwood, where most of the White residents live, is almost completely encapsulated by the horseshoe-shaped river system created by the three bodies of water.

The Tallahatchie and the Yazoo run parallel to one another, but like bitter siblings, the two bodies of water flow in opposite directions. Many believe the word "Yazoo" means "river of death," which is fitting, since twenty-nine sunken Civil War ships rest below the river's greenish-brown surface. As if to not be outdone by its rival, the Tallahatchie River was the site where a child's body was found in the mid-1950s. The nature of the murder and the inconceivable torture perpetrated against that child would shake the nation and initiate a change in the destiny of an entire race of people.

But long before that historic event, Greenwood was barely anything at all. With just 308 residents in 1880, the town was a stopping point, a place to take a break, for people using the Yazoo River to transport cotton. Mary Carol describes early Greenwood as "a rickety shantytown of saloons and sheds." However, an increased focus of the US government on flood control between 1880 and 1920 meant that more and more people were able to purchase farmland in the Delta without having to worry that the Mississippi River would come and wash their investments away.

In time, Greenwood was surrounded by small farming communities, and South Greenwood was the center of commerce. At the turn of the century, the view of North Greenwood from the Yazoo was that of a vast, flat landscape that ended only when it yoked with the horizon. All this would change, though, when two investors began buying up land in North Greenwood and building estate-size lots on a street called Grand Boulevard.

The wife of one of the investors felt that since it was named "Grand," the street should offer more than flat, rectangular plots. With the help of her husband, she traveled along the edge of the Tallahatchie River and placed markers on young oak trees she wanted to have uprooted and moved to North Greenwood. In the end, a thousand trees were replanted along Grand Boulevard. Decades later, the boulevard would be defined by those towering oak trees, turning the street into a Greenwood landmark. Years later, in a *New York Times* article, the US Chambers of Commerce and the Garden Clubs of America would name Grand Boulevard one of the "10 Most Beautiful Streets in America."

The Delta was quickly entering a period some would later refer to as the Second Cotton Kingdom, and Greenwood positioned itself right at the center of it. In 1917, the town drastically shortened travel time to major cotton markets when it debuted a new train station on the Illinois Central Railroad, commonly referred to as the "Main Line of Mid-America." To capitalize on the new opportunities made possible by the station, more and more cotton men flocked to Greenwood. So many offices opened on River, Front, and Market—the streets that ran parallel to the Yazoo on its south side—that the area quickly came to be known as Cotton Row.

After studying the photographs taken during that season of innovation and newness, Mary Carol observed,

> It's not necessarily an attractive community, with piles of coal littering the dirt roads, oxen parked on the main thoroughfare, dirty plumes of smoke rising from steamboat stacks and muddy, ragged riverbanks winding through town. But there's an air of vibrancy and optimism evident in these photos, the sense that this place was on the verge of something huge, something that would carry it along to prosperity in the next century.

From 1900 to 1920, Greenwood was the fastest-growing community in the entire state of Mississippi. "Profits from cotton production and all its secondary industries brought an influx of money rolling through Greenwood's banks and out into the hands of grocers, haberdashers, milliners, hoteliers, doctors, and lawyers. With those abundant funds came an architectural revolution."

South of Market, behind Cotton Row, was Washington Street, where new, one-story homes with front-facing gables, modest front lawns, and wraparound porches were popping up. On the wide, dirt roads of Walthall, Main, Howard, and Fulton Streets—all of which ran perpendicular to Cotton Row—new businesses were opening almost daily. The streets were often crowded with cars, horse-drawn carriages, men in three-piece suits, and ladies in ankle-length, light-colored dresses who carried umbrellas to protect themselves from the Delta sun.

In 1914, a man named W. T. Fountain opened Fountain's Big Busy Store on Howard Street. From where it stood, Fountain's bright red building, with thirty different departments in its 22,500 square feet of selling space divided among three floors, was a symbol of prosperity not just in Greenwood or the Delta but for the entire state of Mississippi. "Every year," Sara Criss wrote in her memoir, "[Fountain's] would put a large curtain over the side window until Thanksgiving afternoon, when they opened it for everyone to see what the new toys were that year."

Several blocks south of Howard Street, on Carrollton Avenue, Quinn Drug Company erected a long, dark brick building that took up almost an entire block. A Jewish couple, Mr. and Mrs. J. Kantrovitz, shortened their name to Kantor and built their own department store across from Fountain's. The building, which they called the Adeline, was made of white marble and brick. Others opened hardware stores, shoe stores, fine-dining restaurants, and jewelry stores. There was even a chiropractic office that went up, as well as a 10-cent only shop. In 1921, Charles and Marie Lusco opened Lusco's Grocery Store just south of Carrollton, on the corner of Johnson and Main.

What began as a grocery store eventually turned into a place for men, well-off members of the planter class, to gather in the small storeroom to drink an illegal alcohol concoction that Charles Lusco made himself. The locals called it *Dago Red*. The term *Dago* was a racial slur for Italians, many of whom were settling in the Delta.

Just when the grocery store was really becoming a success, the family was rocked by three tragedies. First, the grocery store burned to the ground. But Charles and Marie didn't waste any time worrying about what was lost. Instead, they quickly purchased another, much larger building on Carrollton Avenue, a few blocks from the train tracks, and opened Lusco's Restaurant in 1933.

Then, their oldest daughter, Marie, whom everyone called Dear, was married to a fireman and raising a family when her daughter died of pneumonia. The entire Lusco clan was devastated by the loss. The final blow came when, while still mourning their daughter's death, Dear's husband suffered a heart attack while he was battling a blaze. The people of Greenwood said he must have died of a broken heart. Dear was left with children to raise and no skills besides working in the restaurant. So that's what she did. She joined her parents in the business. Eventually, her two sisters came on board as well, and they continued to thrive in the restaurant business even after Charles and Marie passed away.

Even though everyone knew the Lusco family, not everyone chose to dine at their restaurant. For example, Sara Criss's father worked at a cotton oil company, one of the many businesses that sprang up in response to Greenwood's growing cotton industry. Yet, for reasons he kept to himself, Sara's father differed from most of his peers in that he didn't make going to Lusco's a tradition for his young family. But Sara never felt like she missed out on anything. As the town continued to grow, circuses and traveling shows would come to Greenwood at least once a year. The traveling entertainers would set up a large tent in a vacant lot and offer educational classes, plays, and minstrel shows throughout each day. For much of the nineteenth and early twentieth centuries, wildly popular minstrel shows portrayed dimwitted, ever-jolly Blacks dancing, wisecracking, and performing plantation songs. Minstrels solidified the image of the happy, simple-minded slave and were often performed by Whites in blackface.

Mary Carol acknowledges that the way her mother remembers her town's history doesn't quite encompass the entire picture. She writes that "Greenwood and the Mississippi Delta, in the 1920s, was a harsh and brutal place for many of its inhabitants, white and black, but . . . for Sara, looking back from 1990 to her childhood, Greenwood was a magical town, set squarely in the center of the universe, and peopled by kind and quirky characters."

One of those "quirky characters" might have been Tom Hunley, who was the inspiration for one of the most iconic and lasting images of stereotypical poor, simpleminded Southern Blacks. A man named J. P. Alley was living in Greenwood during the early 1900s when he walked past Hunley, an ex-slave, mopping the floor of an office building. The two had a brief conversation that somehow humored Alley. He decided to create a comic sketch based on Hunley, which he called Hambone's Meditations. Hambone spoke broken English and shared with readers half-baked philosophical ideas. Eventually, the cartoon was syndicated and the caricature of Tom Hunley became a part of national consciousness. Two cigar companies used Hambone in their logo and the image appeared on numerous "plates, clocks, tins, cans, and glass jars."

In 1943, another character of note rose out of Greenwood and onto the national stage. A young Black kid who'd grown up forty minutes outside of Greenwood got the chance to play his guitar live on the radio. The station, WGRM, was broadcast from the second floor of a building on Howard Street and marked the introduction of B. B. King to the airwaves. Inside of ten years, King would become one of the most important and influential figures in R&B, producing songs that regularly appeared high on the *Billboard* charts, touring and performing almost nonstop, and founding his own record label.

It's no wonder that Sara saw magic in her town. It must have seemed as though anything that came out of Greenwood was destined for greatness. Mary Carol put it best when she observed that "looking back at those days, captured by these long-discarded cameras, there is a pervasive sense of pride and energy infusing the streets of Greenwood, a belief that the good times were just going to roll on forever."

A Not-So-Magical Town

Similar to where Booker lived when he was young, a good number of the Blacks who called Greenwood home in the 1950s and '60s were living in areas the locals referred to as "the country." These were plantation communities on the outskirts of Greenwood.

On weekends, Black and White "country folks" would gather up their families, along with their minimal weekly earnings, and head into town. Before noon on a Saturday, it often felt as though Greenwood's population had doubled with the mass of people that flooded the downtown shopping district. Once they arrived in town, though, Blacks and Whites went their separate ways.

Author Sara Criss describes this division by explaining that in Greenwood, "we had a totally segregated society. There were no black employees in stores or businesses except in janitorial and maid capacities. Blacks did not go to white restaurants, theaters, and other places of entertainment. Public swimming pools were for white only and black only. They [blacks] did not use the City Park or participate in any of the summer recreation programs except in their own part of town, which had one park, a swimming pool, and a summer playground program sponsored by the Park Commission. The schools were totally segregated, as were the churches."

Johnson Street, just a few blocks from Booker's Place, marked the farthest north that Blacks were allowed to freely travel in Greenwood, and the street was the heartbeat of Black commerce. Blacks bought clothes at Stanley's Department Store or Kornfield's, had their shoes fixed at Collins Shoe Shop, and saw films at the Dixie, the Black-run movie theater. There were places to get hot dogs where only Whites could enter, but Blacks could wait outside and order through the window.

On Friday and Saturday nights, almost all the stores on Johnson Street stayed open late to accommodate the Blacks who crowded into the shops and eateries. Someone walking down the street during those bustling hours would get a sampling of whatever sounds were trending in Black music at the time, intertwined with the boisterous voices of friends gathered together in small cafés to exchange news and gossip. It was in these late hours when the economic difference among Blacks really showed. There were Blacks who could afford not just the food at Booker's Place but the complete experience. Booker's patrons had nice clothes, cars to get from here to there, and cash to buy the booze they brought in with them, and they weren't saving up all their money each week for a single night out. Blacks who could afford to go to Booker's Place were in the minority, because the level of poverty in their communities had reached catastrophic highs.

Segregation and discrimination greatly limited their employment opportunities. Good paying jobs for Blacks were so scarce that the very idea of moving up the economic ladder was almost mythical, little more than fodder for children's bedtime stories. Most of the jobs for Greenwood's Black middle class were service positions in the homes of Whites.

Most Blacks barely made enough money to feed and clothe themselves and their children. Finding decent housing was a constant problem. According to historian Charles Payne, "Eighty-two percent of Negro housing in [Leflore] county was substandard, which in the Delta could mean sub-any-human-standard. Nevertheless, Negroes living in tar-paper shacks with one or two light bulbs would regularly receive higher utility bills than White families in modern homes." In 1960, the average White family in Leflore County was bringing in $5,200 a year, just below the national average of $5,600, while Black families in Leflore averaged an income of $1,400 annually.

In a moment that illustrated what those numbers actually meant for daily living, a young Black veteran returned to the Delta in 1946 and was deeply disturbed when he visited a family "where there were fourteen children, half-naked, without a bed in the house, with no food, burning cotton stalks to keep warm." Greenwood resident attorney Alix Sanders mentioned that while not all Whites hated Blacks, many did. "All you had to do to qualify for the hatred was to be Black. And being Black meant you were not free to do a lot of little things." Race dictated "the language you used, the tone, where you worked, how you walked, what you did." Sanders explained that Blacks were "trained at a real early age" how to act in a way that would be acceptable to Whites. These social rules were not required of all Blacks.

In a sort of caste system, Whites in Greenwood had different expectations for different types of Blacks. Sanders recalled that some of the things Booker was able to do "would not have been tolerated from a Black of quote lesser standing." Sanders described owning a business and driving a nice car as things Booker was allowed to do when other Blacks were not. Booker "was held in a unique kind of esteem as a business person functioning and making money." Sanders said that while Booker would have been referred to by some Whites as an "uppity nigger, but he was smart enough to never allow himself to be trapped into being cast as an uppity nigger. He could go places and function where lesser Blacks would not go and function well."

Booker had connections. Walter Williams worked at a local car dealership, and he marveled at how Booker's relationships with Whites enabled him to get "help that the average person couldn't get, especially if he was Black." On one occasion, Booker provided Walter with a massive amount of cash as a down payment on a car; the difference was being financed through the local bank, a place where most Blacks would not dare enter.

It would seem that Booker wore an air of respectability, that he had a presence about him that could have cost other Blacks a severe beating. If it was believed that a Black person felt good about themselves, if they came across as holding themselves in high esteem, they might be called "uppity." A Black person with the confidence to make even momentary eye contact with a White person in Greenwood ran the risk of being called "insolent," and potentially of having someone decide to prove to you that you were nothing more than trash.

These were the things Booker never talked about. How he managed to operate a business on the Black side of town, and not just work on the White side of town but to build something akin to rapport with the White elites. It would appear that, like walking on a high wire, Booker was able to make the necessary shifts in tone and stature in order to morph into whoever he needed to be in any given moment.

Local Blacks must have seen in Booker a man who, in a climate of poverty, unemployment, and unchecked violence, was doing quite well financially, in spite of his color. Even if they didn't personally witness the practiced camaraderie Booker shared with Whites, they were certainly aware that his job was a rare one for a Black man. It was a solid, highly respectable, middle-class job at an exclusive restaurant with prices beyond the budgets of many White, mid-income families. This meant that, almost nightly at Lusco's, Booker spent time conversing and laughing with some of the most powerful men in town.

In addition to holding a respectable job far from the fields, it was widely rumored that Booker took home a considerable amount of cash from tips every time he waited tables at Lusco's. This theory was proven correct by the rental properties he purchased and the money he was able to invest in his own restaurant.

After working at Lusco's for two decades, Booker took what he'd learned and opened his own place. Because of segregation, he didn't have many locations to choose from. He decided on a little building at 211 West McLaurin Street. He knew that since his place was on McLaurin, most people would just assume that it was like all the other dives on the street. His business would have to thrive from word-of-mouth; therefore, just like at Lusco's, it was the customer's experience that needed to shine.

To someone driving past, Booker's Place couldn't have looked like much. A Coca-Cola sign with the words "Booker's Place" hung above the entrance, which was a set of wooden double doors, each containing a large window through which sunlight flooded the restaurant. Though the interior was only about thirty feet across and fifty feet in length, Booker managed to create a space that worked both as a full-service restaurant and a nightclub.

When people entered his restaurant, Booker almost always knew them by name. He'd greet them with such warmth it was if he'd been waiting all night for their arrival. He'd ask for updates about sick relatives or inquire about recent travels. After catching up with Booker, his customers would find a place to sit.

Someone going to Booker's with the intention of having a quick meal alone could turn to their left and eat at the long, shiny mahogany bar that ran almost the entire length of the wall. If several friends wanted to gather together, they could use one of the spacious, built-in wooden booths on the right side of the restaurant. For those out on dates, there were the freestanding tables in the middle of the room. Each was covered with red Formica, with its own dimly lit lamp in the center. Then just beyond the tables was a small dance floor for anyone who wanted to move to the music that flowed out of the jukebox located to the right of the entrance.

Booker even found a way to take care of those who needed a secret place to play illegal card games. There were two doors on the back wall, and the one on the right opened into the kitchen—a small space that didn't have air-conditioning but did have a narrow door leading to the outside that was often left open to let heat escape. Somehow, in that tiny space, Booker managed to squeeze in a table that people used for poker and other games. To protect his card-playing clientele, he always had one man watching the front entrance and another keeping an eye out back, so Booker could be alerted if the police were coming.

The other door on the back wall led to a short hallway that had a pay phone and a stool in it. The hallway ended with an entrance to a tiny bathroom containing a small mirror, a toilet, a sink, and just enough room to turn around in.

Booker's Place opened in the morning and offered breakfast to people before they went off to work or school. Midday he sold a sit-down lunch, and even offered a bagged meal for those who didn't have the time to stay and eat. However, it was his dinners that helped solidify his place in Greenwood history. Chitlins, greens that had been cooking all day long, barbecue, corn muffins served with buttermilk, hamburgers, steak, chicken—the list of well-prepared offerings went on and on.

Several nights a week, when the dinner rush was slowing down, the restaurant would turn into a club, and a DJ would bring in his turntable and spin records into the morning hours. The state of Mississippi was dry until 1966, so Booker didn't have a liquor license, but that didn't keep him from selling booze. He sold whiskey to those who wanted it or ice, cups, and sodas to the patrons who brought in their own.

On a warm Saturday evening, the place was usually crowded with people spilling out onto the sidewalks or lining up just waiting for their chance to get in. The crowd itself was a colorful mix of young guys in brightly colored suits, older men in muted tones sporting fedoras, young girls in halter tops and cancan skirts that flared out at the bottom, and older women in dress suits or church clothes. Regardless of age or social status, everybody wanted to go to Booker's Place.

His success earned him resentment—not only from poor Whites who didn't think he deserved to live that kind of a life but from poor Blacks as well who felt rebuffed by the way they were treated when they tried to enter Booker's café. For many Blacks, it may have seemed that even Booker's restaurant was not safe from the caste system Greenwood used to separate acceptable Blacks from the nonacceptable. But he didn't turn down money. Blacks who wanted ice for the liquor they'd bought up the street were welcome to buy it at Booker's Place. Blacks who'd saved up money and could purchase food were welcome there as well. However, if they didn't have money the next week, they could be asked to leave.

On the nights when Booker waited tables at Lusco's, it was often his wife, Honey, who closed up for him. He worried about her because sometimes hungry, poverty-stricken Blacks who didn't have any money to spend would try to enter the restaurant. They'd hang around, asking the paying customers to buy something for them. The penniless would-be patrons quickly found themselves up against Booker's zero-tolerance policy for loitering, most of them leaving without argument.

In spite of her own business acumen, Honey was small in stature and therefore ill-equipped to handle some of the rougher people who wanted to enter Booker's Place. Given the restaurant's location on McLaurin, there was always the danger that Honey could be overtaken in front of the restaurant on the way to her car. Not wanting her to take any chances, Booker insisted that Honey always carry a gun.

She had to protect herself because calling the police wasn't an option. Blacks never knew how an encounter with a local officer would turn out. Even someone like Booker, who had relatively close relationships in the White community, couldn't count on receiving help from the Greenwood Police Force.

A Testing Ground
for Democracy

In Sara Criss's memoirs about her life in Greenwood, there's a section that deals specifically with the civil rights movement. She begins it by saying, "The Civil Rights Era, though generally thought of as being the sixties, really began in Leflore County, Mississippi, in the late summer of 1955 with the brutal killing of a fourteen-year-old Chicago Negro, Emmett Till."

In the summer of 1955, a sixty-four-year-old part-time preacher and full-time sharecropper named Moses Wright was living with his wife and children in Money, Mississippi. During a visit to Chicago to spend time with his niece, Mamie, Moses told her and her son, Emmett, about the wide-open spaces and immense beauty of the Mississippi Delta. Emmett wanted to see it for himself, so he begged Mamie to let him go. After much consideration, she gave in and let her fourteen-year-old son head down to the Delta with Moses and two of Emmett's cousins. Before Emmett left, she cautioned him to remember that life for Blacks in the South was very different than what it was like for Blacks in Chicago.

Once he arrived in Money, Emmett spent his days playing with other kids and picking cotton. One afternoon, Emmett and one of his cousins went into a White-owned store called Bryant's Grocery and Meat Market to buy some candy. The store was owned by Roy Bryant, but on that particular day, his wife, Carolyn, was in charge.

Reports on what happened inside the store are conflicting. Some people claim Emmett whistled at Carolyn. Others say that he had a speech problem and would often whistle to keep himself from stuttering. His mother would later explain that Emmett had trouble pronouncing the "B" sound, and that maybe, if he was trying to ask for bubble gum, he may have whistled to avoid falling into a stutter. Still others said that Emmett spoke to Carolyn, saying something like "Bye, baby," in order to win a bet he'd made with his cousins.

What happened afterward is not in dispute. A few nights later, on Sunday, August 28, 1955, Roy Bryant and his half-brother J. W. Milam went to Moses Wright's house, woke Emmett, and took him into the night. Till's cousin, Curtis Jones, later explained, "I was awakened by a group of men in the house. I didn't wake completely—youngsters, they sleep hard, you know. When they came, my grandfather answered the door and they asked him did he have three boys in there from Chicago. And he stated yes. So, they told him to get the one who did the talking. My grandmother was scared to death. She was trying to protect Bo [Jones's nickname for Emmett]. They told her to get back to bed. One of the guys struck her on the side of the head with a shotgun. When I woke up the next morning, I thought it was a dream."

Four days would pass from the night Emmett was taken before Curtis would hear anything about his cousin. "Wednesday I was over at some relatives' house. We was out there picking cotton. One of my uncles drove up there in that 1941 Ford. He said, 'Curtis, they found Bo.' I say, 'Is he alive?' He said, 'No, he's dead.'"

Emmett's body had surfaced in the Tallahatchie River. It was later discovered that when Emmett was taken from Moses Wright's house, he was tortured through the night and well into the morning.

The fourteen-year-old boy had been stripped naked, pistol-whipped, and had his eye gouged out, and was later shot in the head. Then Bryant and Milam used barbed wire to tie a two-hundred-pound cotton gin fan around his neck before tossing Emmett's body into the Tallahatchie River.

Mamie Till Bradley had already been alerted that her child was missing. It didn't take long for her to learn why he was taken and, as she waited for news about her son, Mamie developed an awareness that she couldn't name or say out loud. She knew deep down that he'd been murdered. Finally the call came, the one that confirmed her suspicions. She would later recall that "when I began to make the announcement that Emmett had been found and how he was found, the whole house began to scream and cry."

Soon afterward, ". . . the order came from the sheriff's office to bury that body just as soon as you can. And they didn't even allow it to go to a funeral parlor and be dressed. He was in a pine box. Well, we got busy. We called the governor, we called the sheriff, we called Crosby, my mother's brother. We called everybody we thought would be able to stop the burial of that body. I wanted that body. I demanded that body, because my thoughts were, I had to see it, to make sure, because I'd be wondering even now who was buried in Mississippi. I had to know that was Emmett."

Amid pressure, the sheriff finally arranged to have Till's body sent by train to Chicago. Mamie met the train and was accompanied by reporters and photographers. While still at the station, the box was opened for the mother to identify her son. A photo was taken that captured Mamie's reaction to what she saw inside that box. In it, she appears to be crying, her hand is on her chest, and she's falling, her body gone limp.

The sight of her son's mutilated body led Mamie to make a decision that would ultimately change the course of history. "I decided I wanted the whole world to see what I had seen. There was no way I could describe what was in that box. No way. And I just wanted the world to see." Mamie decided that her son's funeral would include an open casket.

Somewhere in the neighborhood of fifty thousand people attended the funeral and saw Emmett's bloated body in the casket. Emmett's face was puffy and misshapen beyond imagination. His skin had taken on colors varying from the whitest of whites to the darkest of browns. One could barely make out the child's ears and nostrils. It was difficult to tell where his ripped-out eye had once been. Photos of his body, which for many came to symbolize all that was wrong in the Delta, were printed in Black magazines throughout the country.

The trial took place in September 1955 and included testimony from local Blacks like Moses Wright, who identified J. W. Milam as one of the men who'd taken his nephew. Even before the trial was over, Moses's family had moved north, and he followed soon after. The nation waited with bated breath to see what sentence the two men accused of the heinous crime would receive. The all-White jury took sixty-seven minutes to find them not guilty. One jury member even joked that it wouldn't have taken so long if they hadn't stopped to get a soda. Less than six months after being acquitted, a magazine article came out in which Milam and Bryant admitted the crime, detailed what they'd done, and expressed absolutely no remorse.

Myrlie Evers, the widow of slain civil rights leader Medgar Evers, would later say that "The Emmett Till case was one that shook the foundations of Mississippi, both Black and White. With the white community because of the fact that it had become nationally publicized, with us blacks because it said that even a child was not safe from racism, bigotry, and death."

The murder of fourteen-year-old Emmett Till served as a kind of throwing down of the gauntlet between people of decency everywhere and the insulated power structure that ruled in the segregated South. News coverage of the event ensured that it was hard to ignore. From places both far and wide, people were tuned in to the senseless murder of a child whose only crime was having brown skin.

In a collective state of shock and rage, the nation turned its eyes to the Mississippi Delta, and to Greenwood in particular.

Maybe if they'd been living in a different time, the Whites of Greenwood might have been able to better connect with the national conversation on race. Unfortunately, the message Greenwood Whites received from this national fervor was not one of compassion for Blacks and a concern for their civil rights. Instead, filtered through local leaders with segregationist agendas, the message impressed upon many Whites living in the Delta was that it was once again time to fight. Just like in the war for Southern Independence lost less than a century before, outsiders from the North were once again trying to change the South. Only this time, it was hippies and communists who were coming into their towns to recklessly rip away and destroy the sense of magic and community they'd labored to create.

The members of these communities were, by and large, the direct descendants of the ones who'd braved the Delta when the land was still wild, who'd fought back the river to build their levees, who'd overcome the thick, entangled vines and hundred-foot-tall trees in order to build plantations and to forge a new way of life. When that way of life was challenged, the instinctual reaction of many Southern Whites was to dig in their heels, gather together their love of place, and defy any force that threatened their collective dream.

WITH THIS NEW, UNFLATTERING national attention, the White Citizens' Council ramped up their efforts. Sara Criss recalled that "It was more or less expected of us to pay our $5 yearly dues to the Citizens' Council and to stand behind them." She explained that the director of a local bank was a Council member and he expected all of his employees to join as well.

Greenwood's newspaper was called the *Commonwealth*, and according to Sara, the owner's wife was called into a meeting with the presidents of the three local banks and told that "if the local paper took any stand they did not agree with on the civil rights issue, they would not advertise again in the newspaper. Perhaps this was one reason that later on during all the racial strife the paper did not run any editorials to try to improve the situation or sometimes even to cover a racial disturbance."

Sara also mentioned an incident when one of the Council leaders warned her that if they tried to integrate Greenwood schools, it would lead to rioting. He also "visualized White girls marrying Negro boys if the schools were integrated." It seems that Sara grasped the lunacy of that idea, but she also struggled to know what to do.

She said she "was afraid of the Klan, afraid that if I wrote something they did not like, I would have a cross burned in my lawn, or be threatened, or be included in the hate sheets being distributed, but I was also afraid of the Citizens' Council because their members were my friends and I did not want to incur their ill will, either."

The hate sheets Sara's referring to were newsletters with names like *A Delta Discussion*, *Truth Bulletin*, and *The Nocturnal Messenger*. Their goal was to communicate their agenda and sway public opinion. These newsletters were left on lawns, on doorsteps, and under the windshields of cars for those living in communities all throughout Greenwood and the surrounding area. Black or White, someone in town wanted to make sure that every resident of Greenwood received warnings about what would happen to their world if they chose to integrate. In another entry, Criss reflects on what it was like for her to live through those early years of the movement:

> Even though it was exciting covering the news that was attracting national attention and seeing the top news folks in the country doing their job, it was very draining emotionally because we never knew from one day to the next what might happen to provoke a situation that would bring in Federal troops. Greenwood was so tense, and all of this was so new to us. It was springtime, and during that very difficult period the trees on Grand Boulevard turned to green and the azaleas and other flowering shrubs were in bloom, and it was definitely our prettiest time of year and my favorite time.
>
> I can remember on my 42nd birthday [April 1, 1963] riding down the Boulevard with tears in my eyes for what was happening to our town, saying a prayer that it would soon all be over and that all these agitators would leave town and let us go back to being the same old Greenwood. We did not know that it would never be the same and that many heartbreaking times lay ahead for us.

Sara was right. Greenwood would never be the same. While she was looking upon her town with a sad spirit, longing for "the same old Greenwood," civil rights workers were dreaming of a new one. "COFO leaders promised in the spring of 1963 to launch a saturation campaign for black voting rights in the Greenwood area, which had 'elected itself the testing ground for democracy.'"

Part Five
The Delta

*It takes a stranger driving through the Delta
only an hour or two to see the human misery.*

Neal Peirce

From the Cotton Fields
to the Football Fields

"**I** could snort a little coke and the pain would just go away," my dad said one night when the two of us were on the phone. It was 2009 and he was living in Florida with his new wife. After the birth of my two sons, he'd transformed himself from a distant father into a stellar grandparent. Not only did he send gifts on birthdays and Christmas, he even sent silly cards to my kids on Halloween, Easter, and St. Patrick's Day. He'd leave phone messages for them in a voice disguised to make himself sound scary or just plain goofy.

In the two years since I'd first learned about Booker, my father had been diagnosed with cancer, declared cancer-free, and then diagnosed with an aortic aneurism. During those months of treatments and appointments, I made a request of him—one that would change our relationship forever. I asked him to tell me about growing up in Greenwood, explaining that it would help with my research into my grandfather's life by enabling me to envision the time and place in which Booker lived.

I was lying. I didn't want to admit to my dad that I was growing increasingly fond of him and that I longed for better memories than the ones of him stumbling into the house late at night drunk, conning me out of my birthday money so he could use it to gamble, and making me pretend we weren't home because he was hiding from people he owed money to. If he died before my sons were old enough to remember him, I wanted them to have a little more than that.

My father was born in 1950 in a farming town called Money, Mississippi, the same town Emmett Till was visiting when he was murdered. Located ten miles north of Greenwood, Money had only a few stores, a post office, one school, and a cotton gin. It was deep in the woods, way off the beaten path, and in spite of its name, whether you were White or Black, if you were among the five hundred or so residents of Money, in 1950, you were probably poor. The only people who saw any significant cash in Money were the owners of the handful of plantations located there.

My father's parents, Roosevelt and Josephine Jones, already had two other children when my dad was conceived. For some reason, people around town started a rumor that the unborn baby couldn't possibly be Roosevelt's, who in the end chose to believe the gossip. He left my grandmother, married someone else, and built a new family in the same community as the family he'd left behind. Years later, there was no question about who'd gotten Josephine pregnant, because none of Roosevelt's children looked more like him than my dad, Leroy.

Most of the people living in Money were sharecroppers who lived in houses or shacks located on the plantations that employed them. Most farm managers required each family to have a man living in the house. Because of that rule, when Roosevelt left, Josephine had to move. She ended up finding someone who agreed to let her live on their farm as long as she and her children worked the fields.

It seemed like a decent deal, but it wasn't, because the farm manager was cheating her. At the end of every season he told Josephine that she owed him money, that she hadn't picked enough cotton that year to cover her expenses. One year, she took copious notes so that when the time came to settle up she could challenge his math. After she shared her calculations with him, the manager told her that if she didn't like his math, she could leave, but then added, "I don't know where you gon' go, a woman alone with all dem kids." He was right, of course. Josephine had to accept whatever he gave or did not give.

My dad wasn't sure which came first: the graveyard or the shotgun shack they lived in. He just remembered spending the first nine years of his life playing in a yard surrounded by tombstones. The shack they lived in didn't have indoor plumbing or electricity. An outhouse filled with flies and maggots sat several yards off from the house.

Water for food, cleaning, and bathing had to be collected several times a day from a well that was a long hike away from their home. When my father turned five, gathering water from the well became his job. Everyone had to work, life was hard, and food was scarce. "My mom would do stuff to try to get food," he told me. "She'd go on the side of the road pickin' up pepper grass. It's a green that grows wild. You never hardly seen 'em anymore, but back in the '50s it was plentiful. It was beside the gravel road and every time we ate it, it was so gritty because that sand was on it."

Eventually, Josephine remarried. With a man living with her, she was able to move to a better plantation on the other side of Greenwood, into a new house with electricity and indoor plumbing. When the farm manager demanded that Josephine's kids miss school to work the fields, her new husband refused. He told the manager that the children weren't going to miss a single day of school to pick cotton. Any picking they did would have to be done after school or on the weekends.

On this new plantation, when the kids weren't picking cotton they were playing all kinds of sports. Before my dad was even in high school, people began to notice his uncommon athletic ability. In the coming years, after decent coaching, encouragement, and constant practice, my father became known all over Greenwood as someone who was going somewhere.

"We started to win games and my name started to get around," he told me one night on the phone. "I was in the newspaper and it started to take off, and my stepfather, he used to tote all of my pictures around in his pocket and he'd say 'That boy going somewhere one of these days.'"

By the time he was in tenth grade, his coach informed him that he was one of the best players in the country. College scouts began coming into Greenwood to take him out to lunch. Some offered him money; others let him drive their cars even though he didn't have a license.

My father's body seemed designed for sports. For starters, he was incredibly tall. When he finally stopped growing he measured in at a full six feet eight inches. In spite of his height and his muscular physique, he was also fast and agile. Football, a game of speed and strength, seemed designed specifically for him.

There was just one problem. He struggled to read. In the backwoods of the Mississippi Delta, no one knew what was wrong. His illiteracy became a source of shame, something he tried to hide. His inability to read on grade level meant that he wasn't going to graduate from high school on time. As an adult, he'd learn that his reading problem had a name. It was called dyslexia.

A lifetime later and he still sounded upset about those early years. "When I got to twelfth grade I needed a half semester of English, but they didn't offer it during the summer. So I had people from UCLA, Notre Dame, Ohio State, Michigan, I had all of the fifty major colleges offering me scholarships. I got a letter from everywhere. People came to Mississippi who had never been to Mississippi before. And once they found out that my grades wasn't good, they never came back."

Norfolk State was the one school willing to sign him. Their coach made arrangements for my father to graduate during the summer from a local high school in Virginia. The only stipulation Josephine insisted on, before sending him off with a few pieces of clothing rolled up in a paper sack, was that all seven of my father's siblings receive free-ride scholarships to Norfolk State as well. He would finally have the means to lift his family out of poverty. And not only that, playing at Norfolk State got him one step closer to his dream of playing for the NFL.

When he lived in Greenwood, eating at Booker's Place was financially out of reach for him. But when he was back in town visiting from college, my dad decided it was high time for him to experience the place he'd heard so much about. When he entered the restaurant, it was late in the evening, and, according to the rules, he was too young to be there. Familiar with Booker's reputation, he was fearful that he'd get kicked out, but hopeful that his height would make him look older or that his small-town celebrity status would make Booker want him to stay.

He sat down in a booth and watched as Booker, not one of the waitresses, approached his table. Booker stood next to my father's chair, looked down at him, and asked, "Well, what do you want to eat?" My dad figured Booker was irritated because he knew the young football player was trying to sneak his way in in spite of his age, but the barked greeting was the only punishment he gave my dad.

Back in Norfolk, things continued to go well for my father until 1972, when his stepdad died. His mom immediately lost her job as a sharecropper because she no longer had a man living in the house with her. Without warning, Josephine was suddenly a widow, unemployed, and about to be homeless. My dad started spending more time away from school and more time in the pool halls hustling

THE SONG AND THE SILENCE

so that he could pull together money to send to his mom and siblings. The money he made in a few nights was enough for Josephine
to feed herself and her children for weeks. All this hustling meant
spending even less time on schoolwork and in classes. His teachers
were unwilling to pass him if he wasn't even making an effort.

Facing a season on the bench at Norfolk because of his grades
and concerned about how to help his mom, my dad dropped out of
college and accepted an offer to play with the Canadian Football
League.

The life my father experienced in Canada was unlike anything
he'd imagined. "In Canada, a man is a man is a man." He'd finally
left behind racial prejudice. He could go where he wanted to go,
eat where he wanted to eat, and no one asked him any questions
or treated him as if he didn't belong. It wasn't until he was living in
Canada that my father realized just how racist Greenwood was.

He played for the Edmonton Eskimos from 1973 to 1975. NFL
scouts regularly flew to Canada to watch his games. He was confident that he'd get signed to play for the pros as a first-round draft
pick. Toward the end of his second season, all that hope vanished
during a simple play on a wet field.

"I was going to make a tackle," he explained, "and it was wet and
I slid. I had the guy that I was throwing down in front of me. Some
kind of way I slipped and slid, he ended up on top of me. But I'm
still standing, I'm almost on the ground but I'm still standing. I'm
crunched down and I can't move. Now the pile is falling on me; I was
in so much pain that I kicked my leg, and when I did that I broke my
ankle and I wrenched my knee and I screwed my back up."

Afterward, he was told he'd never play again. The scouts were
gone. Word went through the NFL that he was finished, too injured
to play, but he fought back to recovery. He was able to play again,
but he was never able to deliver the same level of performance. His
dream of being an NFL star was fading fast.

Miraculously, the Rams invited my dad out to Los Angeles, where they tested his body to see if he really could play. They bent his leg in different positions and made him run on a treadmill. My father laughed when he told this to me and said it reminded him of the scene from the movie *Rocky IV* when the Russian boxer was on the treadmill and punching machines to show the media how strong he was. Throughout all of this, my father was in pain, but he ran and smiled and told jokes because he had a family to provide for.

The Rams picked him in the second-round draft, and then subsequently traded him to the San Diego Chargers. My father had a decent career, but I could sense he believed that if he'd gone to the NFL before being injured, he would've been one of the greatest players of his generation, maybe even a household name.

When I was in high school, after my parents had separated, my mother told me once that the light left my father's eyes when he began playing for the Chargers. He never wanted to say anything to disparage his team, but I got the sense that he didn't feel the level of racial equality working in San Diego that he'd felt in Canada.

In our nightly calls, he told his story to me with sighs to illustrate his shame and punctuate his regrets. Everyone believed my dad did poorly in school because he was lazy. Teachers accused him of just wanting to coast by on his athletic talent. What left me speechless was that, after all these years, he believed it, too. Even though he'd been diagnosed with dyslexia in adulthood, he thought that if he'd worked just a little harder, he could've done entirely better in school.

I knew enough about dyslexia to know my father was wrong. Even after working with tutors as an adult, he could still barely read. Over the years, I'd seen him struggle to make out simple labels in the grocery store. And in the dark days, when I was a little girl and my father was ruled by his addiction, there were times when he wanted to steal money from my mom's checking account. His literacy levels were so low that he had to get my sister to forge my mom's signature, even though her name was printed right there on the top of the checks.

There are varying degrees of dyslexia, and his was quite severe. No amount of staring at secondhand textbooks discarded from the White schools could change the pathways in his brain. No matter what the stakes were, it was unlikely that he would learn to read through sheer will. He needed someone to slow down and take the time to understand the way his mind worked.

I'd always been told a fairy-tale version of my father's ascent from poverty to a world of riches. In actuality, he knew from the time he was a boy that he had to play his cards right and hone his skills so he could find a way for his family to escape hunger. As a boy, he watched each night as Josephine removed tape from the tips of her fingers, made raw from picking cotton. She winced as she cleaned and rewrapped them. He knew she couldn't pick cotton for the rest of her life.

The minute people recognized his uncommon athletic ability, whether spoken or unspoken, he became the hope for his family's future, and he didn't disappoint. After his stepfather died, my father bought his mother a house, where she lived until she passed away.

Maybe it was the weight of responsibility placed on a boy who couldn't even read that led my father to feel the best years of his life were the ones that came before football. "It was a rough ride but I loved it, the cotton field," he said. When he was little, he worked the fields, played under the burning sun with his siblings, swam in a pool of water made by a natural dam, and was too young to see that his family was barely surviving, subsisting on the edge of life.

When he got older, there was pain, both physical and mental. Once he went pro, it seemed to him that people only cared about whether or not his body was well enough to play—if his tendons would hold together for a few more tackles. My father spent most of his life slamming his body into other men, wrapping his arms around them and then flinging himself—with his human cargo in tow—as fast as he could into the hard earth while people cheered.

When his career was over, he turned to substances to silence the physical pain that remained. And it worked. By the time he cleaned himself up, the family he'd built was long gone.

When I was a girl, I thought I wasn't interesting or engaging enough to capture my father's attention. After those calls, I understood that when I was growing up he was overwhelmed, struggling to make it through life. He'd gone from extreme poverty one day to having enough money to buy multiple cars with cash the next. He'd gone from the cotton field to the football field with no one to help him make sense of it all. As a father, he could've done better, but I no longer believed it was my fault that he didn't.

Fever

I never quite knew how to relate to other Black people. At some point during my childhood, I think my parents realized I was having problems fitting in, so they did what they could to help. One year, my mom bought me a Black Cabbage Patch doll named Garnet. It was supposed to be exciting. Cabbage Patch had finally made a product for all the little Black girls who wanted their dolls to look like them. My mother was beaming when she gave Garnet to me. The look on her face told me that she believed she'd solved a major problem.

I didn't know what to say. I'd never seen an uglier doll than the one I was holding in my hands and I'd never heard of such a strange name for a girl. Aside from Garnet's color, I couldn't find anything different about her from the White Cabbage Patch dolls. Her hair, her lips, her nose, and even something in the structure of her cheeks still seemed White to me. I didn't believe the toy makers had made a new, Black doll. I was convinced they'd taken a White doll and just made it darker. Garnet was the perfect symbol of a hand-me-down life. No matter how much money my parents had, they couldn't make the world think of us first.

My mom kept trying to fix it. When she thought I wasn't listening, she whispered with my dad about what to do. When I reached middle school, they had a radical idea: Have her bussed to a place where they look like her, an inner-city school where she'll be the same. There she will thrive.

So one day I got on a bus and left my affluent, predominantly White neighborhood and traveled through the military housing, the business district, the industrial part of town with its pungent odors, and into a neighborhood with two-room houses, where pit bulls roamed the streets. I was dropped off at a school where the children were locked in or bad people kept out by thick, towering black bars that enclosed the campus. Immediately, I noticed I was the same color as most of the kids at my new school, but race was the only thing we had in common, and pretty soon they noticed it, too.

With my proper English and love of Phil Collins, I was accused by my new classmates of "acting White." It didn't help that when my mother visited campus she drove a shiny Mercedes Benz, wore high heels, scarlet-red lipstick, and carried a different Louis Vuitton bag every time.

Many of my classes were populated with kids who had parents in prison, loved rap, knew drug dealers and gang members, wore gold chains, had relatives who'd been shot, and fiercely hated the police. What really separated us, though, was that they were comfortable in their skin, as if they had stepped out of a world where Black really was beautiful.

I didn't get their jokes; I'd never heard of the chips they liked to eat or the grape drinks they gulped. At my old, mostly White school, I'd been different because I was Black, but at my new school I was different because I wasn't "Black enough."

In the summer of 2010, I found myself thinking a lot about my discomfort with other Blacks because I was planning to travel to Greenwood. During one of our nighttime calls, my dad asked me if I'd bring my husband, Milton, and the boys to an upcoming family reunion. When I told him that we probably couldn't afford it, he offered to pay the kids' airfare and to find a place for us to stay with family.

My cousin Rena agreed to put us up. She was married and had one daughter. I hadn't spoken to her since the visit to Greenwood with my sister almost fifteen years before. We pulled up in front of Rena's house on a warm evening in June 2010. I didn't know much about architecture, but I knew that Rena's house was old in a special kind of way. The house had a sense of history, as if it owned itself and the people inhabiting it were just passing through. Inside there were two bedrooms, a claw-footed tub in the bathroom, and a spacious kitchen. Her husband and her daughter were there, as well as my father and his brother Roosevelt, Rena's father.

After saying hellos, I went back out to the car to make sure we hadn't left behind sippy cups or insect repellent. My father came with me and we talked about plans for the weekend. Rena's husband leaned his head out the front door and asked us what kind of pizza we wanted for dinner, and I said, "Vegetarian." The two of us proceeded to have an awkward back-and-forth exchange in an effort to understand each other. He thought I just wanted a cheese pizza. My father finally interrupted and told him to ask for tomatoes, mushrooms, and peppers. Rena's husband took one last look at me, shook his head, and ducked back into the house.

When I was finished getting everything out of the car, I went back inside, where everyone was sitting close together on a couple of couches. Throughout the room, wild blueberries were gathered in candy dishes and plastic bowls of varying colors as if on display. They were on the coffee table, side tables, shelves, and a computer desk. Rena kept offering them to us. She'd gone out and picked them herself.

The problem was that, as a rule, I never ate freshly picked fruit. I was a city girl and believed I could only trust food that had passed through the legal regulations imposed on grocery store conglomerates. But since I'd already failed at the simple act of ordering a pizza, I wanted to find a way to fit in, so I decided to take my chances and taste the berries. After all, considering how many bowls of them were scattered around the room, it seemed that Rena ate them all the time, and she was still standing.

I put a few berries in my mouth and bit down. The juice that gushed from their outer shell tasted like nothing I'd ever had in my mouth before. They were remarkably sweet but not cloying, and they had a flavor so far from the blueberries I'd eaten in my life that I almost felt as if I were sampling a new candy from Willy Wonka's Chocolate Factory. I reached for the bowl to grab another handful, but Bishop had taken it for himself and was stuffing his face so fast that his lips were already bluish-purple.

While we waited for the pizza, Rena gave me a tour of the house. We were back in the kitchen when we finally started catching up on each other's lives. Rena had attended a university in New York, but after a few years there she got sick—really sick. She was diagnosed with lupus. She moved back to Greenwood to be close to family and never looked back. Rena worked at the middle school. When she mentioned this, I thought about Vera saying the schools weren't integrated when she was young, but that was decades ago. I wondered how things were now.

"So, is there a lot of diversity at your school?" I asked while Rena began to wash the dishes. She shook her head and said that her school was around 95 percent Black.

"When we move into White neighborhoods, they just move out. Everything's still segregated here. They put their kids in private schools."

Over the next several minutes, while Rena talked about life in Greenwood, I went through a series of shifting thoughts and emotions. My immediate response to her claim that her school was still almost completely segregated was that she was obviously exaggerating. Then an image flashed in my mind of a Black person trying to make life sound harder than it really was in order to justify their own complacency. But Rena was smart; she'd lived in New York, so certainly I could trust her assessments.

As I watched myself climb that ladder of judgment, I was shocked by my own thinking. Even the fact that Rena's college career was the detail that made me consider her to be a trustworthy source was something that brought me instant shame. If she'd never left Greenwood, would I be more inclined to believe she was exaggerating?

My most vivid memory of Rena was from a night out during that summer visit when I was eleven. Rena was the only cousin old enough to drive, and she'd taken me, my sister, and another cousin out to the store. Everyone got something, including Rena. She bought herself a Kit Kat. I can't remember who started it, but one of us mentioned how much we loved Kit Kat and asked Rena for one of her bars. She said, "Sure," and handed it over. Then someone wanted another one, and then someone else wanted yet another one.

Rena only got to eat one out of the four bars in her Kit Kat, and she didn't complain at all. She was in the driver's seat and I was sitting behind her on the backseat wondering about this curious girl who'd just given away all her candy.

It's true that I knew very little about Rena, but none of what I did know would logically lead me to believe that she'd lie or exaggerate about anything. Where had those assumptions come from?

The pizza arrived, and while everyone was grabbing a slice and talking about life, I kept thinking about how quick I was to disregard Rena. I thought back to my childhood. Was my image of her connected to the narrative of Black life I'd been taught in my all-White schools in the 1980s? The sense I had was that the civil rights movement was a good thing that was effective, achieved its goals, and was definitely over. Now, everyone just needed to move on. Anyone who continued to speak about relations between the races or the quality of life for Blacks had a chip on their shoulder.

But it wasn't even Rena who'd brought up race relations, it was me.

Maybe I just didn't want to believe that things were still so bad. Or maybe I had an underlying yet unassailable conviction that anything amiss in Black communities was a result of inherent defects in Blacks themselves. Whites had done all they could do, and it was time for Blacks to pull their shit together.

I was disgusted with myself.

As if he was channeling my inner frustrations from across the room, my three-year-old, Dexter, suddenly threw up. I figured he'd just eaten too much. We rarely ate pizza, so he may have just overdone it. I apologized and cleaned up the mess. Then he threw up again. After the second time, Dexter tried to crawl into my lap. I picked him up and moved over to the couch, where he laid his head on my thighs. It was warm. I mentioned this to the group and Rena jumped up, ran to the next room, and returned with a brand-new thermometer, still in the plastic. We took his temperature. It was 103 degrees. I always broke Bishop and Dexter's fevers with Motrin. Rena sent her husband to the nearest store to get some.

I gave Dexter the medicine and waited an hour. I took his temperature again and it hadn't changed. Another hour went by, and there was still no change. Not only was it late in the evening but we were at least an hour and a half from Jackson, where I figured there was a decent emergency room.

After discussing this with Milton, he looked down at Dexter and asked, "Why can't we just take him to urgent care or a hospital here in Greenwood?"

All I could think about was what had transpired several years earlier when I'd traveled back to Greenwood for my grandmother's funeral. I'd become almost violently sick after eating a serving of creamed corn. After about eighteen hours of constant vomiting, I finally asked my mother to take me to the hospital. Instead, she called her sister, the only one who'd never moved away from Greenwood, to see what we should do.

She insisted that my mom not take me to any Greenwood doctors. She said I'd end up worse off than I already was. Instead, she recommended a few home remedies and over-the-counter meds. We followed her suggestions, and soon I was at least well enough to travel back to Phoenix.

When Milton inquired about why we couldn't just take Dexter to a doctor in Greenwood, I said, "Because my mom told me not to go to the doctors here. She said they're backward." Without even looking around the room to gauge the expressions on everyone's faces, I knew they thought I was overreacting. I knew this because even I could hear how ridiculous I sounded.

I stayed up with Dexter for hours after everyone else had gone to sleep, giving him medicine, taking his temp, only to find that it wasn't going down. His temperature was climbing. This had never happened with Dexter before. On the few occasions when I'd failed to break Bishop's fevers, I'd always taken him to urgent care. But this night, I was in Greenwood. I felt panicked—panicked enough to call my mom.

We hadn't spoken in months and she'd only met Dexter once, so I wasn't even sure if she'd answer. As I listened to the phone ringing, I remembered myself as a little girl lying on the living room couch with a hot towel on my chest. Then I thought about the metallic smell of the iodine she used to drench my sister's tonsils with. Both treatments had been effective.

"Hello," she said groggily.

"It's Yvette. Did I wake you?"

"That's okay. What's up?"

"I'm in Greenwood—"

"Oh, that's nice."

"And Dexter is sick, he has a fever. Can I take him to a doctor?"

Suddenly sounding very awake, she said, "No, absolutely not."

"Okay, Mom, I need you to tell me one of your home remedies, something passed down to you."

"You need to give him an alcohol bath," she said.

"A what?"

"An alcohol bath." She said it again in a louder voice, like she thought I hadn't heard her.

"How do I do that, Mom?"

"First, you take off all his clothes, and then you take a bottle of alcohol, pour a good amount of it onto a washcloth, and rub his whole body with it. Rub it in real good. Don't miss a spot."

"Okay," I said, waiting for her to go on.

"Okay," she echoed, and then, "Call me in the morning to let me know if he's any better."

"I will. Thanks."

I looked up and explained her instructions to Rena, who immediately went to grab alcohol and a washcloth.

When she returned, I carefully removed Dexter's clothes and kissed his little hands and arms as I did so. His skin was a golden brown, so I always told him that he tasted like chocolate. He looked up at me as if he was wondering what I was doing, so I kissed him and whispered, "Yummy, brownies," then, "Mmm, chocolate pudding."

I did what my mother had instructed me to do, rubbing the alcohol all over Dexter's perfect, warm brown skin. When I finished, I put his clothes back on, and then leaned back. He put his little head on my chest, and I could feel the heat of his breath on my breast as he fell asleep.

An hour later, I took his temperature again. The thermometer beeped and I pulled it from under his arm with my eyes closed, afraid to look. His fever had broken. Tears stung my eyes. I squeezed him to me, but he'd already fallen back to sleep. I sat there and cried. Even before I called my mom I'd known Dexter would be okay. After all, it was just a fever. Even still, I cried because I felt relieved, but also because I felt guilty.

That night my mom had reached back into her memories to hand me a remedy, one she'd received decades earlier. From her ancestors—my ancestors—my mother learned about the healing powers of alcohol baths, olive oil, and iodine. But if one of those individuals were somehow brought back to stand in Rena's house to help me with Dexter, how would I have responded? Would I have trusted them, or would I have questioned the veracity of their treatment ideas the same way I'd done with Rena's description of segregated schools?

THE NEXT MORNING, I woke up with the sun shining on my face. My kids were already awake and in Rena's care. When she had heard them stirring, she'd gotten out of bed, washed their faces, fed them homemade blueberry pancakes, and put them in front of the TV so they could watch cartoons. My dad and his brother were going to spend the morning shopping and cooking for a family dinner later that evening. My morning was wide open.

I called my mom to thank her and to tell her that Dexter was alright. We made small talk for a few more minutes. I didn't really know what to say, and I sensed she didn't, either. We said we'd talk again soon and then quickly ended our call. I made plans to meet with Honey Wright, the woman Booker married after he divorced my grandmother. The two of them were together until the day he died. I still felt reluctant about looking deeper into Booker's life because I was fearful it would end in disappointment, but I was curious. Though I knew it could turn out he'd had no idea how important his words were or he was just blowing off steam and not really thinking about his statements, more and more I felt as though I just needed to know. His entire life felt like a secret that had been kept from me, one I was slowly beginning to unfold.

Honey and I had a few brief conversations before I arrived. Over the phone, her voice was cryptic, like it came from someone in the final stages of death. Every syllable she produced seemed to take considerable effort.

When I arrived at Honey's house, I found it to be small but thoughtfully kept. A garden of delicate, light-colored flowers hemmed her home in with understated beauty. On her porch were plants and two plastic chairs that were both free of debris and dust. The rest of the street didn't look as nice as Honey's house. Few, if any, had flowers in front, and the porches looked as though they were about to fall down.

I climbed the steps leading to Honey's front door. This visit marked the beginning of my Booker Wright research in earnest. My heart pounded as I rang the bell. I took a long, slow, deep breath to calm myself, but then almost gagged because I reeked of mosquito repellent. I was rubbing my nose, trying to get the scent out of it when I heard the front door open. I couldn't see inside because my view was blocked by a black iron security screen.

"Well, hello, there," I heard Honey say. I knew it was her because I recognized that labored voice.

"Hello," I said in response. When she opened the security door, I stared at her in silent surprise. If I hadn't heard her voice through the screen, I would never have believed the woman standing before me was Honey Wright, because nothing about her belied effort. A few years shy of her eightieth birthday, Honey Wright was strong and effortlessly beautiful.

She was short and slender, with skin so light it was barely brown at all. Aside from a few strategically placed freckles, it was clear and thin, almost translucent. Dark, girlish curls fell carelessly onto her unwrinkled forehead, and the corners of her plump lips turned up into a warm, easy smile. A simple dress with bright flowers barely hid Honey's well-kept figure. Her brown eyes were warm, she was feminine, and her posture was strong. I sensed she knew her beauty was there, even understood its power, but had grown bored with it. I felt self-conscious as I stood in front of her in wrinkled gray linen pants and a sweat-stained blouse.

Honey's real name was Mildred, and even though everyone seemed to use her nickname, I wanted to be respectful, so after saying hellos I asked, "Should I call you Mildred?"

"Of course not," she said as she leaned forward and wrapped a long, slender arm around my waist, pulling me into her darkly lit home. "Everybody calls me Honey."

Hanging on the wall in her front room was a picture of Booker. It was a photograph treated to look like a painting. In the portrait, Booker had a small, *Mona Lisa*–like smile on his face. I knew Honey had married again after Booker died, and her second husband had also passed away, but I didn't see any of his photos hanging on the wall.

We spent close to three hours together that day. She shared with me what she knew of Booker's television appearance, which wasn't much. She told me about the food they served at Booker's Place and how Booker had to go to Lusco's in the afternoons. Then she told me a story of loss and longing that was more profound and more beautiful than I could have imagined. It was the story of Booker and his mother, Rosie—how they were lost to each other and then how they were found. What I didn't know as I sat in Honey's living room taking in the horrible circumstances surrounding Booker's upbringing was how much more meaning and depth the story would have for me as I continued in my journey to understand what life was like for Blacks during those years, and what his two minutes of television had actually cost him.

Town on Fire

The details of how Emmett Till was murdered, coupled with the farcical nature of the trial that followed, made the entire event both unbelievable and unforgettable. Rich or poor, White or Black, the torture and murder of an innocent child and the subsequent release of his killers marked a shift in thinking throughout the nation; it was a horror that defied all reason, an event that could not be forgotten.

There had always been tension in Greenwood, but previously it was primarily experienced by Blacks who had to struggle to build lives for themselves and their children amid the constant threat of violence. They obeyed not only the segregation rules known as the Jim Crow Laws but also had to submit to the unspoken, unwritten laws enforced by lynchings and other acts of violence. For Blacks, Till was a stark reminder of what could—and would—happen when those unspoken laws were broken.

Greenwood Whites, on the other hand, allowed themselves to believe that the silence of the Blacks in their midst, the reason they didn't complain about segregation or the unspoken rules, was because Blacks didn't mind them. Actually, it was common for Whites to lament the national attention with statements like, "Our Blacks are happy."

After Till's murder, the tensions that had previously been felt so deeply by Blacks began to wade into the White community. The town of Greenwood was now on the radar of national news crews who were searching for stories about the burgeoning civil rights movement. They were not disappointed.

In her memoir, Sara Criss recalled a night, in June 1963, when she was watching television with her husband and "[Medgar] Evers came on with a rather strong plea for Negroes to register to vote. At the time we commented that he certainly was brave to appear on TV with such remarks knowing how many White people there were listening who were developing a growing fear of racial disturbances. Then on June 12 we were in Birmingham on a short trip and awoke to the morning news with a bulletin that an NAACP leader in Jackson, Medgar Evers, had been shot and killed."

Nine days later, Byron De La Beckwith, a well-known Greenwood resident and a member of the White Citizens' Council, was arrested for the murder of Evers. The following year, two hung juries failed to determine De La Beckwith's guilt and soon afterwards all hell broke loose in Greenwood. Marching, picketing, and arrests became common occurrences. Shortly thereafter, people from far-flung parts of the country began pouring into town to challenge Greenwood's way of life.

Then on July 2, 1964—less than a year before Booker's interview with Frank De Felitta—the Civil Rights Act, signed into law by President Lyndon Johnson, made the segregation of public places illegal and "heralded the beginning of some of Greenwood's most trying times."

Greenwood Whites were torn between two desires. They wanted to stand in defiance of the Civil Rights Act, a law they believed was misguided at best and dangerous at worst. But they also longed to maintain the community they'd built. They were desperate to find ways to make it feel as if their world was not really changing at all. The odds were stacked against them, not just because of the Civil Rights Act but also because of the numbers.

The powerful in Greenwood had always been outnumbered. Before the Civil War, in the Southern states it was common for just a handful of White men to manage a plantation with hundreds of Black slaves. This created a population imbalance that continued even after slavery was abolished and White planters decided to embrace the sharecropping system. In this new system, similar to slavery, one White family could own a farm with multiple emancipated Black families living on their property as sharecroppers, "a form of life Blacks repeatedly said was only marginally better than slavery."

By the 1960s, Greenwood's population was around twenty-two thousand, and it was almost an even split between Blacks and Whites, with Blacks outnumbering Whites by only about seven hundred. However, when the farming communities that surrounded Greenwood were added to the equation, it was an entirely different story. Leflore County had a population of 47,142 people, of whom 16,699 were White and 30,443 were Black. Even though Whites made up only 35 percent of the overall population, they owned 90 percent of the land.

The passing of the Civil Rights Act threatened the Southern way of life, the collective dream, that Greenwood Whites had grown accustomed to living. If taken literally and executed immediately, the federal law could cause a sudden influx of Blacks making their way into White stores, churches, schools, neighborhoods, their very lives. Whites in Greenwood responded quickly, railing against a change from the outside that felt too quick and too radical.

Eight days after the law passed, the local chapter of the White Citizens' Council released a statement urging business owners to resist integrating. The Council went so far as to promise financial support from the White Citizens' Legal Fund "to anyone involved in litigation for refusal to serve Negroes." It would appear that local Whites were paying close attention. Almost immediately, several of the restaurants, which had previously been for Whites only, converted into private clubs where only members could enter.

Sara Criss noted a number of other drastic, spur-of-the-moment decisions Whites in Greenwood were making in order to avoid having Blacks flood their world:

> As soon as the Civil Rights Bill was passed the city ordered the municipal pool closed, along with the Youth Center and the Library. We had had the best city recreation program in the state with a full-time director, and this signaled the end of all of that. Hundreds of children had learned to swim under Red Cross instruction each summer, and closing the pool meant the end of that program.
>
> There had been all sorts of instructional programs for children at the Youth Center, such as baton twirling, dancing, exercises, etc. All of this, too, ended. The Library opened three weeks later, but all of the chairs had been taken out so that no one could sit down in there.

Even though it was only closed for a week, the idea of losing the swimming pool was just too much for some Greenwood citizens to bear. A few of the town leaders figured that if restaurants could become private, then certainly the city pool could as well. Within a week's time, the Kiwanis Club reopened the pool as a private club. According to Sara, "This venture did not last long, as it was too expensive for the club, and the pool finally remained closed. At one point the Junior Auxiliary tried opening the Youth Center as a private endeavor, but this too was not successful."

One of the Whites who had the most trouble after the act was passed was the man charged with managing the Leflore Theater, because Blacks had set their sights on integrating it. Night after night they showed up and attempted to enter. These efforts often ended in arguments, and sometimes in violence.

The manager of the movie theater was stuck between a rock and a hard place. His parent company fully expected him to comply with the new federal law, but many Whites in Greenwood were determined to do otherwise. For the most part, Whites stopped going to the Leflore Theater after the Civil Rights Act passed, because of the nightly commotions. Nevertheless, there continued to be at least a few local Whites in Greenwood who wanted to see movies and really didn't care what color the other patrons were. Sara Criss writes about how that perspective played out for one prominent member of Greenwood society:

> Thatcher Walt, who was editor of the *Commonwealth*, decided he did not want to be intimidated and kept from going to the theater by the roughneck whites and agitating Negroes and so attended a movie there. While he and his family were out of town the next weekend, someone shot into his home. Not long after, he resigned his job and moved to Florida, saying he no longer wanted to live here. It was that bad. The decent, respectable citizens who comprised most of the population were caught between two groups who were trying to stir up trouble.

The passing of the Civil Rights Act wasn't the only event unsettling the waters in Greenwood. The summer of 1964 was also the Freedom Summer, a season in which Blacks were really beginning to mobilize in a concentrated effort to get the vote. But it wasn't just local Blacks pushing for change. Volunteers were pouring into the South from all over the country to help with their mission. Meanwhile, Whites who were angered by this activity responded with all kinds of violence. Sara said that "there were almost daily reports of Negro churches being burned." Greenwood had gone from being a family-centered town to a combustible, unpredictable battleground. Reporters from all over the country were coming in to document the discord. Sara, a young mother at the time, had gone from living in a quiet, idyllic town to living in one that felt like a war zone.

Both Blacks and Whites in Greenwood felt the powerful tide of change as it slammed into their town. But how the experience played out for Blacks was quite different.

A Force to Be
Reckoned With

In the 1960s, the streets of Greenwood were run by an all-White police force who served the good of White Greenwood while creating what some called a "reign of terror" in Black Greenwood. One resident made a habit of peering down alleyways on Saturday nights just to see which Blacks the cops had chosen to terrorize and beat for no reason other than to remind them, and everyone around, of the extent of their power.

One of the first Black attorneys in Greenwood, Alix Sanders recalls that the police department was made up of poor Whites who were "abusive to Blacks," and specifically "abusive to lower-class Blacks." To many people, it seemed that the local police department's primary job was to stop integration. Another Greenwood resident said of the time that "there was no protection given to Black citizens, especially when you were attempting to assert certain civil rights, you became an enemy that the forces would have to deal with. The police department was engaged full-time in those kinds of things— to maintain the segregated system that was in place in that day."

In 1962, a Black activist named Sam Block moved into Greenwood to open an SNCC office. When he went to the courthouse to learn more about registering to vote, he was greeted by the sheriff, who asked, "Nigger, where are you from . . . I know you ain't from here 'cause I know every nigger and his mammy." He then instructed Sam to pack his clothes and leave town for his own good. This was just a harbinger of the resistance Sam and the Black residents of Greenwood would face in their efforts to gain the vote.

According to Charles Payne, in Leflore County in 1961 "almost 100% of Whites were registered to vote, compared to just 268 of Blacks (2%). In the seven years since the *Brown* decision, only 40 Blacks have been allowed to register."

Ironically, some of the reasoning behind the vehement fight Whites put up against giving Blacks equal voting rights was probably best described by Sam Block at an SNCC conference in 1963, when he acknowledged that they were:

> [A]sking the people in the Delta to do something which they don't ask of any white person anywhere else. . . . And that is to allow Negroes to vote in an area where they are educationally inferior but yet outnumber the white people and hence constitute a serious political threat. Because in every other area of the country, the Negro votes are ghettoized—the Negroes elect their leaders, but they don't elect leaders to preside over what we could call a numerically inferior but educationally superior white elite.

Block was exposing a circular problem in the movement. Blacks struggled to obtain quality educations for a multitude of reasons, including not being allowed to send their children to school because planters wanted them in the fields, little support for teachers, an imbalance of dollars allotted to Black children when compared to White children, and, not least of which, the fact that their schools had still not integrated. Blacks needed political representatives who would protect their right to an education. The only way to get those representatives was to vote.

When Sam Block first arrived in Greenwood, it wasn't just Whites who showed resistance. Sam's efforts to get Blacks registered was met with a hard concrete wall of fear. Blacks were so afraid of all that Sam and his colleagues represented—the violence they were sure to face in their efforts—that Greenwood Blacks crossed the street if they saw Sam coming in their direction. The fear of registering to vote wasn't a hyped-up fear.

It was well-known that in Brookhaven, just over a few hours' drive from Greenwood, a Black man named Lamar Smith had been shot dead at ten in the morning in front of the courthouse where he was helping Blacks complete absentee ballot forms so they could vote without being threatened at the polls. In spite of his murder taking place in front of multiple witnesses, no one was ever charged. The reality was that any White person who felt strongly about Blacks not being allowed to vote could go to any extreme to stop them without the threat of prosecution.

In spite of the cold reception Sam received from both Whites and Blacks, he and his colleagues continued to canvass, and one by one, Greenwood Blacks began joining the movement. By the end of 1962, everything had changed. The civil rights movement efforts in Greenwood were like a well-oiled machine. On almost every single block in the Black neighborhoods were people who were supportive of the movement and willing to help on the many occasions when SNCC workers were fleeing from violence.

In February 1963, four Black-owned businesses were firebombed, and when Sam Block claimed that the fires were arson, he was arrested for making statements to disrupt the peace in Greenwood. On the day of his trial, over a hundred Black protestors made their way to city hall in what some said was the "first mass protest by

Greenwood Blacks in living memory." Sam was sentenced to pay a fine and spend six months in jail.

Later that month, two hundred Blacks went to the courthouse to register to vote, and that same night, members of the KKK fired a machine gun into a car carrying three SNCC workers, severely wounding one. In the coming months, Blacks who went to the courthouse to register to vote were met by helmeted police officers with attack dogs and nightsticks. That summer, a young historian and activist named Howard Zinn visited Greenwood and described the SNCC office as having "the eerie quality of a field hospital after battle."

In the midst of Greenwood's volatile, racist environment, Booker continued working at Lusco's and running Booker's Place. Aside from allowing activists and movement workers to eat at his restaurant for free and having his building vandalized by Whites, Booker seemed to have gone through those years relatively un-scathed. The White Citizens' Council seemed to be everywhere, in everything, trying to keep Blacks from making any form of progress. It's likely that their members were aware that Booker entertained movement workers, but what, if anything, the Council did about it is unclear.

There was one afternoon at Booker's Place when he wasn't around but the restaurant was still open. The last of the lunch crowd had shuffled out, so the restaurant was pretty empty, with the exception of the staff, who were cleaning and preparing for the dinner rush. The restaurant door opened and a White police officer came in. Usually when people entered Booker's Place they'd pause and look around to decide where to sit or to see who was there. But this officer acted as if he was entering his own home. His gait didn't slow as he crossed the threshold and walked straight back toward the kitchen without acknowledging any of the workers he passed by.

He entered the kitchen, walked over to the stove, and put his hand in a pot of turnip greens. At that time of day there was almost always a pot of greens, with chunks of ham hock, cooking on the stove. When the dinner rush began, the connective tissues and tender chunks of muscle would have melted into the greens, giving them a succulent, mouthwatering flavor. When the officer pulled his hand out of the pot it held a juicy piece of ham hock. He continued to stand over the stove and began to eat it. Then, while his mouth was still full, he began to make meaningless small talk, as if to further humiliate them by eating their food with his mouth open.

The officer was tall, with the kind of cheeks that always looked deeply flushed, like they'd just been pinched. He stood there in Booker's kitchen talking about nothing while the juice from Booker's greens ran down the sides of his hands and onto the floor.

One night, several Blacks gathered at a grocery store owned by a local police officer, and four people were arrested. Sara was in the station and "John Handy, a light-colored Negro who had been involved in other incidents during the summer, was standing in the station when Curtis Underwood, one of the policemen, lost his temper and gave him a heavy blow right in his stomach."

During that same summer, 1964, Silas McGhee got into an argument with a Greenwood cop over how his car was parked. The officer became outraged by Silas's disrespect and said that someone should "blow his brains out." Later that night, while sitting in his car with the window down, Silas was shot in the face from just a few feet away. While he was slumped over on the seat, waiting for death to come, he heard a woman's voice over the police scanner he'd installed in his car. She was calling out in celebration, "They got the n—! They got him!"

A Self-Portrait

Frank De Felitta met Booker Wright at Lusco's during an unseasonably cold winter in 1965. At the same time, two states north, river waters were rising higher and higher. The waters would continue to swell until they created a weather event that would come to be known as the worst flood in the Upper Mississippi in recorded history. But weather wasn't on the filmmaker's mind. He was still young, and arrogance ran through him like a delicious spice. Frank was years away from developing age spots or an appreciation for the ominous ways of nature. When the filmmaker interrupted the waiter's life, he was a different man from the one who, four decades later, sat on the other side of the camera to tell the story.

There's a black-and-white photo of Frank taken during his trip to the Mississippi Delta. In it he's standing, or perhaps balancing, on uneven debris in front of an ashen-colored, abandoned plantation house that's in wild disrepair. The structure has no doors or windows and is leaning on thick, wooden pillars. Tall weeds clutter the foreground and tangled wooden boards that may have once been a balcony hang precariously just a few feet above his head.

In this scene of utter ruin, Frank is wearing an unwrinkled suit and tie, smoking a cigar, and maintaining a cool, relaxed posture. He has broad shoulders, hair as black as ink, and dark, knowing eyes that look directly into the camera. Everything about him reads as effortless except his expression, which is intense and focused, just shy of showing irritation, as though he's willing the photographer not to screw up the shot.

Though Booker and Frank were from vastly different worlds, they were equals in many ways, not least of which was this quality. Be it a blessing or a curse, both of them had something living just beneath the surface, creating both an air of greatness and of great solitude.

Frank, who was neither tall nor wide, managed to exact an imposing presence as if he took up more space than the product of his height and weight. With a personality that blended authority, charisma, and curiosity, he was the kind of man who longed to follow his instincts and was unsettled when not doing so. But those times were few and far between because Frank was savvy enough to pull together the resources to embark on almost any adventure.

The son of Italian immigrants, Frank grew up in New York City. In his early twenties, he became a pilot, flying large transport planes in World War II. At the end of the war, he was asked to fly US officials to Europe.

For three months we were to tour all of the concentration camps that we could get into and there were about 100 of them. And it was a dreadful time when they were exhuming bodies.

And I, as a youngster, had to see things I never believed I would ever see. The death of the Jewish people came home to me. I knew very little about Jews and what have you and I didn't know what the war was about at the time, I was just trying to labor through it. But I learned. It was a great lesson to have to go through horrid camps and see their methods of killing, their method of burning them in ovens, huge ovens.

It was the most hateful time of the war, the worst time of the war. That was by all means the most terrible experience I've ever been through in my life.

When Frank returned home to New York, it quickly became clear that the experience had changed him. The simple, mundane trivialities of life now struck him as not only meaningless but also heartless, because he, and everyone around him, knew that somewhere in the world people were being tortured, starved. Like a man running underwater, Frank's efforts to build a new postwar life pressed up against the density of what he had learned but could not accept about mankind: There were individuals in the world who would harness all their talents to engineer ways to destroy innocent people, and there were others who would stand by and watch.

It took two years, but Frank managed to drag himself out of the darkness. First he became a writer and then a filmmaker. He moved up in the industry, and by the late 1950s, he held a position at NBC that enabled him to work full-time creating two documentaries a year.

Frank was a lover of jazz and thought it would be interesting to explore on film how jazz music was influenced by blues and ragtime traditions in the American South. This project took him deep into the Southern states, where he visited with and filmed Black sharecroppers. Each morning at first light, men, women, and children dressed in shapeless rags made their way out into the vast cotton fields. As the day wore on, the heat grew more aggressive and the humidity more intense, yet they remained in the fields until the unforgiving sun took back the last of its rays. Then the workers returned to their shacks, where they consumed meals made from scraps before collapsing, exhausted, only to wake and do the whole thing all over again the next day.

Frank filmed them as they hummed and sang the blues. Their sound, like prayers offered up in a godless temple, touched upon a dark sorrow. In their music was their struggle, wrapped up and translated into a melodious cipher.

All of it—the people, their sound, their sorrow, and the suffocating heat—held Frank in a sobering embrace, confronting him with emotions he hadn't experienced in close to a decade. At some point on that trip, he turned to his producing partner, Fred Ramsey Jr., and, referring to the hopelessness surrounding them, he asked, "Why is this happening?"

Fred thought for a moment, and then tried to offer an answer. "Well, Frank, you can't change the world—believe me, the world is always gonna be this way; you gotta understand it."

To which Frank replied, "Well, maybe if we do something, we can change it."

When he returned to New York, that brief and seemingly insignificant exchange stayed with Frank, and he continued to have a desire to, as he put it, "Do something." A few more years would pass, but eventually a plan began to unfurl itself in Frank's mind—a plan that led him straight to Booker Wright. He decided to make a documentary about the civil rights movement. Always the maverick, Frank did the opposite of what most of his contemporaries were doing at the time. He decided to stay away from the Black story, choosing instead to examine the mind of the White Southerner.

Frank started conducting research and quickly found that the place he wanted to go to was the one he was continually being told to avoid, because that place had been transformed into a veritable war zone.

In 1962, President John F. Kennedy nationalized the Mississippi Guard and sent them, along with US Army military police, US Border Patrol agents, and five hundred US Marshals, to Oxford to squelch the violence that was stirred up when one Black man named James Meredith tried to go to school at the University of Mississippi. At one point, there were so many troops in the small town that it felt as though they outnumbered the residents. Charges were later dropped against him, but the governor of Mississippi, Ross Barnett, was fined and sentenced to jail time for his involvement in trying to stop the integration of the historic school.

In spite of all that was happening throughout the state, the situation in a small town called Greenwood, eighty miles south of Oxford, was markedly more intense. By the mid-1960s, almost daily the KKK and other local Whites were shooting into the homes of Black residents and firebombing stores as a way to punish, warn, and frighten those accused of registering to vote or attending movement meetings.

In March 1963, Martin Luther King Jr. expressed his concern for the town in a telegram to President Kennedy. King warned of the possibility of an event similar to the one that had taken place at the University of Mississippi at Oxford the previous year:

DEAR MR. KENNEDY, THE SITUATION IN GREENWOOD MIS-SISSIPPI HAS DEGENERATED SO THAT I HAVE NO ALTER-NATIVE BUT TO APPEAL TO YOU AS HEAD OF OUR NATION TO PERSONALLY INTERVENE ON BEHALF OF THE SAFETY AND PROTECTION OF CITIZENS AND WORKERS INVOLVED IN VOTER REGISTRATION. TODAY THE REV. D L TUCKER WAS MERCILESSLY BRUTALIZED BY POLICE DOGS. HARRASSMENT [sic] CONTINUES BY POLICE AND THE HOODLUM ELEMENT DURING VOTER RALLIES AT THE LOCAL CHURCH. IN SPITE OF OUR PERSISTENT COUNCIL FOR THE PEOPLE TO REMAIN NONVIOLENT I FEAR THAT IF SOMETHING IS NOT DONE IM-MEDIATELY TO RELIEVE THIS HEINOUS SITUATION, A NIGHT WILL SOON COME DARKER THAN THAT NIGHT IN OXFORD. NOTHING COULD BE MORE DETRIMENTAL AND EMBARRASS-ING TO THE IMAGE OF AMERICA IN THE WORLD COURT OF NATIONS.

A few months later, on the evening of June 11, President Kennedy gave what would come to be known as his famous address to the nation on civil rights. He called upon every American to examine their conscience in regard to the opportunities afforded to Blacks. He cited several statistics to shed light on the low quality of life that most Black Americans were unable to escape because of widespread discrimination. Legislation "cannot solve this problem alone," he said. "It must be solved in the homes of every American in every community across our country."

Hours after Kennedy's address, Medgar Evers was getting out of his car and preparing to walk into his Jackson, Mississippi, home. His wife and children were heading toward the front door to greet him when Byron De La Beckwith, a prominent member of the Greenwood community, shot Evers in the back in his driveway while his children were on their way out to greet him.

The following year, De La Beckwith was tried twice for the murder of Medgar Evers, with both efforts ending in hung juries. Mississippi's White community gathered around to support him. His bond and legal defense were funded by the White Citizens' Council, the group that was determined to stop integration, and the former governor of Mississippi interrupted one of the trials to shake De La Beckwith's hand.

These were the types of things Frank heard during his initial months of research. However, the stories didn't serve as a warning; instead they increased Frank's fascination with Mississippi and with Greenwood in particular. Frank's interest in Greenwood morphed into a kind of hope. To Frank, Greenwood burned like a far-off torch in a desperately dark and endless night. Frank believed that if he could examine Greenwood, look closely at the thoughts and attitudes of its White citizens, that he might find and expose the roots of hate.

"All the people—camera, sound people—came out of *NBC News*. That was a kind of must," Frank recalled. "So it was difficult, when I wanted to make the Mississippi story, to find a crew that was willing to go. I offered a couple of cameramen an opportunity and they turned me down. I finally got Joe Vadala, who's a marvelous cameraman who was"—Frank paused as if searching for the right phrase—"interested in risking his life in Mississippi."

In time, Frank was able to pull together a crew, and in 1965 they traveled the almost 1,200 miles from New York City to Greenwood, Mississippi. At first, Frank had trouble getting Delta Whites to go on camera with him. Many felt they'd been misrepresented by the national media, who, in their minds, had disregarded the sincere affection that flowed between Whites and Blacks. Most local Whites either believed that the violence and unrest that had settled into their town was being exaggerated by the media or that, if it was true, it was being caused by agitators who'd infiltrated Greenwood.

Slowly, with gentle persuasion in intimate, one-on-one conversations, Frank tried to convince Greenwood Whites that his film project was different, that his intent was to simply record and then present their thoughts to the nation. He explained that his only goal was to offer them a chance to go on camera and present their arguments for segregation. It worked. Within a few weeks, Frank was becoming a known factor in the small town, and people were beginning to open up to him.

The filming of the documentary occurred without incident. As their work was ramping up and they were getting more and more interviews scheduled, Fred Ramsey—the co-producer and consultant—suggested that he and Frank go out to dinner at one of the town's most popular restaurants, Lusco's. Fred had eaten there before and encouraged Frank to go so that he could hear the restaurant's famous Black waiter, Booker Wright, recite the menu. Frank refused, reminding Fred that he wasn't in Greenwood to film Black people, because the whole premise of his movie was to examine the attitudes of White Mississippians. But Fred wouldn't relent. He insisted Frank set aside at least a little time to visit the historic restaurant and meet its most endearing waiter.

Frank finally acquiesced, so one night the two men did what countless others had done before them: They walked down Carrollton Avenue toward a redbrick building with the name "Lusco's" painted next to a set of double glass doors. They passed through the entrance and stood in the restaurant's large foyer with the hope of being waited on by Booker Wright.

Inside, well-to-do Whites were standing around waiting to be seated. Black waiters dressed in white moved quickly and efficiently about, carrying plates and calling out orders. Even from where he stood by the front door, Frank could smell Lusco's succulent steaks sizzling on the grill.

After a few minutes, the two men were led to a table covered with a white linen cloth, matching napkins, plates, and silverware. A heavy Black man approached the table and greeted them. The waiter had a wide, bright smile, wore black pants, a matching bow tie, and a white chef's coat, and he had a crisp white towel slung over his arm.

"How ya' doin' tonight?" he asked, bowing with a slight bend at the waist. "My name is Booker."

"I've heard that you have a special way of reciting the menu for White people. I'm a White person, and I was wondering if you would do it for me." Booker smiled, ignored the awkward clunkiness of Frank's request, tilted his head back, and in a warm, raspy voice started his one-man show.

"We don't have a written menu. I'll be glad to tell you what we're going to serve tonight. Everything we serve is à la carte," as he spoke, his words strung together into a song, and he swayed from side to side, barely stopping to take in a breath.

We have fresh shrimp cocktail, Lusco's shrimp,
    Fresh oysters on a half shell, baked oysters, oysters Rockefeller, oysters almandine, stewed oysters, fried oysters,

Spanish mackerel, western sirloin steak, club steak, T-bone
steak, porterhouse steak, rib eye steak, Lusco's special steak,
Broiled mushrooms with the flavor of garlic,
Tight spaghetti and meatballs,
Soft shell crab,
French fried onions, golden brown donut style.
The best food in the world is served at Lusco's.

Booker finished with the flash of a smile, and Frank realized
that not only was he clapping, he was laughing in spite of himself. The waiter reminded Frank of something from long ago, a
Black minstrel show. In Booker, Frank saw the embodiment of
the Negro on the stage. He didn't know how he'd use it, but Frank
knew he wanted to film the waiter performing the menu for his
documentary. To his delight, Booker was quick to agree to go on
camera.

As the two men continued to talk, a short, dark-haired Italian
woman approached the table. "If you're planning on doing anything
with your movie with him, forget it," she said, indicating that Frank's
reputation had preceded him. "I don't allow any cameras to come
into this place. This place is off limits to you. You come here to eat
and that's it."

Frank put on his most charismatic smile and tried to win her
over, but she wasn't having it. When she walked away, Booker leaned
over to the filmmaker and whispered, "Listen, you want to get my
picture? I got a place. We can do it there."

Frank agreed, so the following day he made his way to the Black
side of town to a street called McLaurin that was littered with worn-
out clubs and eateries. He pulled up in front of Booker's Place and
went inside. Once the crew had finished setting up their gear, Frank
asked Booker to recite the menu. The waiter did it almost the same
way he'd done it the night before, bringing a powerful and joyful

energy into the small space. This time however, when his song came to an end, Booker didn't stop.

While the camera was still rolling, the waiter made a profound shift. Without missing a beat, he abruptly came out of character—at once revealing that his persona had been false and that beneath his song and smile ran a current of tortured emotions. As if deftly stepping from behind a carefully constructed veil, Booker turned to his side and said, "That's how I talk because that's what my customers, I say 'my customers,' be expecting of me. When I come in, this is the way they want me to dress," he said.

Then he changed his voice and said with angry authority, "Booker, tell my people what you got."

He returned to his own voice and said, "Some people nice, some is not. Some call me Booker, some call me Jim, some call me John, some call me nigga! All of that hurts, but you have to smile. If you don't"—he raised his voice again—" 'What's wrong with you, why you not smilin'? Get over there and get me so and so and so and so!' "

He went on, "There are some nice people. 'Don't talk to Booker like that. Now, his name is Booker.' Then I got some more people come in real nice, 'How you do, waiter, what's your name?' Then I take care of some so good and I keep that smile. I always learned to smile. The meaner the man be, the more you smile, although you're crying on the inside or you're wondering, 'What else can I do?'

"Sometimes he'll tip you, sometimes he'll say, 'I'm not gonna tip that nigga, you don't look for no tip.'

"Yes, sir, thank you." Booker was using own his voice, but it was softer, placating. " 'What did you say?!?' " Then, while bowing as if to pacify an aggressor and in a voice so soft it was almost a whisper, "Come back, be glad to take care of you."

Continuing to replay the scene, he went on, " 'Don't talk to him like that, that's a good nigga, that's my nigga.' Yessir, boss, I'm your nigga." He nodded, smiling idiotically.

Then he returned to himself. "I'm trying to make a living. Why? I got three children. I want them to get an education. I wasn't fortunate enough to get an education, but I want them to get it, and they're doing good. Night after night, I lay down and I dream about what I had to go through with. I don't want my children to have to go through with that. I want them to be able to get the job that they feel qualified for. That's what I'm struggling for. I don't want this and I don't want that, but I just don't want my children to have to go through what I go through with." His smile was gone. He changed back to the angry voice again and said, "'Hey, tell that nigga to hurry up with that coffee!'"

His voice softened, barely louder than a whisper, and he said, "I'm on my way." Later, when the camera was still rolling, Booker slumped over in a chair, and as if he was singing a commercial jingle he said, "Just remember, you got to keep that smile."

Mississippi: A Self-Portrait aired nationwide on the evening of Tuesday, April 5, 1966, on NBC during a time when TV watchers had fewer than a handful of channels to choose from. Newspapers throughout the country carried stories about the documentary, and almost all of them mentioned Booker's touching yet disturbing monologue. In two minutes of television, the duplicitous heart of racism was laid bare, and while the nation was watching, the Negro on the stage sang a very different song.

A Moralist

The night *Mississippi: A Self-Portrait* aired marked the culmination of one of Frank De Felitta's most ambitious projects. Almost an entire year had passed between the evening when Frank filmed Booker Wright and the night when the waiter's image was splashed across televisions screens in homes throughout the nation.

During that year Frank experienced a lingering disquiet about Booker's scene. As a filmmaker he knew the raw vulnerability Booker exhibited made for wonderful television. As a concerned citizen Frank understood that Booker's scene offered up a snapshot of the inhumanity of segregation, an image not diluted by screaming crowds or conversations about critical legislative change. And as a human being, Frank had seen enough of Greenwood, Mississippi to know that those two and a half minutes of footage had the potential to upend Booker's world and to put the waiter's life in grave danger.

After recording Booker's scene, Frank had provided the waiter with his phone number and told Booker that he could delete his interview from the film if Booker changed his mind. Months later when it was getting close to their airdate and Frank hadn't heard from Booker, he reached out to him directly. Frank wanted to give Booker one last chance to have the scene removed and maybe even to quiet the worry in his soul, but the waiter refused.

In the days before *Mississippi: A Self-Portrait* aired, newspapers across the country were publishing stories about it. Like the film itself, many of the writers of these stories were clearly attempting to examine and understand the race issue in the Southern states. Several articles included excerpts from the film. When considered in its entirety, most reported that the documentary was balanced; however, some of the printed excerpts from the film may have sounded less so. Taken from Frank McGhee's voice-over, a few of the excerpts sounded like the musings of an inquisitive scientist describing White Mississippians as if they were a strange, difficult-to-understand species. Johnstown, Pennsylvania's *Tribune-Democrat* included the following from McGhee's voice-over in the film:

> Put race aside, and most Mississippians are humble, gentle, charming, courteous, hospitable, and humorous people . . . Add race, and many of the Mississippians become fearful and sense doom in the future. They feel they are surrounded by Negroes used as unwitting instruments by outsiders—Negroes who do not realize they are being used in a larger plot to weaken the white race and destroy America. They see themselves as the last defenders of Western Civilization.
>
> The personal concern of nearly all Mississippians for individual Negroes is genuine. It is warm and deep. They feel a responsibility for the welfare of the Negroes they know; care for them in illness and distress; often intercede for them in minor brushes with the law. It's a paternalism, tinged with guilt; an outgrowth of the slave-master relationship requiring subservence of the Negro.

Some of the reports made Frank and Fred Ramsey sound like heroes who'd returned home from a harrowing journey. In the New

Jersey *Trentonian*, Fred Ramsey Jr. described Greenwood as "the scene of the Emmett Till murder and . . . the home of the man accused and acquitted of slaying Medgar Evers. Greenwood," says Ramsey, "is a tough town."

He referred to his three months in Mississippi as "a rough experience for the NBC crew. It was not a congenial atmosphere. We knew at all times that we were being trailed and watched by the Klan."

The Tiffon, Ohio, *Advertiser Tribune* captured a moment in which Frank De Felitta may have been trying to explain how such conditions, such prejudices, such violence were allowed to continue for so long when he said that "Until recently . . . most responsible white citizens of the state who did not approve of the injustices and violence of this closed society remained silent." However, it was a reporter named Eleanor Roberts with The *Boston Traveler* who was able to get the most intimate portrait of how Frank really felt about the motivations behind that Southern silence.

> It is painful for the white man in Mississippi to adjust his thinking . . . They say we're not prejudiced against the Negro, we like him. Yet in the next breath they add, "But why should we integrate our schools?" They complain that Negro children know all about sex and the seamy side of life by six and seven, that it would be bad to have them mix with white children at that age. But they refuse to "recognize that the Negro child's lot is a direct consequence of the white man's actions."
>
> What emerges in this documentary is a degree of inflexibility in their thinking. They find it hard to realize that their attitude towards the Negro is morally wrong.

"Every time I go over the film I get more depressed," but by the end of the article the filmmaker acknowledged that "there is also a feeling of sorrow for the southern white man who is embroiled in this untenable situation."

It's difficult to know if word of these articles made their way back to the residents of Greenwood by way of calls from distant relatives or friends. The *Greenwood Commonwealth* only included a listing of the film with other shows scheduled to come on television that day. Regardless of whether or not Greenwood Whites were excited or apprehensive about the documentary, they treated its airing as if it was an important event.

The night *Mississippi: A Self-Portrait* aired, Booker was waiting tables at Lusco's, and as usual, the restaurant was packed with customers, many of them members of the planter class. When the documentary came on, people began crowding around the extra-large black-and-white television in the foyer. Frank had edited the film in such a way that Booker's scene delivered a potent punch, a wake-up call of sorts sent out to viewers around the country. But in Greenwood and inside Lusco's that night, the punch was not a wake-up call. It was a devastating, leveling blow.

In an article that appeared in the *Houston Chronicle*, Ann Hodges described exactly what was happening in the film before Booker shared his personal story. To set it up, Hodges quotes McGhee's assessment that many of the Whites he'd interviewed saw themselves as "the last defenders of society as they have always known it." The article proceeds:

> To prove McGhee's thesis, the program interviewed a number of leading Mississippi citizens, including a group at a business man's luncheon . . . "It is difficult for me to understand why the entire country is so intent on integrating our schools," said one of them. "We don't hate Negroes. We love them as individuals."
>
> But their conversation was negated by the powerful appearance of **Booker Wright**, a Negro restaurant owner, whose candid words packed a potent message: "Some White men are nice and some are mean." He smiled. "Some call me

Booker and some call me nigger. All that hurts, but you've got to smile. The meaner the man, the more you smile. Why do I do it? I got three children. I don't want them to go through what I go through. 'Come here, nigger, get that coffee,' yes sir, but remember, keep that smile."

The film was cut to make Booker's words act as a direct response to the claim of Whites that Blacks in the Delta were happy to live in shacks, go to dilapidated schools, and live with the constant threat of violence. That night at Lusco's the response to Booker's words was swift and harsh. The customers he was serving began calling out, proclaiming that they didn't want Booker to be their waiter. Then the phone began to ring. Some of Lusco's longtime customers were calling in to say they never wanted Booker to wait on them again.

In the rising noise of the restaurant, Booker turned to its owner, Miss Marie, and said, "Well, I think it's time for me to go."

The dark-haired woman looked up at him and simply said, "Yes, Booker, I think it is."

In the days that followed, newspapers from Washington State to Florida carried stories about Frank De Felitta's cinematic achievement. Percy Shain of the *Boston Herald* began his article by saying, "It is hard to believe that NBC could go into the heart of Mississippi (I use the word heart advisedly) and draw from it an hour-long documentary of inspiration and hope and feeling in exploring the race issue."

A reviewer with *RTD* said the documentary was "easily the best of its kind ever done on race relations in the Deep South." Danbury, Connecticut's *News Times* called it "a superb documentary which actually succeeds in telling both sides of the Civil Rights battle in a state which has the deepest traditions of the old South."

The Flora, Illinois, *News Record* described the film's tone as "a lesson in controlled good taste and careful diplomacy," and the *Atlanta Journal and Constitution* called it "a many-sided and many-faceted exposition of Mississippians' thinking," and ended the piece by declaring that *Mississippi: A Self-Portrait* was "television journalism at its best." Many of the newspapers reported on a sense of hope that ran through the documentary. A writer with the Sharon, Pennsylvania, *Herald* spoke of how the film sought to "keep in mind the compassion that is necessary to solve all such entangled human dilemmas."

The majority of the stories mentioned specific scenes, and many of them referred to Booker. A newspaper out of Fort Wayne, Indiana, reported that, in an extremely telling moment, "Booker Wright, Negro restaurant owner by day and waiter by night, tells how he plays 'Uncle Tom' and keeps smiling so that he can earn the money to give his children an education."

Another Indiana paper described a "wrenching moment when a Negro waiter named Booker Wright recited—in beaming, cadenced pride—a long and complicated menu, then for a moment bared his soul." Another simply expressed that "the words of Booker Wright . . . offered material for additional exploration." A critic for *Newsday* reported that one of "the most telling segments of the film" was when "a Negro waiter [was] recounting his 'Uncle Tom' technique," and the *Boston Herald* made note of "the Negro waiter who told what was really going through his mind while he bowed and kowtowed to his clientele."

The *Philadelphia Inquirer* described that in the film, "Several prejudice-denying Whites insisted that all Mississippi Negroes have always been very 'happy,' but one of them, a waiter, gave moving testimony of what lay behind his fixed smile."

The *Journal and Courier* out of Lafayette, Indiana, focused an entire article on Booker by taking six paragraphs to print, word-for-word, what he'd said about his relationships with his customers. The *Seattle Times* reported that "unforgettable were the comments of a Negro who worked in his own restaurant by day and moonlighted as a waiter at a White restaurant. He insisted that however insulting his White customers might become, the one thing he had to remember was to 'keep that smile.'"

For a moment in time, people throughout the country were abuzz with the words of an illiterate Black waiter from a small cotton town who'd managed to capture their hearts. Hodding Carter III would describe Booker's scene as "the most stunning, absolutely pitch-perfect, straight-on rendition of one humiliation that was his regular existence as a waiter in that place which was of course the seg's favorite place . . . When I saw it, I thought to myself, 'He's a dead man.'"

It turned out that Frank was right on all counts. Booker's scene made for excellent filmmaking: It gave people insight into the deep emotional pain caused by segregationist policies, and it also put Booker in danger. Whether motivated by the initial broadcast or the way it reignited nationwide critiques of White Southerners, not long after the film aired, a White cop overtook Booker one night when he was alone. The officer beat him—pistol-whipped him, to be precise. As far as anyone can tell, Booker never spoke of the broadcast or the beating, not even to his children.

Possibly because so few Blacks owned televisions, *Mississippi: A Self-Portrait* appeared to have gone unnoticed in Black Greenwood.

Almost thirty years later, when John T. Edge was conducting research on Lusco's for an assignment in a graduate seminar class, he found that when he asked people "about the civil rights movement, almost without exception people told me that they remembered Booker being interviewed on the NBC news."

Many Whites who believed they'd shared true friendship with Booker were insulted by his explanation that he only spoke the way he did to make his customers happy. It was a detail they could not or would not get beyond. They felt defrauded. They found out on national television that the one Black man they trusted, the one they saw as upstanding and respectable, had built relationships with them out of a kind of counterfeit affection.

By the end of the twentieth century, scholars viewed Greenwood, Mississippi, as a critical town during the civil rights movement. It was a town Martin Luther King Jr. visited, a place of marches, murders, and triumphs, but for local Whites it was a single man who'd gone on television and spent two minutes sharing how he felt, who was remembered long after others were forgotten.

When John T. finally saw the footage, well over a decade after he'd completed his research, he considered why Booker's moment may have been so profound and so memorable. "Booker was not necessarily an activist, maybe Booker was a moralist. Because if you think about what he did, he spoke about how he was being treated and what he wanted for his children. He made a basic moral argument. 'I'm being mistreated. My children don't have the opportunities they should have. That's what I want for the future.' That's a basic moral argument."

Apparently, this simple notion was powerful. Several of the Whites John T. interviewed expressed that it was when Booker unloaded his emotional burden on the national news that "the civil rights movement came home for them; that was the moment of impact for them."

Part Six
Mothers

It wasn't my surface most defiled.

Eddie Vedder

A Crack in the World

When I spoke with John T. in 2007, he'd heard stories about Booker's news appearance, but he hadn't seen the footage himself. From what he described, I imagined a classic "man-on-the-street piece," in which Booker was randomly stopped by a newsman who put a microphone in front of his face, and then Booker—out of anger or without thinking—made provocative statements about life in the Delta. That's what I believed for four years until I had the opportunity to see it for myself.

I made several attempts to find the footage he'd appeared in, but always to no avail. When I first learned about Booker from John T., I started a blog where I'd post a few times a year with random updates about my search. Then in April 2011, I was contacted by a man named David Zellerford. He said he was a good friend of a filmmaker named Raymond De Felitta whose father, a retired filmmaker named Frank, was the person who'd originally filmed Booker in 1965. David had found my blog and said he had the footage of Booker appearing on *NBC News*. A few days later, he emailed the video file to me.

When I sat down to watch the footage, I tried to prepare myself for the shock of seeing my grandfather and hearing his voice, but I was completely unprepared for how much he revealed about himself.

After watching Booker's monologue for the first time, I heard myself say, "This isn't what I thought it would be. This isn't what I thought it would be."

My grandfather had lived a humiliated life, and whatever he experienced was so bad that he lay awake in bed at night fearing that his own children might have to go through the same thing. When Whites who thought they were friends with my grandfather referred to him as "my nigga," he had to degrade himself by taking on a high-pitched, idiotic voice and proclaiming, "Yes, I'm yo nigga."

It broke my heart. I was so proud of him. And I knew that he was not an accidental activist, because his interview wasn't spontaneous. It was clear from the lighting, the camera angles, and the setup that the moment was well planned. My grandfather had the chance to think about what he would say. He took a calculated and courageous risk.

But why? He wasn't a full-time, speech-giving activist funded by a nationwide organization. After the broadcast, he wasn't going to be walking through town with strong Black men who'd pledged to keep him safe or moving on to give another speech in another city. Booker pulled back the curtain on his own town. He exposed the people he worked with and whose tips had helped fund his dream of restaurant ownership. He knew he'd have to face them, and he had to know they wouldn't be happy.

It was just a moment—a beautiful, thoughtful, well-executed moment—of stark honesty in which one man who had nothing to gain removed the mask of his everyday existence to show his most basic, raw humanity, and in doing so, he was able to touch the most basic, raw humanity of everyone who saw it. Long before reading any of the news articles that came out, long before listening to anyone else describe the impact of Booker's words, I understood their power because of how the piece touched me not as a granddaughter but as a human being.

But the question remained: Why did he do it?

I viewed the film footage over and over again, each time noting something different. One time, I noticed how closely my son resemble Booker. At the time, Dexter was four, and his thick brown skin was taut over his cheekbones. Whenever Dexter smiled, the skin on his cheeks got thinner and took on a lighter shade, making his face appear to light up from the inside. Booker's face did the same thing.

Each time I watched him say, "Well, that's what you have to go through with, but remember, ya gotta keep that smile," I'd press pause and gaze into his eyes. I wondered what it would have been like to have known him, to have grown up with him in my life like my mom had. That thought always led to the sinking realization that, sooner or later, I was going to have to connect with my mom to share this with her.

My mom, sister, and baby brother had all moved to Phoenix a few years after I did. Even though we were within an hour's drive of one another, we almost never interacted.

The previous fall, after eighteen months of silence, she'd called to ask me if I wanted to bring the family over. She was looking at her calendar and she mentioned meeting on November 15, then said, "No, how about November 22?"

"I'm not sure about that day, November 22," I responded.

"Oh?"

"No . . . well . . ." I held out for as long as I could, but it didn't help her memory. Finally, I said, "That's my birthday, and I don't know what Milt has planned." It had been years since she'd called or sent a card, but I never thought she'd forget on which day I'd been born. Each of those little occurrences, those minor slights, was a cut made with the finest of blades. The more time I spent with her, the more likely it was that I'd bleed out. We didn't get together that time, and I was glad.

In the days when I was watching Booker on video over and over again, I knew I'd end up sharing it with her. Although I was reluctant to connect with my mom, I was also curious about how she would respond to the video. When I first told her in 2007 that I was looking into Booker's life, she said wonderful things about him, but seemed to feel somehow cheated out of what the two of them could've shared, because she never quite got along with Honey.

Every time I watched my grandfather talk about his love for his children. I thought of my mother. I'd imagine myself being there when she watched the video for the first time. I wanted to see her face when she once again saw his. But I was afraid that I'd mess it up somehow. Maybe I'd say the wrong thing and upset her. I figured it would be easier for both of us if I just emailed the video file of Booker's television appearance, but I didn't have her email address. Four days after I first watched it, I decided to call her from the car when I only had a few minutes to talk. As I dialed, I was half hoping she wouldn't answer.

"Hello." She sounded as though she'd rushed to the phone. I wondered if her caller ID let her know it was me. My heart lifted. Maybe she'd missed me.

I asked her how she was. Fine. She asked me how I was. Fine. She asked about the kids. Getting bigger. Then, silence. Before the awkwardness could overtake us, I decided to tell her why I'd called. I felt a little guilty, though, because it dawned on me that she may have thought I was calling to say hello or even to reconnect.

"Remember a few years ago when I heard about your father appearing in the news?" I sounded like I was introducing a studio audience to a mystery that would begin *after these messages*.

"Yes," she responded, with an equally cryptic voice.

"Well, the man who filmed it has a son, and his son's friend called me and sent me the film." It was clunky. I should've rehearsed.

"And it's Daddy?" I'd never heard her use that word before.

My voice softened. "Yeah, Mom, it's your dad, Booker Wright."

"Oh my God," she whispered.

"I can email it to you, if you'd like to see it."

"Yeah." She was distant. "Send it to me." I could see the lines popping up on her forehead. I pictured her lips next to the receiver, moving without sound coming out. I wondered if I hung up right then whether she would even notice.

I spoke louder, hoping to bring her back. "I don't have your email address, Mom. I can write it down."

"Why don't you and Milt and the kids come over for dinner?" Her voice was airy, like she was in a dream.

"Sure," I heard myself say. "When would you like us to come over?" My hand, the one holding the phone, did a violent, involuntary shake. Normally I would say yes and then act as though we'd set up a time at some later, never-to-come date. Maybe some part of me was calling her bluff, seeing if she'd actually have us over.

"How about the third Sunday in April?"

"Sure."

She gave me both of her addresses, email and home. I wrote them down in the car, and when I got back to my house, I emailed her the video file.

I closed my laptop. In the time and silence that had grown between us, I'd removed my mom from the parts of my life that mattered to me by not telling her about them. She never asked and I never offered details about my children, my marriage, my work, my neighborhood, my friends, my hobbies, or anything else. Every new thing that came into my world made me more of a stranger to her because she had no knowledge of it. While I hadn't intentionally constructed the distance between us, I enjoyed being free from feelings of rejection. I'd forgotten to miss her, and I'd stopped being paralyzed by her absence.

I glanced at my closed computer and wondered if I'd left the back door to my life unlocked.

WE WENT TO MY mom's house on a Sunday afternoon. When she opened the door, I couldn't believe what I saw. She had changed so much. She'd lost a lot of weight and looked tired, older. She was wearing a wig and lipstick, but no other makeup. Her eyes looked like someone else's. Throughout the afternoon, she maintained a warm smile and made awkward jokes that Milton and I were quick to laugh at.

Bishop was excited about meeting my mother. He acted as if she was a new toy, something he wanted to spend hours playing with. Every time she asked either of the boys a question, Bishop would answer with a lively smile dancing on his lips. Dexter was quiet. When she hugged him, he pulled away and leaned into me and told me in a whisper that she smelled funny.

I felt strange around my mom. To me, motherhood was invigorating. I loved my sons with a love that was more than love. I often told them that if my affection for them was a sound, it would be so loud that it would leave a crack in the world. Everything on earth would shift, skyscrapers would collapse into the sea, sleeping volcanos would erupt, and rain would cease to fall because my love for them was greater than any planet could contain.

When I tickled them, I'd say between giggles, "Remember how big my love for you is." When they were drifting off to sleep, I'd lean in close and whisper, "My love for you knows no bounds." When they were wiping their mouths on their sleeves, I'd kiss the tops of their heads and say, "I can't believe how lucky I am to have you as my sons."

Becoming a mom had awakened a strength in me that I hadn't known before. Mother love is primal. Indestructible. Yet here was this woman who'd become a stranger to me because she didn't feel like picking up the phone and dialing my number. I pushed against the temptation to feel all the things I'd felt as a girl—that something must be profoundly wrong with me, something so terrible that it could destroy the most powerful thing in the universe, a mother's love.

As we ate our lunch, a familiar feeling was coming. I could sense it, smell it in the air like a wave moving toward land. Worthlessness wanted to wash me away. Seeing my mom live a life without me, as if she'd never given birth to me, was painful. I couldn't detect anything in her tone, in her eyes, or her movements to indicate that she'd missed me at all. I focused instead on what was wrong with her. I searched for her flaws so that I could convince myself that I didn't want her love anyway.

The kids finished eating before we did, and my mom said, "I've got a new movie, *Rio*. How about I put it on for the kids?"

"That's okay, I brought toys for them," I said. I didn't like for my kids to watch too much television and they never watched movies before I'd researched their content on different parenting sites. Plus, letting her know that my kids were smart enough to entertain themselves felt like a jab to her parenting abilities. I started pulling their toys out while my mom walked over to the television. She turned on *Rio*. Bishop rushed over to watch it and Dexter followed suit.

"It looks like they want to watch it, Yvette," she said. I tried to smile as I repacked their toys. My mom, Milton, and I continued to eat while the kids watched the movie. Milt talked about his students and we listened intently. I was thankful someone else was there to keep my mom and me from falling into silence. I wanted to ask questions about Booker and about Greenwood, but I hadn't written anything down and, for whatever reason, sitting there that day it felt strange to talk about Booker or Greenwood. The two of us never talked about race or about anything vaguely related to it. That

Booker's story was centered on his experiences as a Black man in the South was undeniable. So, even if we did want to talk deeply about him, the roles we'd assigned for ourselves over the years made it almost impossible. My mother and I did not talk about race.

Most of the afternoon it felt as if we were together but trying to avoid land mines. The conversation never dipped below the surface. When the credits on *Rio* began to roll, Milton and I began gathering the children's things. Bishop and Dexter said good-bye to their grandmother. When we were walking to our minivan, my mom followed. She and I made promises to do it again.

As we drove away, I thought about the afternoon I'd just spent with my mom. We were family, but we communicated as if we were citizens from warring nations, loyal to the cause, turning every single interaction into an opportunity to fight or defend.

Had we ever been close? I thought about the moments I'd shared with my children when they were newborns, the ones they'll never remember. Moments of tenderness, cuddles, holding up their heads when their little necks were still too weak to do it on their own.

Surely my mother and I had moments like that. There must have been a time when we were citizens of the same nation, before the ground we were standing on began to shift. When did we become so different?

When I'd gone back to Greenwood, almost a decade before, I'd walked into a JCPenny and was greeted by a cashier with bright eyes and a shocked expression on her face. "You must be Kathereen's daughter!" It took me a second to remember that was how people in Greenwood said my mom's name: "Kath-er-een."

We still looked like sisters, but my mother was reared in the South and had chosen to raise me in the West. In California, where the sun is always shining, I never understood why she turned so many things into a cause to fight for, why she saw race in simple everyday interactions when I did not. The tectonic plates below our feet had shifted.

Now we were standing on either side of an angry sea, staring at each other from distant islands.

I thought of Booker. The way some of his customers spoke to him, their tone and demeanor, and oftentimes their choice of incendiary language, were all drenched in racial stereotypes, power, and hate. If he was a stranger and he'd come to me to share the pain he felt because of the treatment of his customers, would I have understood, or would I have accused him of taking a small thing and making it about race?

A Specific Kind of Pain

The lunch at my mom's house brought back so many things for me. I'd forgotten how difficult it was for us to be around each other. I'd also managed to forget how much I used to long for her affection. I spent almost every day in April 2011 wondering not so much what I'd find as I looked deeper into Booker's life but how those findings would make me feel. The only way I knew how to make it through life was to look away from family pain. Yet here I was embarking on an effort to stare it right in the face.

A few weeks later, I met the two men responsible for sending me the footage of Booker, Raymond De Felitta, Frank's son, and one of his producing partners, David Zellerford. They flew into Phoenix for a day so that we could meet and talk over breakfast. David was slender, with thinning blond hair. Raymond had a thick mane of wavy salt-and-pepper hair. Everything about Raymond—from his smile to his tone of voice to the warmth in his eyes to how he talked by waving his hands in large arcs—was disarming. He was quick to laugh at himself and told stories about conversations he'd had with famous people like John Travolta and Mark Harmon with a casualness that made it seem normal. We hit it off.

Just as I was wanting to learn more about Booker, Raymond

was also curious about who his father had been four decades before when he'd made the choice to travel into the Delta to capture the deeper story of the movement. Raymond told me that *Mississippi: A Self-Portrait* only aired once because some of the affiliates in the Southern states complained about the content. So, aside from the people who'd been watching that night and the members of Frank's family, no one else had seen the film since the day it aired in 1966.

Afterward, Frank made a few more documentaries for NBC before becoming a full-time novel writer and filmmaker. When Raymond was a kid, Frank would often call the family together to have them watch his documentaries, since there was no longer an audience for them. Whenever he showed the Mississippi film, he would say, "Watch this, look at what Booker gave me. Look at what he did for me." So, Raymond had grown up with Booker's name as part of his childhood, knowing that it was connected to the man his father used to be.

Toward the end of our lunch together, Raymond reached over, touched my arm, and said, "I want to make a documentary about Booker's life, and I don't want to do it without you." He explained that we'd conduct research and interview people, only we'd be doing it on camera. I was ecstatic.

While we ate, Raymond shared what his father had told him about Booker and their encounter in the 1960s. In turn, I decided to share with Raymond what I'd learned about Booker from his second wife, Honey. I told him about how Rosie had lost Booker, how Booker longed for her his whole life, and then how Booker finally found his mother.

AS HE GREW OLDER, Booker often found himself wondering about the type of woman his mother was, what kind of person would abandon her own child that way. Had she been young? Single?

Slowly, he began to pull together what little he knew of her. Since it was while they were still living in Grenada when the Wrights discovered Booker on their doorstep, the young restaurant owner figured that his mother was probably also residing in Grenada at that time. Grenada had a population of about four thousand residents in 1930, when Booker would have been about four years old, so it was possible—not likely, but possible—that someone in the Black community might recall a woman who had a child one day and then didn't the next.

In the 1960s, Blacks from all over Mississippi often traveled to Greenwood, and most made it a point to visit Booker's restaurant. There was one young woman who frequently made the trip from her hometown of Grenada to go shopping, and she always made it a point to stop in at Booker's Place. Each time she came in, Booker would ask her if she knew anything about his mother. Her answer was always "no" or "*I* don't know, sir." She would remind Booker that *she* wasn't old enough to have known his mother, but Booker was undeterred. Eventually, he wore her down. One day when he asked the girl about his mother, she gave a different reply. This time she said, "I'm gonna ask my mother when I go back. I don't know, but she might know."

Elated, Booker asked her to have her mother call if she did happen to remember anything that might be useful in his search. "She can call me collect," he said repeatedly. When the girl went back to Grenada, she provided her mother with the few details Booker had given her about the woman he was searching for.

Her mother said, "Yeah, I know this lady."

The following Sunday, the girl's mother called from Grenada and spoke to Honey. She explained that years ago, there was a man trying to date two girls at once, and one of the girls may have been Booker's mother.

"Where did that woman go?" Honey asked her.

"She went to Gulfport somewhere," the woman told Honey, "but she [Booker's mother] got a sister, a daughter or somebody live up the street up there." After they hung up the phone, the woman asked around and was able to find out where Booker's relative worked. Her name was Julia, and she was a teacher at a school in Grenada.

When Honey saw Booker again, she told him everything she'd learned on the call. He said, "You call her back and tell her we'll be up there in the morning. Tell her we'll go there about seven o'clock."

The next morning when they woke up, Booker told Honey to "call and tell everyone they don't need to come to work because it might be twelve o'clock before we get back, and we can open then." Honey made the calls; then she and Booker got in the car and drove to Grenada, arriving at 6:45 a.m.

When they pulled up to the house, Honey said, "Booker, we can't go to nobody's house this early. Everybody don't get up as early as we do, now." So the two of them drove around, and when it was seven o'clock, they knocked on the woman's door. She told them that she thought Julia was either Booker's mother's niece or cousin.

"Will you come with us?" Booker asked.

"Yeah, I'll go with y'all," she said. The three of them loaded into Booker's car, went to the school where Julia worked, and headed straight for the principal's office, where they asked if they could speak to her. The principal took the three of them down to her classroom. He had them wait in the hall while he went inside to let Julia know that someone was there to speak to her.

After a few moments, Julia came out, and right there in the hall, Booker shared with her the few details he knew about his mother. Julia remembered that her own mother had told her years before that her sister's son had had to go to the doctor to have a sore lanced. While Booker had no recollection of Julia, he still had a vague memory of the lancing procedure.

"Well, do you know where she at?" Booker asked.

"Yes." Julia told him that his mother was living in Chicago.

"Has you got her number?" Booker asked.

"Yeah, but it's a neighborhood number where she gets her calls at, and she work. I don't think she'll be home until five o'clock in the evening; that's when she get off."

"Well, you give her my number, tell her to call me, call me collect. I'll pay for it," Booker replied, and then turned to Honey and said, "I'm going back to Lusco's and I'm gonna tell 'em that I won't be at work today."

That evening, while he waited for Rosie to call, Booker was a bundle of nerves. The telephone at Booker's Place was back near the bathrooms. It was a public phone, and anyone could make calls on it using their own money. As five o'clock approached, Booker took a seat on the stool next to the phone. A few times, customers came back to use it, but Booker looked up and said, "No, y'all can't use the phone now. Can't use the phone."

The clock struck five o'clock, but the phone did not ring.

"It's five o'clock, she ain't called," he said to Honey.

"Well, maybe she got to get off of work maybe and come home," Honey replied. "Give her a little time." But he wanted her right then.

About thirty more minutes passed, moving as slow as molasses, before the phone rang. Booker looked at Honey and cried, "You answer it!" Honey picked up the phone and nodded at Booker. It was her. It was Rosie.

Booker began to cry. He took the phone from Honey, and after a few words said, "I thought you didn't want me and just throwed me away, I never would see you no more."

After several minutes he said, "Look, I'm a let you talk to my wife, now you give her the telephone number and everything and you call me collect. Look, when you coming down here?"

Rosie told Booker that she'd have to wait at least two weeks before traveling to Greenwood because she had to give notice at her job before taking a vacation.

"Well, you just come on, I'm a send you the money and everything," Booker told her.

Honey said, "Look, people can't just do like you think they can. That's her job. She got to let them know."

Booker handed Honey the phone, and she spoke with Rosie, who was also crying. Then Honey handed the phone back to Booker, who talked and cried, and then handed the phone back to Honey. They did this over and over again.

When Honey was on the phone with her, Rosie tried to explain that she never wanted to leave Booker.

"I understand," Honey told her.

"Well, he doesn't," Rosie cried.

"He's just upset because he's been wanting to see you so much," Honey said, trying to soothe her. "Night after night he always talked about he wish he could find his mama. He reckon his mama was dead, his mama didn't care nothin' about him."

But Rosie explained to Honey about the White man that was coming to whip her and how she feared they might also whip Booker.

After a few more minutes of conversation, they said their good-byes. The following night Rosie called again and told Booker she'd made the arrangements with her job to take time off, and Booker told her he would send her the money for her trip down to Greenwood. Mother and son talked for so long that night on the phone that Honey finally said to Booker, "Now you got to let her go to bed, 'cause she got to get up and go to work in the morning."

The next day, Honey went to the bank and withdrew travel money for Rosie.

Every night, until she left Chicago for Greenwood, Rosie and Booker spoke on the phone and reviewed the plans for her trip.

Finally, the day came for Booker and Rosie to meet face-to-face. He invited a crowd of people to a party he was planning to throw at the restaurant that afternoon. He and Honey prepared dishes all morning long, but at 3:00 p.m. they closed Booker's Place and, along with one of their friends, got in the car and headed for the train station.

When the train pulled in, Booker began making his way toward it, pushing past people so that he could be in front when the doors opened. There was something comical about the way Booker just assumed that his mother would be the first one off the train. His unrestrained eagerness was almost childish, clearly hopeful, and infinitely sad.

Finally, Rosie stepped off the train, already crying. She went to Booker and the two clutched each other and stood there, in the middle of the platform, crying together. There were people around them, some who were waiting for friends to arrive and others who'd just disembarked and needed to find their luggage. Many of those people slowed down and then stopped to watch Booker and Rosie. The two held each other as if they feared someone would come along to tear them apart again, as if by holding each other they could communicate all the love they hadn't been able to share before.

The minutes ticked away. At first Honey was impatient, wondering how long Booker and Rosie would keep this up. Then she noticed that the friend who'd come along with them had started to cry as well. She stopped thinking about how much time was passing by and started thinking about family. She figured she might've felt the same way if she hadn't seen her own mother for so many years. She realized then that some people just don't know how important it is to have a family. Even if all you have is a cousin here or there, that's still a blessing. People might argue, but you can't take it to heart, not if it's family. To her surprise, Honey found herself crying as well.

Thirty minutes would pass before Booker and Rosie finally let go of each other. They climbed into the car and headed for Booker's Place. When they arrived, the food had been laid out nicely. Booker took a plate and served Rosie. He wanted her to get the first bite of every dish. And even though all the guests invited already knew what the occasion was, Booker kept introducing Rosie to people and saying, "This my mama," as though finally being able to say those words felt so good that he wanted to do it again and again.

After lunch, Booker, Rosie, Honey, and the friend who'd gone to the station with them all climbed back into Booker's car and headed to Clarksdale so that Rosie could introduce Booker to some family she had there. They stayed in Clarksdale talking, laughing, and telling stories until seven o'clock the next morning.

Instead of heading back to Greenwood, Booker wanted to take Rosie to Grenada to see Julia, the woman who was responsible for bringing the two of them back together. On the way there, Honey sat in the front passenger seat, while their friend drove the car. Booker and Rosie were on the backseat where they sat together silently crying and kissing each other.

It was difficult for me to tell the entire story to Raymond without tearing up. I knew what it was like to feel rootless, like you don't belong to anything or anyone. Booker spent his entire life feeling unwanted by his mother and unworthy of her love. The moment that I always tried to picture in my mind was the one of him sitting on a stool and crying into the phone. He was at Booker's Place, the place where he was king, but in spite of all of his success there was something broken inside him that could be healed only by what he learned on that phone call. He was wanted. In that one call, in that one moment, he found redemption. He opened up the envelope of his boyhood heart, and his mother filled it with a story of never wanting to let him go. She had not chosen to abandon him. She had not left him on a doorstep. I felt that Booker and I had similar longings, a song sung in two-part harmony, our voices so close that a listener could never discern where his stopped and mine started. I understood what it was like to feel a loneliness that can only be cured by having family, by having someone who makes you feel tethered to the world.

When I finished sharing the story, Raymond was silent for several beats as if pulling his thoughts together. David looked from me to Raymond and back to me, and then said he didn't think the story was relevant to the documentary. I didn't agree with him, but I also knew that my emotional attachment to my grandfather's story made it difficult for me to have an objective perspective. I figured I'd have time to think more about it later. I took a sip of my cold coffee, and the three of us went on to discuss when we would be able to travel to Greenwood together.

Then, as if something finally crystalized in his mind, and as though we'd never stopped talking about Rosie and Booker, Raymond looked at me with searching eyes and said, "You know, that kind of hurt stays with you. I've met people who are extremely successful and talented, but they never find peace or feel like they have any value at all because their parents didn't love them. That's a very specific kind of pain. It can be crippling. No matter how old they get, or no matter how smart they are, most people never get over feeling rejected by the people who're supposed to love them the most."

A History Lesson

Raymond and I were equally in awe of Booker's story, but we both needed to understand so much more about life in the Delta before we began conducting interviews for the documentary. So, for the next six weeks, I committed myself to research. A professor at a local university suggested I read a book called *I've Got the Light of Freedom*, by Charles Payne. In his book, Payne lays out the conditions, both social and economic, of Black lives in the years before the civil rights movement and then goes on to describe how it was local people who had the courage and the drive to keep the movement alive. Payne's book centers almost entirely on Greenwood. It was an amazing read and I pored over it. I read other books as well, books about the flood of 1927 and narratives of Blacks who'd lived in the Delta before, during, and after the civil rights movement.

I saw a photograph in which a Black woman's body hangs lifeless, suspended from a bridge over the still and tranquil waters of a river. Her son's body hangs next to hers. Mother and child lynched together. Standing on the bridge is a crowd of White men, women, and even some children looking toward the camera, posing for the photograph.

I read an excerpt from a speech Abraham Lincoln gave in January of 1838 after a visit to Mississippi in which he said, "Dead men were seen literally dangling from the boughs of trees upon every road side." He was most likely exaggerating to illustrate an important point: The state of Mississippi was a place of violence.

I was familiar with the Jim Crow laws of the South, but the more I read, the more I was convinced that Mississippians played by their own rules. These rules, though largely unspoken and unwritten, were taught and reinforced by violence, causing Blacks to lead lives of constant vigilance. After hours of research I distilled the rules down to six major themes:

Never tell a White man he's wrong. One night, a Black man named James Gooden was resting on his front porch after having worked all night at trying to restore the levee after the flood of 1927. A police officer pulled up and called to Gooden, ordering him to get into the truck so that he could go work at the camps. Gooden said he'd just returned from work, but the officer didn't care. After a fruitless discussion, Gooden got up and walked into his house. Though uninvited, the officer followed him inside and shot him. Gooden died a few days later.

Never appear to be disrespectful. In 1934, a seventy-year-old tenant farmer named Henry Bedford got into a verbal disagreement with a White man about land. The man felt that Bedford had spoken to him disrespectfully, so he, along with three others, beat him until he died.

Never be accused of committing a crime. In 1936, when Roosevelt Townes was in his mid-twenties, he was accused of murdering a White man. A mob of three hundred or more that included women and children tortured Townes with a blowtorch for over an hour, during which time each of his fingers and both of his ears were burned off, one by one. Later, Townes was set aflame while still alive.

Never be too prosperous. In 1944, a sixty-six-year-old minister named Isaac Simmons farmed 278 acres of land that he owned outright, some of which had been in his family since 1887. White men began making claims to some of his land. Fearful that what he owned might be taken out from under him, Simmons sought advice from an attorney.

Word of the visit got out, and Simmons was assaulted on his own property by six armed White men. He was shot to death in front of one of his sons, who was beaten and told to evacuate the property. When the son returned to claim the body, he found that his father's teeth had been knocked out, his arm broken, and his tongue cut out. I found this story so disturbing that I wrote about it on my blog. A woman who read the post contacted me and said she was a descendent of Isaac Simmons. She told me that even though her family didn't live on the land stolen from Simmons, they did still have the deed that he'd tried so hard to protect for them.

Never be in the wrong place at the wrong time. In 1949, a man named Malcolm Wright, his wife, and five of his seven children were traveling down a road in a mule-pulled buggy. Three White men, traveling down the same road in a car, had trouble maneuvering past Wright's buggy. They became angry, got out of their vehicle, and dragged Wright, who was unarmed, down to the road. With a bumper jack, one of the men beat Wright in the head repeatedly in front of his family, who watched in horror as Wright's skull caved in and his brains oozed out onto the side of the road.

Never touch a White woman. In 1951, a Black man named Denzill Turner had an epileptic seizure at a bus stop. The White men who witnessed it didn't understand what was happening, so they assumed Turner was drunk and that he was allowing his body to flop around so that he could touch White women. The police were called, and when they arrived, they accosted Turner. After a brief struggle, the officers shot him in the head.

These incidents weren't the only ones I read about, nor were they the worst. Charley Shepherd's lynching lasted for seven hours and ended with him being set on fire. "The mob saw to it that his mouth and nose were partially filled with mud so that the inhalation of the gas fumes would not bring his agony to a premature end." He burned alive for forty-five minutes before finally his "agonized fighting at the ropes and flames" subsided.

According to Charles Payne:

Such mutilations—parading dead bodies around the town, shooting or burning bodies already dead, severing body parts and using them for souvenirs, using corkscrews to pull spirals of flesh from living victims or roasting people over slow fires—were as much a part of the ritual of lynching as the actual killing. They sent a more powerful message than straightforward killing would have sent, graphically reinforcing the idea that Negroes were so far outside the human family that the most inhuman actions could be visited upon them.

During those six weeks, there were times when I felt as if I was drowning. I didn't want to read anymore, I didn't want to see even one more photo of a Black person being beaten, but I couldn't stop. I needed to learn as much as I could before going down to Greenwood. I needed to understand the world Booker knew so that I could understand him, and then present his story in the film.

Part of what struck me about Black life in the Delta was that the horrors seemed to occur exponentially. After decades of being mistreated, humiliated, sexualized, spoken down to, and forced to do menial jobs, so many Blacks then had to stand by and watch loved ones get beaten to death. Their lives were compounded by one trauma after another: the daily trauma of racial abuse, and the physical trauma of being beaten without cause. I stumbled upon an article about the long-term effects of trauma and how repeated emotionally traumatic events can influence an individual's biochemistry, causing not only psychological scars but also chemical changes that influence how someone interacts with their environment. These chemical changes can imprint themselves on genetic code, allowing the remnants of trauma to be passed down from generation to generation.

My mind was spinning.

I didn't know what to do with all this information I'd learned. It made my soul rage. The stories of loss gave birth to a fire inside me, one that I feared I'd lose the ability to control.

More and more, I thought about the cliché of the angry Black man or woman. I decided that while emotions like anger, bitterness, and even shame aren't altogether uncommon in the human experience, something different—a darker cousin of those emotions—takes over when the hurt is inflicted by someone with power. When those with power abuse it, the ones hurt have no means for retaliation. They can't hurt the powerful the way they've been hurt. When the powerful inflict wounds, it often takes place in the open, within the confines of socially accepted—though morally depraved—behavior.

They wore suits when they lynched you. They drank illegal whiskey from a clean glass. They delicately wiped their mouths on monogramed handkerchiefs after they spat on you. What is left for you to do? You have no resources or purchase of power to tip the scales. As a matter of course, your very essence is socially unacceptable. You have no suit, and you drink moonshine from a dirty mason jar. Your handkerchiefs are handed down, withered, and stained in blood.

Occupying this space in the world is damning. It's a place where the soul is under pressure that builds and builds with each infraction, but there is no room to explode. The explosions happen on the inside, within the soul, making it burn itself up from deep within.

That type of pain, from the flippant and the powerful, withers away all that was good inside of you. After being humiliated day in and day out, what do you have left? Does the fiery pain burning in your soul steal oxygen from your ability to hope, to dream, maybe even to love? How do you accept degradation with a smile and still tell yourself that you're better than that, than the way they're treating you all day, every day? How do you believe that you're different from the way everyone sees you?

Men were treated like boys and women like whores, and then they returned home to their children. Mothers knew they could not protect their sons from being overworked and exploited. Fathers knew they could not protect their daughters and wives from sexual harassment and even rape. What remained in their hearts that they could gift to their children?

Even my mother's explosive rage over my striptease took on new meaning as I learned about the world she'd grown up in, where a woman with a brown body was often a commodity. One Southern governor claimed it was impossible to actually rape Black women, who were viewed by some like dogs in constant heat. In 1944, when Recy Taylor was gang-raped by six White men who all acknowledged what they'd done, two grand juries declined to indict.

I thought of my father and wondered how his life might have been different if he'd been taught to read. Booker was such a charismatic person and an astute businessman, and I wondered who he would have been if he'd been born in a time and place where race really didn't matter.

I wanted to face the guilty, the perpetrators of injustice. Were all White Southerners responsible for what they'd allowed to happen in their world? What does it take to be complicit in a crime? Malice or intent? What about foreknowledge?

When I was a little girl and my teachers or the talking heads on TV discussed racism, inevitably someone would comment that racism was about ignorance. Everyone would nod, and that seemed to be the end of the conversation. But what kind of ignorance? People who lacked book knowledge, who never went to college, who couldn't balance a checkbook? Or were they ignorant of something else? Was it an emotional ignorance, a deficit? Maybe something in them had been severed, some ability for human compassion, empathy, kindness had either been cut off or simply failed to properly form.

That's what I wanted to understand. That's what I wanted to get from Greenwood. I wanted to see Booker, to feel his presence, yes. And then, with the sense of him locked inside me, I wanted to expose the underbelly of darkness I was certain was alive in the Delta. I wanted to shed the brightest of lights on the evil that would enable a person to take their own children to watch while a mother and son were thrown from a bridge, to watch their bodies twisting as they struggled to breathe—and then to capture it in a photograph with pride. What the hell was wrong with these people?

Not long before I was scheduled to fly out, I learned that Raymond and his production team had managed to set up an interview with Noll Davis, who, they informed me, had been a president of the White Citizens' Council. Davis was one of the five men seated at the round table in the scene that preceded Booker's in Frank's original film.

For the life of me, I couldn't figure out why he'd agreed to meet with us. Regardless of whether or not his politics had changed, he certainly had to know the world around him was different and that, all those years ago, he'd stood on the wrong side of history. Davis had to expect that we'd hold him accountable for who he'd been and for at least some of the damage and fear that was spread by the Council. Maybe he wanted to apologize or even clear the record by minimizing his involvement. I decided that whatever he wanted to get from our meeting was incidental.

As I prepared to go to Greenwood, I was filled with so many emotions—excitement, anxiety, sorrow, and rage. I wanted to face Noll Davis and others like him because, in my mind, those who'd taken part in the terrorizing and degrading of Blacks or watched it take place in their small towns were soldiers with an inhumane, ungodly mission. Every single one of them represented the people who'd robbed my grandfather of his dignity.

Weeks later, when the trip was over and I'd returned to my life, I would look back with amazement at the determination that surged inside me as I packed my bags, said farewell to my children, and boarded the plane that would take me down into the Delta. In retrospect, it's almost incomprehensible to me that I'd had such confidence and such clarity before I went to Greenwood, because I had neither when I returned home.

On June 15, 2011, when I stepped off the plane in Memphis, Tennessee, and began looking for the car that would take me down into the Delta, I thought I understood the South and the nuanced relationships between Blacks and Whites because of what I'd read in a few books. I believed that redemption could be found through vengeance, and that an absolute truth was just waiting for me to uncover it. Greenwood would prove me wrong on every count.

Part Seven
The River's Eden

For me, forgiveness and compassion are always linked: how do we hold people accountable for wrongdoing and yet at the same time remain in touch with their humanity enough to believe in their capacity to be transformed?

bell hooks

A Place to Descend To

When I landed in Memphis in the summer of 2011, an associate producer picked me up at the airport and drove me into Greenwood. The drive down into the Delta was more beautiful than I remembered from when I was a little girl. The freeway was surrounded by impossibly tall trees with leaves that boasted every imaginable shade of green, from a dull, almost navy-blue green to greens so vibrant they seemed to sparkle. I was in awe.

There's something irreverent, almost defiant, about the Delta. Even the name "Mississippi Delta" isn't correct, because it's not a delta at all. A delta forms at the spot where a river meets the sea. The Mississippi Delta is actually an alluvial plain, created by the Mississippi River racing downhill and depositing her collection of sediment. It occurred to me that I was traveling on land that had been collected from waterways throughout the continent.

After driving for two hours, we finally pulled up to Greenwood's courthouse. It was a grand and picturesque two-story building with a white clock tower rising from its roof and standing like a beacon for the town. We went inside to connect with Raymond and the film crew. My dad was already there, and after greeting each other and meeting the rest of the crew, Raymond told us he'd like to shoot the first scene at Booker's Place.

The drive there was sobering. The Black section of Greenwood looked like a postapocalyptic ghost town. It had a scent I couldn't place. I imagined it to be a mixture of rusted train cars, drop biscuits, Crown Royal, cigarettes, and sweat. Every few blocks ended in an empty lot where Black men sat in broken lawn chairs, some without shirts, most with alcohol. The men and sometimes women stood on corners drinking their brew and looking out at the world through glassy eyes. With bare chests, shoulders with shirts hanging off of them, eyes bloodred with blank, black marbles in the center of them, they watched us. As our cadre of cars approached, their joyless laughter would abruptly stop, and they'd look at us as if we were aliens.

Street after street was filled with abandoned buildings next to ones still in use. They did not have "For Rent" or "For Sale" signs on them, but wooden boards covered many of their windows. A few of the empty buildings had windows that were uncovered, and as we drove past I peered inside and saw refuse, materials left behind. It felt as if those empty spaces were looking back at me, desperately trying to scream in spite of their sentences to life in silence.

At first, I thought all the scattered businesses that remained open were struggling to stay afloat. The signs that held their names were often so worn they were almost unreadable. Many of their windows and doors were coated with filth. I began to wonder if the businesses could get away with looking so worn down because the people living in that community had so few options.

The roads we drove down were filled with potholes, some so large that we had to greatly decrease our speed when driving over them to ensure that we didn't damage our vehicles. The day was just beginning, and I already felt hopeless. I remembered that this whole thing started because I believed that my two-year-old son needed to understand his history so he could feel proud. I almost laughed out loud at the thought as we turned onto McLaurin.

The stretch of McLaurin Street where Booker's Place was, which had once been hopping with clubs and businesses, was all but deserted. All the clubs had been torn down except for Booker's Place, which had stood empty for years. It didn't close immediately after his death, though. Honey managed the place with the help of family for as long as she could.

In the end, Honey had to sell the building when bone spurs in her feet made standing all day physically impossible. It was actually her doctor who told her that she had to give it up, and it broke her heart. By then, though, Booker's Place had already fallen from grace. The quality of the food had diminished, and the place no longer attracted customers from all over the state. Eventually a church bought it. They were planning to turn it into a youth center.

We parked down the street so the cameraman wouldn't get our cars in the shot. Even after all these years, the Coca-Cola sign with the words "Booker's Place" was still there. It was missing some of its glass, but it was there. Raymond didn't want us to go inside because he wanted to film that the next morning. He just wanted my dad and me to walk down the street together while my father shared whatever memories came to mind.

My dad left Greenwood as a football star. Whenever he returned, people remembered him. Even people who'd never met him had heard the story about the local boy who made it all the way to the pros. We'd only been on McLaurin for about twenty minutes when more and more cars began driving by, each one moving slower than the one before it. Some of the drivers rolled their windows down to shout, "Hey, is that you, Leroy?" He'd walk over, shake their hands, and then introduce me, all while the cameras were rolling. Part of me wanted to tell my dad to stop so that we could begin the work of making the documentary, but I knew how much this meant to him. It was one of the few blessings of football he could still claim.

As my father and I stood together on McLaurin Street, under

the Delta sun, neither of us knew what was coming. That was one of his last happy summers before all the concussions he'd blown off as nothing finally caught up to him.

THE SUN WAS JUST beginning to go down by the time we left Mc-Laurin and headed over to a church on Howard Street. Even though we were still on the south side of town, Howard Street was lovely. It was located a block north of Johnson Street, which in decades past had represented the farthest north Blacks were allowed to travel in Greenwood. The building that had once housed Fountain's Big Busy Store had recently been renovated and turned into a five-star hotel and a trendy bookstore with a coffee shop on the top floor. I later learned that the owner of Viking, a company known for making high-end kitchen appliances, was a Greenwood native, and he'd recently put a lot of money into Howard Street in a revitalization effort.

We drove up to the Church of the Nativity, which was old but well kept. It had a regal look to it. It was once the home church of Byron De La Beckwith, the man who assassinated Medgar Evers. We were there to participate in a meeting of a group called the Bridge. Charlott Ray, one of the members, explained that the group was created because "since the civil rights movement, we've developed basically two separate cultures here in Greenwood. We have the black culture and we have the white culture. They don't go to the same schools, they don't go to the same churches, they don't tend to deal with the same businesses downtown. So, you've got two totally separate groups in this tiny little town that need to be meshed."

She wasn't describing Greenwood of the 1950s, she was describing Greenwood of 2011. The people who were at the Bridge meeting that night were a blend of Whites and Blacks and a mix of socio-economic levels; most appeared to be over fifty. We had food set up, and people mingled for the first few minutes. Then the meeting was called to order and everyone made their way to folding chairs facing the front of the room.

After being introduced, Raymond stood up in front of the crowd and explained that we were making a new documentary to revisit the one his father had made in the mid-1960s. We also wanted to highlight and uncover as much as we could about Booker Wright. He introduced his father's film and we screened it for them, to get their responses to it and to see what they remembered about Booker.

The film Frank made about the South was a triumph in many ways, in part because it captured not only hate but fear and confusion as well. It illustrated just how far people will let themselves go to avoid a painful truth. Frank's film revealed that a lot of the Whites living in Greenwood during the movement didn't want to pick sides. They wished the problem would just go away or solve itself without them having to lose the way of life they'd grown so accustomed to.

One of the most powerful scenes in Frank's black-and-white film takes place in the home of the Grand Wizard of the Ku Klux Klan. It begins with his three very young children climbing all over him while he sits in a chair, laughing. It's an idyllic image, reminiscent of a Norman Rockwell painting of what a loving father and a solid family should look like.

Later, Frank interviewed him without his children, and at one point he said, "According to history, the Klan saved the South. And I believe if it's to be saved again, the Klan will save it." He went on to explain his belief that God might be using Klansmen to turn back the enemy.

Looking back on the film with the clarity of the forty-plus years that have passed since it was made, the Grand Wizard's words sounded insane. But the man Frank interviewed was wearing dress pants, had a lovely home, and appeared to be a man of influence. He spoke without arrogance, as if he was explaining an accepted truth to an outsider. In some ways, it was his lack of passion that made the moment so disturbing. During his segment, there were a few sounds of disapproval from the audience, but most remained silent.

I was waiting for another scene to come up, one that always left me feeling somewhat undone when I saw it. A man wearing a gray suit and a long face appeared on the screen. He had dark hair and looked to be in his forties. He spoke with an air of humility and caution, as if wanting to be honest and clear while doing no harm. Cigarette smoke rose up from off screen and floated in front of his calm expression. "Now what happened here in Mississippi happened all over the South," he began, "and that is until 1954 there was no great outcry from the intellectuals, from the teachers and columnists about the morality of this type of social structure. Then all of a sudden, in 1954, this decision," he said, referring to the *Brown vs. Board of Education* ruling that made school segregation unlawful, "not only changed the whole concept of the social order but what it said was in effect that we had been living in sin for all these many years.

"And this thing became really a moral issue," he continued. "Now this was quite a traumatic experience for us in the South, and I think it was for the rest of the nation, to be told all of a sudden that what you've been doing, what you've been believing in, the way you've been living all your life, and the way your parents lived before you and forebears, is not only wrong but immoral is quite a shock, and unfortunately it's easy to understand why the attitude of Mississippi to this new order of the day, this new change, was one of inflexibility and one of defiance."

Every time I watched that scene, I had the same thought. He was talking about family, about having the thing that tethers you suddenly brought into question. The South is a place of heritage. Where

I lived, people moved to a different house every five or six years, but many of the Delta's residents were still living in the very house and on the very land where their parents had lived, and their parents before them. For some, the idea that the values they'd believed in, relied upon, and built their own families on were not only wrong but shameful and that their beloved ancestors were monsters may have been too painful to bear, an idea unassimilable to their sensibilities.

Whenever I looked into the unassuming face of the man who spoke those words, I wrestled with how to file away his testimony. Unlike the Klan Wizard, this man was difficult to dislike.

A few moments later in the film, five White men are seated at a table in a restaurant, and a man in voice-over says, "This is Carnaggio's Restaurant. Gathered here are five men, representative leaders who speak for Greenwood. They voice the orthodox liturgy. Hardy Lott, the attorney who defended Byron De La Beckwith; Mayor Charles Sampson; Noll Davis; Stanley Sanders; Robert Wingate."

The voice-over drops out and Hardy Lott can be heard saying, ". . . bothered me and it has all of my life, and that is the fact that people in other sections of the country are thoroughly convinced that we are prejudiced against colored people on account of the color of their skin."

Wingate responds, "I think you're absolutely right. On the contrary, there's a very warm feeling on the part of most Southerners toward . . ."

The voice-over cuts in, "This is a private club; Greenwood avoided integrating its public accommodations by converting public eating places into private clubs for Whites only. No Negroes enter here, except as servants."

Wingate went on, ". . . the plantation owner had a colored person who had worked for him for a number of years but had gotten too old to put in a day in the field. He didn't run him off, he didn't fire him—he left him with a home, he gave him food, he gave him clothes, and he gave him a place to live his life out in peace and contentment."

Noll Davis added, "There are many instances where these older colored people are still living on plantations, charged no rent, they do no fieldwork or no other kind of work. They're still looked after, carried to the hospital, and helped out in many ways."

Wingate nodded and said, "We wouldn't do that if we didn't like 'em."

Lott interjected, "But what they would come back with always and say, 'If that's true and you not prejudiced against 'em, why do you want to keep your separate schools? Isn't that prejudiced?' Of course it's not."

Then Sanders explained that, "It's difficult for me to believe that the American people, being as we know—we're a part of them—being fair-minded people, would want to impose on any area of this nation a situation in which illiterates"—here the camera captures Wingate nodding and smiling—"would be allowed to vote."

Lott agreed, "That's true," he said. You can build the schools as we have and provide the teachers, but you can't go round and get 'em by the neck and make 'em solve an education. That's something they have to do for themselves. It's difficult for me to understand why the entire country is so intent on integrating our schools."

The camera shifted again to Sanders, who said, "I think that they feel like we do not have adequate schools for our colored children. And I think that it would change considerably the national attitude if people could come in and see our colored schools."

Then the voice-over cut in again and the screen was filled with images of Delta schools. "It's true, many Negro schools do look adequate. It's also true many were built belatedly to give equal facilities in a vain effort to keep separate facilities. Josephine Haxton gives an unorthodox view."

As images of schools continue to move across the screen, a

woman's voice is heard saying, "I don't know a great deal about the Negro school system, because of course White people don't know too much about the life of Negroes in the towns they live in. The problem of getting qualified Negro teachers in the Negro school systems, I understand, is very hard. Probably the Negro student who graduates from the best Negro high school in the state doesn't have as good an education as a White child in a comparable school simply because the teacher's not as good, because he has been raised in a deprived environment and he hasn't had as much to bring to his education."

The scene returned to the restaurant, where the five men were still discussing the problems with integration, and Hardy Lott was explaining how he opposed integration because of how deeply he cared for Blacks. Then Booker Wright came on and simply told the world how he felt.

The positioning of the scene makes Lott, Wingate, Sanders, Sampson, and Davis all look like fools. They were proclaiming that all their Blacks were happy. They went so far as to look into the camera and make what felt like a challenge: find someone who disagrees with that. Frank did; he found Booker.

After Booker's scene, a slow-talking man who was out fishing with his son came on the screen. His eyes were filled with concern. He was clearly wrestling to find a way to reconcile his desire for Blacks to have equality with how the change would impact his children.

"I've lived in this Delta all my life, my parents before me, my grandparents. I've hunted and fished this land since I was a child. This land is composed of two different cultures—a White culture and a colored culture, and I've lived close to 'em all my life, but I'm told now that we've mistreated 'em and we must change, and these changes are coming faster than I expected, and I'm required to make decisions on a basis of a new way of thinking, and it's difficult. It's difficult for me, and it's difficult for all Southerners." The camera moved back and forth between the man's face and his son's, a boy who looked to be in his early teens. He didn't nod or gesture while his father spoke, but his eyes were wide as if he was soaking it all up.

His father continued, "An example: Recently, after church, I went to my favorite inn for dinner. I was met at the restaurant door by a waitress, and she said, 'Maybe you better not come in today, the Negroes are here.' I went anyway, and why shouldn't I? I have known 'em all my life. They nursed me. I've eaten the food that they've prepared, they helped raise my children and raised me. I could see no harm in that. I still don't. There are some facets, though, of integration and such that I'm opposed to. I'm still opposed to integration of schools, particularly on a grade-school level.

"Now these children of grade-school level know all about life. They know more about the seamier side of life—sex—than most White high school children, and I think we'd be doing a disservice to our children if we mixed 'em too early. But I'm in agreement with the theory that all men are entitled to equal protection under the law, to dignity, and I'm willing to see these things happen in Mississippi and in the Delta and in the rest of the South."

I squirmed in my seat and looked around the room. It was silent. Everyone was watching. That was another scene that was tough for me. The idea that Blacks were inherently more sexual was wrong, but that man believed it—wholeheartedly believed it. He did not have resentment or hatred toward the people he believed to be oversexed; he even wanted them to have better lives. He was just concerned about the future for his own children.

When I'd first watched Frank's film, my own children had been asleep upstairs. At the time, I was homeschooling and one of my sons was getting close to finishing first grade, but he was still struggling to read three-letter words. Everyone told me not to worry and that sometimes boys read later than girls, but I had a father who was illiterate. My younger brother was twenty eight years old and still having difficulty reading, even though he'd attended public schools. He had a kind personality, and people would hire him knowing he had struggles with literacy, yet not comprehending just how severe they were. His bosses would try to give him small jobs that required little reading, but he couldn't complete them. I was in a panic about my brother's future, and I could tell, even from a distance, that my mother was as well.

So, when my own son hasn't been able to sound out the word "sun," even though he was approaching seven and I'd done years of phonics with him, images of my father and brother would creep into my mind, gripping me with panic. I would have done anything, become anyone, to help him learn to read and to shore up a good future for him. Many nights I lay in bed crying, wondering what to do.

That's what I thought about every time I watched the man by the river. When he expressed that it was concern for his children that kept him from embracing change, a part of me understood. If I believed—truly believed—that an act or a new law would keep my child from having a chance to learn to read, I would rage against it. If people called me a racist, backward, or ignorant, I wouldn't have cared. If activists came into my community, I would have ignored them if I believed it would protect my children and their future.

Every time I watched Frank's film, I felt uncomfortable because of the man by the river. Was the seed of his complacency and unwillingness to help Blacks a twin to a seed living in me? Did love for my children mean that I had something in common with monsters?

Descendants of
Master and Slave

The screening of Frank's film ended. I pulled myself out of my head to look around the room and gauge the reactions of the audience. People were clapping, nodding their heads, and whispering to one another. Raymond went back up to the front of the room, where he thanked everyone and then introduced me. We asked the audience to respond to Frank's film but also to share any memories with us that they had of Booker.

The first person to speak was Anita Batman, a White woman with soft, short blonde hair that gently caressed her face. Behind glasses, her large eyes looked out with an almost constant expression of wonder. Softly, but with confidence, she said, "He was the nicest man I ever met."

Then, a White man named Hiram Eastland stood up to my right. He was wearing cream-colored pants, a matching shirt, and a blue business suit jacket. "I wasn't privileged enough to know your granddad, Booker, but in many ways I'm glad he brought us here together tonight, and I have to say about this documentary that I was really struck by his story, how historic it is. It actually shows the beginning of open-mindedness to change.

"I was struck by the fact that that White man in many ways was put in a position of quickly realizing how ideological it would be to not go in and have dinner with these people that had helped feed his children, who had helped raise his children. I can totally identify with that; I have a Black mother just like I have a White mother." As he said that I glanced around the room as if the expression on a stranger's face might provide clarification. But as Hiram went on, I realized that he'd had a mammy, a Black woman who worked full-time as a nanny in a White family.

"And she was always determined she was going to the cotton field to compete with her sisters, and she took me with her, and some of my fondest memories are being there in the cotton fields with her and her sisters and her making me take a nap on the top of her cotton sack. I wasn't even taller than that chair right there, and I can remember looking up through the cotton, so I know where he got those feelings to make that decision even back in 1966."

Before Hiram finished his last statement, a Black man named Bill Ware stood up. Bill had short hair and was wearing glasses and a Hawaiian-style button-up shirt. He said, "Let me talk about the hostility I have after hearing this man talk about Black women who neglected me to raise him. That's an awful, awful, awful experience, especially if you're a young Black boy running around the streets of Greenwood. My aunt [and] my mother earned two dollars a day working on Park Avenue or Grenada Boulevard or wherever they were. We suffered the indignity of having parents who couldn't spend [the] time that they wanted to spend with us."

I looked around; the faces in the room were without expression. I sensed that Bill's story was no different from ones they had either heard before or lived themselves.

Bill went on, "I'm told that my granddaddy was freed at nine years old. How does a nine-year-old survive in the hostile county that we had in Mississippi and Leflore County? I respect the Bridge and what it does, but I still reflect often on how it could've been had things been different. Now, Anita tells me we watched the same guys rolling out the cotton to load them on barges to roll down the river. She skips the part where I was on the south side of the river and she was on the north side. We found ways to separate ourselves. I'm not so sure that we don't now."

Smiling and nodding with affirmation, Anita responded, "Well, when Bill and I got to know each other, we started saying, 'Remember when this and remember when that' and he was there and I was there; we didn't even see each other, but we lived a very parallel life growing up at the same time in Greenwood." Then she began reflecting on the film. "I guess one thing that really touched me—and it's not what the film meant to do—is I saw people I loved, and"—with her hands clasped to her chest—"I loved Booker and I love Stanny Saunders and I love Hardy Lott and I love Charlie Sampson; his wife taught me fifth grade."

When Anita was young, one of her best friends was one of the Lusco daughters. Many days after school or in the summers, she and her friends would play inside Lusco's while the adults were trying to get everything ready before opening the restaurant up for dinner. During those days, she got to spend a lot of time with Booker. She said that he "would keep up with us and slip us snacks, and he showed us a great deal of kindness, as did some of the other men that you showed. You're left with a feeling of, it was a really bad system, and you could see good people working well within a system that needed changing and you could see bad people working badly within a bad system that needed changing . . . There were a lot of good people caught in a system that was flawed, and they were with the best of will trying to work their way through it."

I felt myself nodding. I wanted to believe that, too, that it was just a handful of radicals who were to blame for one of our nation's darkest periods. The idea comforted me because it meant the majority of people weren't as evil as the deeds they allowed to happen in their midst. The idea also terrified me, because it meant most people lacked the will to do what they knew was right.

Then a Black man stood up. "My name is Edward John Miller; I'm from Money, Mississippi." My father's hometown. I felt myself paying closer attention to him, thinking he might have some real anger, but instead he said, "The Delta is one of the best places in the world to live . . . regardless of where you live you gon' have some difficulties, but one thang about it, one certain amount of us, once you start getting promoted, getting better jobs, you start putting your own people down 'cause you beginning to think you getting a little better than them. And you start to think if you can't keep up with them and be in they style and then it gon' be that kind of situation probably wherever you go at."

He'd opened another door—conflict between Blacks. Before I could really even process what he'd said, Hiram Eastland stood up again and turned to Bill Ware. "I just want to say that I'm really sorry it offended you that I'm talking about my Black mother, but that's just the way it was and that's the way it is. In fact there's a whole movie just filmed here in Greenwood called *The Help* about this whole phenomenon, and what I'm about to say, I'm saying for Rosalie Lackey, because she would spank me if I didn't say what I'm about to say.

"The truth is that I wouldn't take anything in the world for that relationship and that love, and I truly believe that because of relationships like that all over the Delta and all over Mississippi and all, it was people like my Black mother that planted those seeds of love that they were speaking about . . . that helped bring about that change. I love her like I love my own mother. I was there when she passed away, and I was holding Lie's hand this past November just like I did my White mother, and she knew she was dying. I did not know this until I got to her services, but she specifically requested to ask that my brother and my sisters and I be put on the services as her children."

Bill Ware sat in his chair and said, "No apologies needed," without looking at Hiram. I wondered if Rosalie Lackey felt as though she was able to be more of a mother to Hiram than to her own children, if she had any. I also wondered if Hiram was right. Mammies probably did help to humanize Blacks for a generation of Whites who were forced to swallow laws that expanded the rights of Black people.

I'd read *The Help*, and I knew the movie had been filmed in Greenwood the previous summer. The more I thought about it, Hiram's use of the phrases "White mother" and "Black mother" struck me as curious and beautiful. Curious because, as a mother myself, I didn't know if I'd allow any other woman to have such a precious place in my child's heart. But it was a thing of beauty to me that while Rosalie was away from her own children, she was able to give so much love to Hiram, a man whose uncle, Senator James Eastland, had once handed out a document in which he proclaimed Whites had the right to pursue "dead niggers."

Another Black man stood up. His name was Troy Brown, and he said, "I'm still pissed off." This was followed by clapping and people saying "Mm-hmm." It was the loudest response to any of the statements that had been made so far.

As Brown continued, I got the impression he was enjoying his effect on the crowd. "The very people that are talking about 'love fest,' the very people that were oppressed in that film, are oppressing Black people right now, and they're the same color. All you gotta do is just change the color of those White folks and make 'em Black. Something has gone wrong."

He'd been looking to the crowd, but then he turned to face me where I was still standing in the front of the room. "I'm happy that you're here, because I want you to know, when this film is being shown again, that I'm holding my children responsible. I don't want you all to be able to look back fifty years from now and see the same thing, I want it done. I want it gone. I don't want to see little kids that have a substandard education. It's my generation that's having this problem with wrestling with my parents to give us the responsibility; they don't want to let it go. They continue to want to live in the past.

"There are people right now that don't want Black and White . . . This organization is called the Bridge, and there are people on the Bridge who don't want you to cross. Our wall has not come down yet in Mississippi. There are still some people who have to work those menial jobs . . . Your grandfather was better off because he owned his place. No Black gas station here; maybe one Black restaurant left."

He was working the room, looking around and gathering its energy. He continued in a voice that reminded me of a comic delivering a punch line. "The Indians sell soul food!"

This brought loud laughter. "And the very people that we had this big push, big civil rights push to put Black folks at the table politically so that we can have some of the economic power—our average political leader's car costs more than the house of the people they represent." He said it again, only this time with even more emphasis, clearly pronouncing each word so there could be no misunderstanding.

"Their car that they drive cost more than the average house of the people they represent. You can't be in the majority and still blame White folks . . ." He continued as my thoughts wandered off. A local Black political leader, Senator David Jordan, was in the room that night. Was his comment about politicians driving expensive cars a shot at the senator? Brown was looking at me again.

"Unfortunately, I don't think your [grandfather] would be so proud, because he went through the humiliation that he had to go through so that his children wouldn't have to go through—and you know what? Some kids of that generation are still going through the same thing, and I wish I could apologize to your grandfather myself."

As Troy Brown came to the end of what felt like a sermon, a

thin Black woman stood up and said, "I just have a question. You're saying the documentary is about the change that has happened since sixty-six until now. And I've lived the greater part of my life here, and as I look, there isn't a whole lot of change." She explained that when she was a child she wasn't allowed to shop in certain parts of downtown Greenwood because of the color of her skin.

She went on to describe life after integration. "Now, sure, we're welcome to come over here, but what's here for us?" She described Whites moving across the river and taking the vitality of downtown Greenwood with them. In comparing the Greenwood of the sixties to the Greenwood of today, she said, "It's the same soup served in a different bowl. It hasn't changed." As she sat down the room was filling with noise, some people agreeing while others disagreed.

Bill Ware spoke over the crowd. "Things are somewhat different."

The woman quickly responded, "Very little."

Bill Ware went on, "In the sixties, Black folk owned a lot of businesses in Greenwood. When we integrated, we were integrated out of our businesses. There were stores starting at New Zion Church down Johnson Street . . . a drug store over on Carrollton Avenue, a dentist above that. We lost our economic clout when we integrated."

In that instant, I felt the same way I'd felt four years earlier when Vera told me that the schools didn't really integrate. It seemed so obvious that I was surprised it hadn't occurred to me before. In my mind, I saw Blacks rushing with excitement in their hearts and dollars in their hands over to the stores that had once been Whites only. I could not, however, envision Whites doing the same, rushing to Black-owned businesses or taking their children to Black dentists and doctors. Of course, Black business owners would have lost a significant number of customers, not because of the quality of their services or products but because of the joyful surge their customers were experiencing, finally knowing what it felt like to have a choice.

I learned later that Bill Ware had spent several years living in California. Eleven years after the Supreme Court ruled that school segregation was illegal, the schools were still divided along color lines, with Black kids getting the short end of the stick in regard to resources and education quality. By the mid-1960s, Bill had children of his own, children he wanted to see receive a solid education. He took his family and moved to Los Angeles, only returning to Greenwood when he was done raising his family.

There were lots of Black families who did the same thing. They were members of the Black middle class in Greenwood. They were people who kids like my dad could look up to. They were role models and community builders, but once the promise of equality continued to get pushed farther down the line and their businesses began to suffer as more and more Blacks took their dollars to White stores, these stellar community members left.

There was one more person who wanted to have a say that night. State Senator David Jordan stood up and said, "You cannot blame anybody but oneself." Just as his words began to leave his mouth I could feel something in the room shift. A few people—just a few— got up to leave, but it was enough. Everyone had been holding on to something, trying to undo it, to work it out, to understand it, but when the senator stood up, I had the sense that some people just stopped trying. Somehow, he'd managed to remove all the air from the room.

"I am responsible for myself," the senator went on, "and my family, and to help others as well. But if you do nothing and wallow in despair and blame everybody else, that's cursing the dark. Light a candle. I remember in the Black community when most of the homes were rented homes, but they had flower yards. They had pride. They had flower yards and they had swings and they kept that place neat.

"Now that generation is gone, and they have turned it over to the next generation and they've torn it up completely. Cars parked up in the yard. So it's a mind-set. You cannot hold anybody responsible for your welfare but you."

The room was mostly silent while he spoke. I got the sense he had few supporters there that night. I knew the senator still held meetings of the Voter's League, which had begun in the early years of the movement. I wondered if Troy Brown, the one concerned about politicians' salaries, had a point. Troy said that the older generation won't let go. One thing was clear: tensions in the room were rising. Even in the silence surrounding Senator Jordan's comments, hopelessness was coming off the people in the room like steam rising off hot pavement.

AFTER THE MEETING WRAPPED up, we drove through the quiet streets of Greenwood, past the buildings that looked as though they'd been built for commerce so long ago but now stood empty, with no signs above to say what they may have sold. Something tugged at me, and I had the feeling of being followed by orphans asking for change that I knew would never be enough to change the course of their lives. The empty, dilapidated buildings pulled at the edges of my sight line, willing me to look at them, to at least acknowledge that even though they were useless now, that had not always been the case.

Almost all the businesses that were opened almost a century before during the Second Cotton Kingdom, Greenwood's season of newness and innovation, had shut down. Most weren't sold, they just closed their doors and went out of business. Even Fountain's Big Busy Store's reign had ended. Greenwood was a marvel to me. Within a few decades, the town had built itself up from just a few businesses to a bustling destination, and then, after the civil rights movement, it took just a few decades for the whole thing to crumble to the ground.

I realized we were traveling over another bridge. We were leaving North Greenwood and heading north on Money Road. We continued to drive out of town into the dark, down a road that seemed like it could and would go on forever, with slight twists here and there, but no streetlights. Rising out of the darkness was a series of buildings that would be our home for the coming week. The collection of buildings turned out to be houses that made up a hotel called the Tallahatchie Flats. The Flats were reclaimed sharecropper shacks outfitted with electricity, indoor plumbing, and not much else. They were named after the Tallahatchie, the stretch of river that ran behind them, the place of that horrible murder.

Though it wasn't Emmett Till's murder that had made the owners of the Flats choose that particular location. There were three places in Greenwood rumored to be the burial site of Robert Johnson, and one of them was a short drive from the Flats. Johnson was a guitarist and singer who Eric Clapton once called "the most important blues singer that ever lived."

His short life, mysterious death, and enormous talent were the perfect ingredients for a supernatural Delta tale. According to legend, Johnson grew up on a plantation, and in spite of having an intense desire for musical fame, he was a terrible, untalented guitar player. One night, he met the devil at the crossroads and sold his soul in exchange for a drastic increase in his musical abilities. His playing improved, but his life did not.

Theories abounded for decades about what caused his death in 1938 at the age of twenty-seven. It took three days for him to die, during which time he suffered in bed, enduring a death so terrible and painful that, according to Johnson's mother, he begged for the end to come more quickly. The most common theory about Johnson's death was that he was flirting with someone else's woman at a bar one night, so her boyfriend spiked Johnson's drink with strychnine.

As if to match the eeriness of Johnson's story, the Tallahatchie Flats were set up in such a way that, when one drives there at night, the shacks seem to suddenly appear out of nowhere. Between the shacks and the road was a vast field, as though the field itself were a stage and the houses were the watching crowd. It occurred to me that if that place was meant to serve as an homage to two great lives both lost in horrific ways, it had definitely succeeded in at least capturing the ghostly, unsettling sense of the afterlife.

I climbed out of the car and looked around. Except for the hum of mosquitos and the rustles and rumbles of our team, there wasn't a sound for miles. I was sharing a shack with three other members of the crew, but I had my own room, which had a dressing table and chair, a double bed, and loads of dust and cobwebs. There was a photo on the wall of a Black woman staring solemnly into the camera. I knew that in the early years of photography, people remained as still as possible while they waited for the exposure to be made. They didn't smile, they just looked. Somehow her expression said more to me than that. I wondered who wanted her to have a photograph taken. Was it her? Was it a child who referred to her as his "Black mother"? Or maybe it was a plantation manager who snuck out at night to rape her while his own wife fumed in their bed.

I knew I wouldn't be able to look at her photo every day for the next week, so I took it down and put it in a closet in the living room.

I joined my housemates soon after. In spite of how tired we all were, we stayed up for a few more hours. They wanted to know about my journey, but they also wanted to understand why I was so passionate about Booker. They sensed the depth of my love for him.

I sat there in that sharecropper shack and told them all about my family. I explained how I hadn't felt truly connected to my family for years, and how I'd felt confused and unsettled about being Black in a world that prized White skin. One of the girls was a student at Ole Miss who'd offered herself up as a volunteer when she heard about the documentary we were making. She told us she was in graduate school and that her area of study was the trauma of the civil rights movement.

She was looking at the lives of people who'd been intensely involved in the movement and then went on to struggle with various forms of mental illness afterward. They'd paid a price not just when they went to sit-ins and marches, not just when they were beaten. They continued paying the price for decades in the form of untreated trauma. Being relentlessly hated had left a mark on them.

When we were finished talking, I climbed into bed, where I stared at the ceiling wondering about the kind of legacy hate can leave behind.

There was a certain kind of night outside my window, one I was unfamiliar with. It was so black and so dark that it looked dense, as if the night itself was a thick, wet fabric hanging from the sky. Talking about my family always left me feeling exposed, as if I'd removed a protective layer. I closed my eyes and imagined a night beyond my walls that was watching me, seeing my vulnerability.

Since the day I had first watched Booker's footage, I'd felt something within myself softening, turning tender again. Over the years, there was so much I'd forgotten, but all this looking back into the past had caused memories to drip into my consciousness from a part of my heart I'd dammed up long ago. They were random at first. I saw my sister and me playing in our backyard as little girls, and my mother running out to tell us that *Grease* was on. My sister and I loved that movie. As the opening credits rolled, my back was facing my mother, but I could almost feel her as she enjoyed the moment. Then at least our happiness was enough to make her happy.

Another time, I arrived home from school, opened the front door, and walked down the hall into the living room, where my mom was sitting on the couch. We said our hellos and I looked over toward the kitchen, where a cake was sitting on a glass cake stand. Of all the desserts she made, my favorite was her lemon cake with added lemon pudding. It wasn't my birthday. It wasn't a holiday. She'd made it because she loved me.

All those memories had been packed up, stored away, and completely forgotten. My mother had been reduced to a handful of stories used to illustrate why I was so lost and all the rejection I needed a lifetime to overcome.

I glanced around the room. Everything felt like it was left over from another time. The curtains, blankets, and pillows had clearly been salvaged from another home, another life. My shack felt more like a museum than a hotel room.

When I was eleven and I visited Greenwood with my sister, we'd stayed with my grandma Doris in the home my mother had grown up in. That house looked a lot like the shack I was lying in. They were both so far from the way I saw my mother. She liked new things, things that shined, things that were custom-made just for her.

I took a deep breath and turned over onto my side, facing the window. As I fell asleep, I remembered a story my mother told me once about when she was a little girl living in Greenwood.

My mother, two of her sisters, and her cousin—another girl— used to all play baseball in the street in front of their house when they were young. A car with White men inside would drive by, slowing down to watch the girls as they played. These same men would come back later in the evening and drive up and down their street again and again.

In time, they began knocking on the door, pretending to be the police. My mother thought they were the KKK. She didn't really know what to believe; she just knew she wasn't safe. One night her sister Vera was doing laundry. She went out to the back porch where the washing machine was and saw a White man just standing there as if he'd been waiting for her. She cried out and rushed back into the house.

Vera was beside herself. She told her grandmother what had happened, but the woman didn't believe her. She got up herself, went to the door, opened it, and looked out. Whatever she saw made her slam the door shut. She began to scream, calling for all of the children to help her hold the door closed.

"When you're little and something like that happens to you," my mother had said to me, "it stays with you. The house was isolated and those men were coming all the time. They used to try to break in on us. They wanted the young girls. I used to be scared in that house. Every time I closed my eyes, I thought I would see something in the dark."

Booker's Place

I woke up in the morning with a lot on my mind. There was so much darkness in Greenwood. Despair, poverty, resentment, differing opinions about exactly what was still plaguing the town and who was at fault. It was true that I'd gone there searching for a story about Booker, but deep down I was also looking for a way to help. I wanted to bring hope to the Blacks who'd walked alongside Booker in his life. All we'd achieved the night before at the Bridge was to reawaken dormant emotions and frustrations, then record the aftermath.

I shut my eyes, wanting my thoughts about yesterday to stop. We had a lot planned for today. This was the morning we were supposed to go to Booker's Place. For the first time, I'd be able to stand in the place where my grandfather had built his own business.

I dragged myself out of bed, showered, and stepped outside. The morning was quiet except for the mosquitos; they were already humming, and even though the sun was barely coming up, the air was so hot it almost sizzled. Beyond the field in front of the Flats, and across the road we had taken to get there, was a wide, dense field of green that ended when it ran into a forest populated by immensely tall trees.

As I stood on the porch of that sharecropper shack, a poem called "The Slave Mother" came to my mind. The poem describes a person who hears a shriek rising wildly. It's a sound of such immense distress that it has the power to "disturb the listening air." The speaker explains that the sound is from a mother whose beloved son was taken from her, ripped out of her arms and sold into slavery. When I first read the poem, I imagined it taking place in a field where Blacks are picking cotton under a hot sun, too tired to even swat at the assaulting mosquitoes.

A cry like that would have to be a dark reminder of just how little hope for change they had, and evidence of the resounding, unending sorrow known only to mothers who've lost their children. I wondered, was it worse to know a child was dead? Or was it worse to have the knowledge that your baby—maybe even at just eight years of age—was being forced to work all day under a hot sun with an empty belly, to know that your child was being beaten without a mother's warmth to provide comfort, to know that the innocence in your child's eyes, the sweetness of your son's smile, and the joy in his running form were all being slowly destroyed.

Members of the crew began pouring out of their respective shacks, where they'd been meeting to discuss the day's technological needs. I watched as they loaded lighting and camera equipment into vans against the backdrop of the fields.

It took multiple cars to transport our entire crew. That morning, almost everyone had left before me so they could get things set up at Booker's Place. Nicki, the associate producer, stayed back to drive me. We headed south from the Flats past the vacant fields that seemed to go on for miles in either direction to Grand Boulevard, with its towering trees and houses with sprawling lawns of pristine green, recently cut shrubs, and wraparound porches. The exteriors of the homes we passed in North Greenwood looked well kept, as if the owners were being careful to maintain their beauty and original architectural details. They were like miniature museums, individual monuments to Greenwood and its legacy of wealth and accomplishment.

The change was not immediate. We crossed the river and saw lots of businesses and homes that weren't any older than the ones we'd seen in North Greenwood, yet they appeared to be more weathered. The farther south we traveled, the faster the change came. The lovely world around us fell away, and we were no longer in a tranquil sea of ancestral homes; instead we were driving past apartment complexes that reminded me of inner-city projects. We drove through neighborhoods with small houses whose porches were barely standing, with screen doors so worn that the fabric hung from the frames in strips, like flaps of skin. Black children were running around and riding bikes. Elderly adults rocked on porches. Middle-aged adults, mostly men, stood around cars parked on the side of the road talking to one another. Everyone stopped to look at us as we drove by.

Finally, we pulled up to Booker's Place. There were several people out front, including crew members who'd arrived to set up lights and some locals who were helping us with the lay of the land. One of the people there worked at the local state college. She was in a conversation with someone from the crew and was explaining that when students graduated, she always encouraged them to leave and never come back. She spoke of one student who went away, got a master's degree, and then returned home with the hope of giving back to Greenwood. She and other faculty urged him to leave, telling him he had no future in Greenwood.

While I eavesdropped on their conversation, I watched as my father made his way over to one of the cars that had pulled up. At first, I thought it was someone else who recognized him and wanted to catch up on old times, but then I realized it was his sister who was driving the car. After talking with her for about a minute, he waved me over. "She saying that," he began. "She saying that a house got shot up last night. The senator's house."

"What?" I asked as I tried to remember who it was the night before who'd talked about how some of the local politicians drove cars worth more than their constituents' houses. The night before it had struck me as being an elegant and powerful way to show the wealth differential, but after driving through South Greenwood that morning, I was pretty certain that my five-year-old minivan would also qualify as being worth more than some of those houses.

I called Raymond over. I watched as he got the story from my dad and my aunt, half-listening as I wondered if we had been irresponsible the night before by bringing up issues that had simmered for decades when we had no solution, no ideas about how to help people heal. After my aunt drove away, my dad explained that the senator's wife had recently purchased a new Cadillac. Apparently, two shots had been fired, and no one was injured.

Raymond turned to me and began walking me through the details of what was about to transpire. Finally, I was going into Booker's Place.

The first time I heard about Booker's news appearance, I'd had a strong sense of him. I could all but feel his fingers moving through the fields of my life, moving stalks aside to orchestrate everything that was coming to pass—learning about Greenwood through my dad's story, all the history of the Delta that had come my way, seeing the footage, and, of course, now making a film. However, in the last few months, I'd felt my grandfather less and less. As I stood on McLaurin, sweating under the sun, which seemed to hang lower and burn hotter in the Delta, I was hopeful I'd sense his presence again when I stepped inside the restaurant.

It had been a long time since anyone had gone inside, so long that the crew had had to pry the door open before I got there. When I entered, I found a place that was nothing like what had been described to me. It was abandoned and picked over. It looked looted. The bar was still there, but I suspected that was only because it was too massive to carry away. All but one of the built-in booths had been removed. There were no tables or chairs, and a beat-up, stained recliner took up most of the space in the small kitchen. There were holes in the ceiling where birds had built nests. Boxes full of water-damaged documents dotted the edges of the restaurant. Part of the floor had been pulled up, and what was left had a color to it that was impossible to make out because it was covered in a layer of dust that had been there for so long it was stuck to the floor like paint.

I wanted to leave the moment I stepped in. There wasn't much to do there besides look around and try to glimpse what had been. I stood where I knew the cash register used to be. It was where Booker was standing when he was shot. I waited, but in the end I felt nothing.

After a few minutes, I left while the crew continued taking interior shots. Then we all went to lunch at one of my dad's favorite restaurants, a little place called Iola's. She served us a meal of catfish and several other dishes, which I'd later struggle to recall because the fish was divine. Light, buttery, crispy perfection. I asked for a cup of coffee, but Iola didn't serve any. I asked my dad if he knew where I could get some coffee. He said he did and then offered to go with me.

Eddie—the man from the Bridge the night before who'd brought up conflict between Blacks—was with us. He and my father were friends.

When we stepped out of Iola's, a shirtless Black man with bloodshot eyes was standing next to the door staring at me with deep intensity. I ignored him, and, with my father and Eddie, walked a few blocks to a gas station. I poured myself a cup of coffee, doctored it up with sugar and cream, paid for it, and then walked outside. The shirtless man was still there.

As we crossed the street, he began calling to me. "Hey, baby. Where you goin'?"

My dad turned around and, looking down from his great height, he cursed and threatened the man. Eddie stepped between them and told my dad and me to keep going. As we walked away, I glanced over my shoulder. Eddie had his arm around the shirtless man and was leading him away. I heard Eddie say, "Remember, man, just this week, we're not gonna bother the people visiting town. Just this week, alright? Leave the White people alone, too. Okay?"

I wanted to ask Eddie about what he'd said, but I didn't know what to ask. I just knew that I was in a place unlike any other I'd ever been. There wasn't any way to prepare for Greenwood. The town would show me what it wanted, in whatever fashion it chose, whether or not I was ready to understand.

WE HAD MULTIPLE INTERVIEWS scheduled for the remainder of the day, but I was beat even after drinking my coffee. I went back to the Flats to take a one-hour nap, which ended up lasting closer to three. When I woke up, I felt out of sorts. Not because I was in Greenwood but because I was beginning to question what I was doing there at all. Raymond, possibly sensing my growing wariness about what we were doing, suggested that he, David, and I grab a bite to eat at Lusco's.

Carrollton Avenue was a quiet street. It, too, looked deserted until we got closer to Lusco's and saw a doorman standing out in front. He opened the door and motioned for us to head into the foyer. While David spoke with the hostess, I took in our surroundings. The restaurant I'd read so much about was illuminated by a dull, once gold light that lingered forlornly like a trapped fog between avocado-colored walls. From those walls came the vacant, defeated stares of mounted, stuffed animals. Random knickknacks were crowded together on countertops and shelves next to priceless, precariously placed Coca-Cola memorabilia. Hanging high above the entrance to the hallway that still held the curtained booths, above the spot where passwords were required to pass, was a stuffed deer covered with so much dust it looked as though it had soot for hair.

The three of us were led to one of the curtained booths. We ordered a smorgasbord of dishes including the Broiled Shrimp in Lusco's Shrimp Sauce, Lusco's Special Salad, Filet Mignon, Pompano topped with Crabmeat, and a chocolate dish smothered in ice cream for dessert.

Raymond and I were stuffing our faces when David went to see if Andy, the great-grandson of Charles and Marie and the current owner of Lusco's, would stop by our booth to say hello.

When Andy peeked his head in, I understood immediately why his wife, Karen, was the media face for the restaurant. He was intensely shy. Andy usually worked in the kitchen, so he was dressed comfortably in well-worn clothes, probably not expecting to be meeting with us or anyone else. He took a step into the booth with half his body on the other side of the curtain as if he was hoping to spend as little time with us as possible. He spoke so softly that it was hard to hear him.

After a round of introductions, Andy said, in all seriousness, that when he was a boy, Booker Wright was his best friend. A declaration of sorts. He included no anecdotes, just stated that simple fact before asking us about how we were enjoying the food. Raymond and I tried to pull him deeper into conversation, but Andy was clearly eager to get back to the kitchen.

Seeing Andy's discomfort made me appreciate all the more the gift he was giving to us. He expressed how much he loved Booker, said they played together, and that the two talked about being best friends. Andy would've still been quite young when Booker left Lusco's.

When he finally backed out of our booth and returned to the kitchen, Raymond and I immediately caught each other's gaze. We both got the clear sense that the grown man who'd just left us was still missing the waiter who'd been his first best friend. Instead of feeling like this detail added to my understanding of my grandfather, it just made things more muddled. Booker had strong feelings toward Greenwood Whites, specifically about how they treated him when he was waiting tables at Lusco's. Those feelings were intense enough to make him risk his life by appearing on the national news. Nevertheless, my grandfather was tender enough to be considered the best friend of a small child, and not just any child. Andy Pinkston was a member of the Lusco family.

When we got back to the Flats, I grabbed a notebook to jot down my thoughts, but every idea that came to mind was contradicted by the one that followed. I lay down on the bed, and as I drifted off to sleep, the only thing I felt certain about was how little progress I was making in understanding my grandfather.

IN THE FOLLOWING DAYS, the research and the interviews were almost nonstop. I continued to learn more about Booker, but still felt as though every new piece of information was something I didn't quite know how to categorize, either emotionally or in terms of how it related to Booker's life story. Almost every interview we'd done since leaving the screening at the Bridge had included at least one detail presented with such nonchalance that it could easily have been overlooked. But like dark matter—elusive enough to escape detection yet heavy enough to weigh down the universe—the details were revealing a different narrative about who my grandfather really was.

One of the people we interviewed was a Black man who was a little younger than Booker. He remembered going to his restaurant and having Booker drive him back home late at night, even though it was way out in the country. In his estimation, Booker had two separate lives—one on the Black side of town and another on the White side.

But even I knew his assessment was too simple. Booker had half a life on the Black side of town and half a life on the White side of town. To Blacks, his success as a restaurateur, coupled with the time he spent with Whites at Lusco's, made him an oddity. He wasn't one of them. To Whites, he was partially invisible, like the thousands of Black residents who didn't make it into the storied beginnings of the town of Greenwood, who lived just beyond the camera's frame.

Later, we met Gray Evans, a retired judge who told us about Booker being severely beaten by a White cop named Curtis. Judge Evans said, "Everyone knew who did it, who had gave him the beating." In subsequent interviews we began asking people if they knew anything about a local cop from the sixties named Curtis, and many of them did. They spoke of a man who had a fierce hatred of Blacks and whose cheeks almost always looked flushed, as though he was in a constant state of either embarrassment or rage.

Judge Gray Evans was certain that everyone in town knew all about the incident, but when I called my mom to ask her if she knew anything about her father being beaten, she didn't. It occurred to me then that Booker must have been an incredibly lonely man.

I also learned that he cheated on Honey more than once, and had children right under her nose. One of his longtime girlfriends was a waitress Honey had to work with several days of the week.

I met Blacks who hated him and people who were more than happy to talk about how mean he was. I met a lot of Blacks who said great things about my grandfather, but some of them would begin disparaging him to the filmmakers the minute I turned my back. Their complaints were the same: He dated a light-skinned girl; didn't let people into his place; seemed uppity.

A Black member of law enforcement even told one of the production assistants that Booker probably deserved to die because he was a jerk.

One of the most uncomfortable moments I had that summer occurred when I sat down with the mother of the man who murdered Booker. I was nervous before the interview. I decided to look at it as a conversation between mothers. As much as I anticipated that meeting, nothing could have prepared me for what I saw when she walked through the door.

The mother of the man who murdered my grandfather had a face like a ruptured womb. It was a collection of twisted lines, broken symmetry, and colors ranging from bloodred to black. The incongruity of her skin tone gave the impression that some parts of her face were in shadow, while lending a strange prominence to others. The left side was lower than the right, and her lips were turned at an odd angle as if she'd had a stroke. Her cheeks were caved in because she didn't have enough teeth to prop them up. Her left eye, having lost a battle with cataracts or some other ailment, was the color of milky silver, like a dense, priceless pearl.

She, too, talked about how mean Booker was, because he often wouldn't allow poor Blacks into his place. She felt that her son wasn't responsible for Booker's death because he died in the hospital. With a shrug of her shoulders, she glanced around the room and said, "God come and got him."

At the end of every single interview, I was exhausted. The interactions were painful. I knew they would play well on film, but they left me feeling emptied out. More and more I just wanted to go home.

One afternoon, I was standing alone in the long driveway leading up to the Flats, looking out at the fields. I was taking a break, trying to clear my head, when a White couple made the drive out to see me. They didn't even climb out of their car. The wife was sitting in the passenger seat. She rolled her window down and took my hand while her husband leaned over to look up at me. They had no idea if I would be there then, if it even made sense to make the drive.

They stayed only for a short while, but they wanted me to know that Booker was a great man. They wanted me to know how much they missed him, how vivid their memories of him were, and that he'd brought them immense joy.

Then they drove away.

Deconstructing a Racist

Of all the things that happened when I visited Greenwood in the summer of 2011, few would stay with me as much as my meeting with Noll Davis.

The scene in Frank's film that precedes Booker's statements was one I'd watched over and over again. The faces of the five men who sat around a table talking about their own generosity and all they were doing to keep their Blacks happy had become quite familiar to me. Three of them were either former or future presidents of the Citizens' Council, wholehearted believers in their mission.

One of them, Noll Davis, wanted to make it clear that many Greenwood Blacks were, in fact, beneficiaries of Southern hospitality. While looking intently into the camera he'd said, "The colored people are still living on plantations, charged no rent, they do no fieldwork, or any other kind of work. They're still looked after, carried to the hospital . . ."

Every time I thought about his statement, I felt irritated. He didn't acknowledge that the reason retired sharecroppers often couldn't care for themselves was because White plantation owners had cheated them out of profits for decades. He didn't acknowledge that because of racist practices, most Blacks couldn't get jobs doing anything else

besides sharecropping. He believed that Whites were actually performing some sort of charity for Blacks. It incensed me.

I'd gone to the Bridge meeting and felt disturbed by just how
much hurt there still was, then went to Booker's Place and traveled through Greenwood to see the decay and hopelessness juxta-
posed against the immense wealth of the remaining members of the
planter class and their descendants. That morning, I was determined
not to lose my focus. The men and women whose lives I'd been reading about were imprinted upon me as I dressed and focused on what
I wanted to achieve when I finally got my chance to talk to Noll
Davis.

On the way to his house, I found myself relishing the idea of sitting down and confronting someone who'd opposed the civil rights
movement, but in my mind, this man very well could've been one of
the ones who'd humiliated my grandfather at Lusco's. I had a whole
host of questions I wanted to ask him that were fueled by curiosity
and not a small amount of resentment.

I saw my meeting with Davis as an opportunity to perform an
autopsy of sorts. I developed a series of questions that I hoped would
allow me to pry inside his mind and uncover the genesis of his racism. I wanted to know what type of language his parents used about
Blacks when he was growing up. Did he play with Black boys and
girls? How did he see people of color represented in the stories he
was told?

My ultimate goal was to one day be able to write about him, and
in doing so, create a portrait of a life that could serve as a cautionary
tale. I wanted to reach down into Noll Davis's memory and wrap a
hand around the moment the seed of racism was planted. I wanted
to explore how it was watered, and then look into his eyes to see that
seed fully grown.

I was going to deconstruct a racist.

Finally, our entire crew, traveling in four separate cars, arrived at the home of Noll Davis. It was one story, surrounded by trees and bushes, with a wide, winding driveway in front that was littered with fallen leaves so wide they made me think of the wasted, dried-out hands of giants. David and Raymond went in first, then the camera and light people, and then me. Davis was standing in his foyer greeting everyone and telling them where the bathrooms were.

The first thing I noticed about him was his height. He was well over six feet tall, with broad shoulders, a sizable head, and a straight, strong stance despite his age. His gray eyes were wet. His voice was deep, shaky at times, and lusciously Southern. He had a classic, beautiful drawl that made "y'all," "reckon," and the delicate dropping of d's and t's seem right, as though that was how English was always meant to be spoken. His cheeks, which were wide and thick, still held a blush. When he was listening to someone, he would tilt his head to the side and lift a hand to smooth his hair down. When it was his turn to talk and he was searching for the right words, he'd rock back and forth on his heels with his large hands in his pockets. Noll Davis was in his eighties, but somehow I had a sense of the boy he was before he learned to hate people who look like me.

The interview was to take place deep inside Davis's home in a space that appeared to function as a family room. It was dark and had several seating options. As I contemplated where to sit, I wondered whether or not Raymond was going to invite me to interview Davis with him. The family room was full of people carrying large pieces of equipment, moving them back and forth. Finally, I was able to see that, across from a high-backed chair that would certainly be used by Davis, there stood a single stool. I knew then that Raymond was planning to conduct the interview without me.

When everything seemed to be in place and Raymond was just about to sit on his stool, I pulled him aside and in a rushed whisper I asked, "Will you ask him about what he was told about Blacks when he was a boy? Did he see or interact with Blacks? What did his parents say to him about Black people?" Raymond shrugged and nodded at the same time.

"Yeah, if I can, sure, yeah, we'll see." Then he turned around.

My disappointment quickly slid away when I realized that, even if these questions weren't asked during the official interview, I could ask them afterward.

The camera was turned on, and a hush fell over the room. Even though there were three lighting technicians, two cameramen, a producer, and several researchers all huddled together between just a few couches, it was suddenly as if Raymond and Davis were in the room by themselves.

To warm him up, Raymond made small talk. Davis had been good friends with John Faulkner, the brother of famed Southern writer William Faulkner. He spoke about that relationship, about growing up in Mississippi and living during a time when people walked everywhere and used notes as promises to pay debts. Eventually, Raymond asked him if he thought Greenwood had changed since Davis had first moved to the town back in September 1949.

"I think the cultures in Greenwood are getting along somewhat better than they once did," Davis said. "I had one that worked for me thirty-five years. I had known him before I even hired him. We got along just fine. We went through the civil rights era in good shape. We had no problem." From where I sat, my view of Davis was blocked by lighting equipment, so I couldn't check his face to see if he knew how ridiculous he sounded when he claimed that he'd been friends with "one."

He went on to talk about the current economic situation in Greenwood. "I don't see the work ethic I used to see. That's what brought the Mexicans in. See, they'll work. Most of our gins are working Hispanics now, rather than . . ." He seemed to be looking for a word, one that didn't start with the letter "n." He finished by saying, "The people that already lived here."

I stopped listening. I was afraid I would stand up and either scream at Raymond for not calling out Davis's blatant racism or that I'd just tear into Davis myself. I wanted to repeat his statements to him, break them down, and explain how dehumanizing they were. I wanted to ask him what the fuck was wrong with him. What had gone so wrong in his development as a human being that he couldn't even hear how backward he sounded? I clenched my fists, closed my eyes, and leaned back into the cushions of his couch. I took several deep breaths in an effort to take myself back to my plan. I would have to wait.

I could hear Raymond and Davis giggling, chatting like old pals, talking about Byron De La Beckwith, but I forced myself not to listen, to not allow their conversation to penetrate my consciousness. I just wanted it to be over. I was looking toward my moment with the racist.

When the interview finally ended, the members of our crew walked back and forth, into and out of Davis's home, to remove the equipment they'd brought in. I stood in his foyer, waiting for everyone to leave so I could do what I had come to do.

The last person to leave was Nicki, the associate producer. She'd stayed behind to take me to the next interview. She must have sensed something, because she quietly slipped outside, leaving Davis and me alone. We stood together in his foyer, engaging in small talk. I was only half there, because the rest of me was examining him, trying to figure out how to begin, how to delve into my provocative questions.

Suddenly his voice changed, and with a hint of authority he said, "Come sit in this chair."

"What?" I asked.

"You should try this chair," he repeated. I looked around. For the first time, I let myself take in his front room. The carpet was a light, pale color, possibly green, and free of evidence that anyone had ever walked on it. Furniture was smartly placed around the room in a delicate balance. On the far wall there was a built-in bookshelf, under which stood a beautiful, well-polished piano. There was a medium-size settee with plump, comfortable-looking cushions that had a simple painting of pastel images hanging over it. The dark wood coffee table that stood in the center of the room seemed faint and feminine; on top of it were several picture books about historic Mississippi homes. I smiled to myself. This was a room for sipping sweet tea in petticoats and starched trousers.

In one corner, Noll Davis stood, pointing at a futuristic-looking beige leather chair. It was long and slender and had lots of buttons on it. "Come on. It belonged to my wife. No one's sat in it since she died four years ago," he said. I heard myself inhale through my teeth. I shifted my weight and found that my hand was in the path of a narrow sliver of Delta sunlight. It was reaching from the sky, across the land, past the leaves in the tree outside, and through a slender slit in the curtains that I could barely make out. I felt as though I was standing in a beam from a searchlight, a very hot searchlight. I moved away, but not before I started to sweat.

"Come on, sit in it. You can turn it on," he persisted.

I walked over to the chair, awkwardly bent over, and sat down, but Davis had more instructions for me. "Lean back in it. Take this remote; you can make it move along your back—look at it," he said, holding the remote in front of my face. "You can make it massage your back, your legs, and so forth.

"And if you want a deeper massage, push that button there." He kept talking. He talked about the chair, about Mississippi, about the weather, and in spite of a hint of unnamed desperation, I found him to be somewhat engaging. Warm and subtly funny, Noll Davis was good company.

As I sat in his dead wife's chair, I began to sense something familiar in his words, his movements, the quick glances he made in my direction. Something about Davis was familiar to me. Somehow I knew him not from Frank's film but from somewhere else. Déjà vu tugged at the edges of my memory, making me feel more and more certain that this wasn't our first encounter. I tried to push this aside, tried to wrap my mind around my questions. I knew that there was something I was supposed to see, but in my selfishness I wanted to coddle my rage. I didn't want to open myself up to anything else.

He was watching me with a contented smile. For a moment, I wondered if he could read my thoughts on my face. I started trying out different buttons on the chair's remote control. I leaned back and closed my eyes, feigning relaxation as I tried to regain the determination that had pulsed through me just minutes before.

But there was something else, something about Noll Davis that felt remarkably familiar to me. My mind sifted through all that had taken place from the time I'd first entered his house. I recalled how he'd welcomed us. Some of the crew members had repeatedly walked in and out as they unloaded equipment. Davis had greeted each of them, every time. He'd nodded or reminded them of the locations of his multiple bathrooms. He even had a joke about using the one upstairs, and he'd delivered it more than once. He'd been delighted, jovial, almost giddy about us being there.

Davis was talking again, but when I opened my eyes, I couldn't bring myself to focus on his words. I looked at his translucent skin, watched as his heavy, thick, pale tongue flopped from his mouth to nervously moisten his lips.

The realization of where I knew him from came to me not in a rush of emotion or in a jolt of recognition. It felt obvious, as if I'd been searching for my keys only to realize they'd been in my hand all along. At first, I was struck by how long it had taken me to see it, to see him. Then I felt dread. I closed my eyes again, as if not seeing him standing next to me could make it not real. Maybe if I kept them closed long enough, I could rewind, go back to just a few seconds before to undo the knowing.

Davis was still talking, but now he was watching me. I smiled so that he wouldn't think anything was wrong as I wondered if he recognized me, too.

Did he know we were the same?

Noll Davis and I were fellow countrymen, members of the same tribe, coupled together by something basic and human. We both knew what it felt like to be lonely. Ours was not the kind of loneliness easily cured by an outing with friends. This was a kind of loneliness that burned the soul—not enough to destroy it, but enough to cauterize all the entrances so that easy, natural connection was almost impossible.

We both carried a loneliness of such magnitude that it left a fissure in the part of us that moved through the world. From that fissure leaked an unending desire and hope to be known, to be tethered, an awkward, gooey shame that soaked through every encounter we had, no matter how random, no matter how short. I watched as he played the role I'd played for so long and was struck to finally know what it looked like from the other side, for people who met me and only wanted a simple friendship but found that I was always in a desperate search for something akin to family; for someone, anyone to pour so much affection into me that I'd become so heavy I'd never again have to worry about floating away.

I knew then why Noll Davis had agreed to the meeting. Having us in his home would mean that, for a few hours one morning, he could defy the silence.

My desire to interrogate him was still there, but it was quickly drowning. I searched my mind, trying to recall what I'd prepared and trying to summon the anger I'd felt, the need for revenge, but I couldn't pull anything together in my head. My thoughts were rushing away from me, receding along with my resolve.

He moved over to the settee and picked up a picture book about Mississippi mansions. He motioned for me to sit next to him, and I felt myself rising, moving over to him, and sitting beside him. What was I doing? How was I going to leave? Davis was tireless. He went on and on, and I listened and nodded and smiled and acted as if we were old friends. I even laughed at his jokes.

How had this encounter changed so quickly? This man, who had been on the wrong side of history during a critical time for Blacks, didn't want this particular Black girl to leave. His loneliness was almost palpable. He wanted company no matter what shade of skin it came in.

In spite of all that was going on in my mind, I couldn't help but notice that Noll Davis's love of Mississippi was profound. He spoke about the state as if he was an impassioned missionary whose life's purpose was to convert me.

Never before had I met someone who so deeply treasured something as simple and as random as a place, a patch of land defined by longitude and latitude. He urged me to visit certain locales and experience particular spaces. He wanted to show me Greenwood through his eyes. He was persistent, and his energy and love for the Delta were without end.

Later, I would have no idea how much time had passed while I sat next to him. It could have been thirty minutes or two hours. That chunk of time with Noll Davis contradicted everything I'd come to Greenwood to do, and for reasons it would take me a long time to discern, something about the moment felt right. Not correct, fine, or okay, but *right* in the way a painful loss can drip with the absolute, unchangeable certainty of preordainment. Choosing to stay with him, choosing to give the pleasure of my company to a man like Noll Davis without demanding that he answer for his past felt like failure, felt like shame, and felt like absolutely the right thing to do.

My eyes darted around the room like trapped animals searching for an exit. I was anxious, because I knew there was no way to leave without it being awkward. Without saying a word, I stood up while

Davis was in the middle of a sentence. His words trailed off and he looked up at me—his eyes wide with confusion. Then a curtain of realization moved down his face, from his eyes to his blushing cheeks and on to his lips, which said, "Of course, of course, I've kept you too long."

We exchanged good-byes that were too warm, considering we'd just met. There was lots of hand-holding, smiling, slowly walking toward the door, more shaking of hands, nodding of heads, and finally more smiling. He told me to come again and I promised I would, but I could tell he knew I wouldn't. We had the same disease, but we were still strangers.

I turned to exit and was blinded for a moment by the Delta sun before I crossed the threshold. I quickly turned my eyes to the ground and made my way to the car, where I opened the door and climbed in. I looked back and, though it felt excessive, I waved to say good-bye one more time. He waved back and then stood there, watching from his doorway as Nicki pulled the car away from the curb and began driving away. I continued to watch Davis, studying his tall frame until the car rounded a bend and I couldn't see him anymore.

As we traveled through the quiet streets, past the thoughtfully decorated houses, I looked down at my lap and tried to process what had just happened.

I'd expected Noll Davis to be a certain way, and he definitely met my expectations. I thought I was going to explode when he implied that Mexicans were getting more work in Greenwood because at least they were willing to work. In my human calculus, any person who would make those types of remarks was instantly disqualified from . . . from . . . from what?

We drove into the sun. I could feel my face moving in and out of shadow as trees blocked the sun's rays and then let them through again and again.

As I considered my feelings toward Davis and the feelings I had toward everyone like him, I thought of a quote from a book I'd been carrying around so much that some of the members of the crew had begun teasing me whenever they saw it, calling it my homework. It was my already-worn-out copy of *I've Got the Light of Freedom* by Charles Payne. The five-hundred-fifty-two-page book was full of sticky notes, documents I wanted to refer to, and thoughts I'd jotted down on dog-eared pages. There was one page in particular that I'd read so many times I'd almost memorized it.

In describing the horrors perpetrated against Blacks by lynch mobs, Payne described those acts as "graphically reinforcing the idea that Negroes were so far outside the human family that the most inhuman actions could be visited upon them." The horrific treatment of people of color solidified the notion that we were less, that our humanity was not authentic, not as valuable or treasured as that of those with White skin. This allowed so many to watch as Blacks were forced to live in squalor, denied the right to attend schools, languishing in lives of hopelessness peppered with violence.

The reality of Black life was tolerable to the average White Southerner, at least in part, because they put us in a box, one that defined us as being unable to contribute to society, as being over-sexed, filthy, stupid, criminal, illiterate, and on and on and on. Just being Black was the only thing required to arouse disgust and suspicion.

I'd felt disdain for Noll Davis long before I met him, long before I even knew his name. White Southerners had been on my mind, in one way or another, since that conversation with John T. Edge four years ago, and even more so in the two months since I'd watched my grandfather's on-camera act of courage.

In the days before we met, I'd been actively coveting and nurturing scorn and hate for all the Noll Davises of the world. To me, he wasn't a man, he was an archetype, a template for a monstrous stereotype. I'd placed him in a box, defined him before meeting him.

How was my behavior any different than that of the racists who defined all Blacks the same way?

Nicki parked the car and went into the next interview, leaving me alone. I felt like I was teetering.

I was supposed to hate Noll Davis. I was supposed to humiliate him the way men like him had humiliated Booker. Instead, I was asking myself why, during my intensive research, it had never occurred to me that lurking behind some of the more vile personalities in Greenwood history, behind the hate, the rhetoric, and even behind the violence, there might possibly be some tiny, infinitesimal traces of humanity.

Noll Davis and I had come together for a brief moment that ended with neither of us getting what we wanted that day. Instead of answers, I just had different questions, and Davis was left alone again. I felt sad for him. He was a tortured man—that I knew for sure. I also knew that whatever punishment Noll Davis may have deserved for what he did all those years ago was being slowly doled out to him without any help from me.

Part Eight
A Twisted Strand

*And so it goes with each generation, a fortunate
and treasured strand for many families . . .
and a never-ending curse for others.*

Mary Carol Miller
"A Cloud of Witnesses," *Daughter of the Delta*

Harmony

Even though Booker's Place was just eight blocks away from Lusco's, after *Mississippi: A Self-Portrait* aired in the spring of 1966, Booker never went back.

He was already reconnected with Rosie by then. She and her four children were regularly traveling from Chicago to Greenwood to visit him. Years later, Booker's half sister, Margurite, would reminisce about what it was like for Rosie to finally have her firstborn son in her life. Margurite was convinced, beyond doubt, that the best years of Rosie's life were the ones she got to spend reunited with Booker. "My mother had some trouble with her children, real trouble. But when he came into our lives, it seemed like she . . . fulfilled her role as a parent and could feel everything that a parent was supposed to feel because she really had it for a while."

Booker's life had turned a corner. He was finally surrounded by family. The commitment he'd made early on to raise his daughters in spite of being divorced from their mother, the promise to always be there for them, was paying off. His daughters continued to spend their summers living with him, and once they reached high school, they began waiting tables alongside their dad at Booker's Place.

When Margurite was in town visiting, she often joined Booker's own daughters waiting tables at Booker's Place. Whenever her children were traveling to Greenwood, Rosie would remind them that life for Blacks living in the South was different. Her warnings echoed the ones given to young Emmett by his mother, Mamie, almost twenty years earlier. When the family made road trips down to Greenwood, Rosie would pack entire meals for them to eat. This way they wouldn't have to venture into any unfamiliar restaurants, where they might encounter danger because of the color of their skin.

When she visited Greenwood, Margurite spent a lot of time with Vera, Katherine, and Gloria—Honey's daughter from a previous relationship. Whenever Margurite and Gloria made plans to go into town, Booker would warn her not to speak to anyone. He told Margurite that she had to let Gloria do all the talking. At the time, Margurite couldn't figure out what her brother was so worried about, because she knew she wasn't going to say anything to offend anyone. To Margurite, the warnings from her mother and from Booker were just adults being overly cautious.

Since he was no longer working at Lusco's, Booker shored up his finances with other businesses, like selling illegal whiskey. His house had a side entrance in the bedroom, and throughout the night, random people would come and knock on that door. In a half sleep, Booker would roll out of the bed, grab a pint of moonshine, and pass it through the window, and when he pulled his hand back inside, it was full of loose change.

When Margurite was staying with him in the summers, she slept in Gloria's room. Each morning, within minutes of waking up, the two girls would be sitting on the floor in Booker and Honey's bedroom counting change. They'd separate out the quarters from the dimes, and so forth. Then they'd line them up and wrap the coins in used, ripped, worn-out wrappers. By the time the girls were finished, their hands were covered in black grime from the dirty coins.

Around this time, the Head Start program came to Greenwood,

and Booker realized that kids living on the plantations on the out-skirts of town wouldn't get to participate in the program because they lacked transportation. Booker bought a school bus and then made a deal with the people at Head Start to transport the planta-tion kids for a nominal fee.

Booker always had a heart for children, maybe because of what he went through when he was young. Honey had a sister whose husband died, leaving her with several children she couldn't afford to feed. Each day Booker would say to them, "Don't you go to school without first coming in here to get your breakfast." Then, as they were getting ready to leave for school, he'd hand them a sack lunch and say, "Don't you go home from school without first coming in here to get some dinner." Margurite got the impression that he kept those children fed for years. Booker even took one of them, a boy named Bo, under his wing by giving him a job at the restaurant and teaching him how to manage it.

Unfortunately, Bo liked to blow all his pay, and never had enough money to buy decent clothes. After watching this cycle over and over again, Booker began holding back some of Bo's pay. The following year, when kids were on a break from school, Booker waited till the end of one of Bo's shifts, handed him a wad of money, and told him to go straight to the store to get some decent clothes.

Lots of Black kids who went to Booker's Place grew used to him telling them to take school seriously and to get all they could out of it. Back then, education was on everyone's mind.

Even though the Supreme Court had ruled school segregation il-legal, Whites in Greenwood had essentially ignored the order. Once again, in an effort to not just have civil rights but to use them, Blacks in Greenwood began making moves to integrate their schools. In the fall of 1967, Black children began trickling into White schools in the single digits. It was clear that, at that rate, it would take another fifty years for the schools to integrate. The Supreme Court intervened, ordering the Greenwood School District and the Greenwood Separate School District to submit a plan "for total integration by February 1 [1970]."

Almost overnight, enrollment of White students in public schools fell by the hundreds; almost all of them began attending local private schools. "Everything changed in 1970," Sara Criss wrote in her memoir. "Sports were soon dominated by blacks, as more and more white students dropped basketball and football and track. Attendance at the ball games dropped, as fewer and fewer whites attended the games."

In the decades before the movement, Greenwood had been a place where almost every local event was a reason to celebrate or throw a parade. "The high school games had drawn huge crowds, and before the present stadium was built with a larger seating capacity, the local men . . . would get up at four in the morning to go stand in line at Roberts Drugstore to buy season tickets to the football games to be sure of getting seats."

While some things were changing, others were still the same. A young activist named Stokely Carmichael was keeping the fire of the movement going. In 1966, he traveled to Greenwood where, while giving a speech, he used the phrase "Black Power." It was the first time that phrase had been used, at least publicly, and people around the nation took notice. Characteristically, the Ku Klux Klan put out a newsletter that included the following content:

Now, we have this message for the Negros of this area. The world first heard the revolutionary cry of BLACK POWER shouted from the mouth of a sunbaked Ubangi named STOKLEY CAR-MICHAEL right here in Greenwood during the "Mississippi March." If any of you should allow your selves [sic] to become intoxicated with this revolutionary brew, rest assured, you will be

*promptly sobered up with massive doses of BLACK POWDER,
already in the hands of we white, Christian patriots. Do not be
fools, black men. We will live here with you in the future as we
have in the past or we will fertilize the soil of our beloved South-
land with your remains.*

Try as they might with volatile words, the White Mississippians' way of life was becoming part of history. The White Citizens'
Council failed in its promise to stop "something they did not understand and could not handle. And that was the determination of
Black Mississippians to change the condition of their life and to
sustain that effort in the face of murder, mayhem, riots, and arson."
Bewildered, beaten, and embittered, Whites found ways to make do
in this new world. Some embraced it; most did not.

If Whites living in Greenwood in the early 1900s had an almost
"exhausting vitality," by the late 1960s they were just exhausted, and
they were not alone. The White response in Greenwood to integration left many Blacks feeling a different kind of sting, a different
form of humiliation. It's one thing to be hated from afar, but to look
into the eyes of people who don't want to put their hands where
yours have been or sit where you've sat might wear on the soul just
as heavily as physical wounds from violence.

Before integration, Blacks in Greenwood had pockets of society,
streets and neighborhoods, where Whites were reluctant to enter.
Black business owners often mentored the young and took fatherless
children under their wings. Many Blacks who grew up in Greenwood before the movement lived in a bubble where everyone they
interacted with looked just like them. They only had to think about
Whites when they went into downtown Greenwood.

By the late 1960s, it seemed as though true change might never
come. With their private schools and private clubs, Greenwood
Whites had managed to take a detour, circumventing integration

altogether. As young Blacks grew older and had children of their own, many felt the promise of the movement had somehow missed Greenwood. Many of them packed up their families and moved out of town.

Booker's primary residence continued to be in Greenwood, but he was also making a life for himself in Chicago, where he often went to visit his mother and siblings. There was something about Booker during those years that wasn't quite right. He seemed unsettled. Unless he was in Chicago with Rosie.

When he was in Chicago, Margurite noticed that Booker was able to completely relax. He'd take Margurite out and show her a side of the city she'd never seen, to restaurants she'd never visited, where they'd eat dishes she'd never heard of before.

"And the money; that man had plenty of money, and he loved money, and, see, that's what I thought would've gotten him hurt. When he'd come to Chicago, I'd always tell him, 'Don't you pull out all that money at one time; you can't do that, you're not in Mississippi.' He was something, he was something. I tell you, my brother was something else, and I enjoyed that brief time, but it was so— what should I say—so full of everything that this family needed at that time. It sure was. He meant a lot to us. He meant a lot to us."

It was when he was in Greenwood that Margurite noticed something odd about Booker. He seemed distracted. Not unhappy. He was distant and quiet. In Greenwood, Booker had a shadow he couldn't shake off.

What she didn't notice was that people all over town were growing in their hatred of Booker. He still had to toss people out, but something in him was changing. Instead of it being a necessary evil, his treatment of poor Blacks turned into an expression of something unresolved inside of him, like something he was trying to expel.

A Black woman who worked at Booker's Place for years to put herself through school remembered him as an angry man who didn't pay her well. He screamed at her for making mistakes, even though he hadn't provided proper training, and he let her walk herself home in the early morning hours through the dangerous streets of Baptist Town while never once offering her a ride. "I just figured that's how he was treated over there at Lusco's, and so that's the only way he knew how to treat people."

Still, Booker's family continued to grow. He fathered two sons, one with a woman in Chicago and another with a woman in Greenwood. He even reconnected with his "adopted" father, Willie Wright, who had grown too ill to care for himself. Booker arranged for him to be moved into a nursing home and began taking his children to visit him.

In his final years, Booker spent a lot of time with Rosie. The thing that eluded him his whole life was finally in his grasp. Booker Wright knew where he came from. He had family—one that seemed to never stop growing. In the early 1970s, his oldest daughter, Vera, gave birth to a child whom Booker cherished. Whenever Vera brought her son into the restaurant, Booker would proclaim, "This is my grandson!" Vera remembers those years with fondness. She was older, out of school, and her relationship with her father had grown from one of parent and child to one of friendship.

The two of them spent hours together laughing and talking. Sometimes, when they were alone, Booker would tell Vera something that would eventually have great meaning to her—something she would hold on to in her darkest hours. "If anything ever happens to me, I want you to know that I've lived my life. I have lived my life."

A Murder Story

Seven years after Booker's news appearance and the last time he'd stepped foot inside Lusco's, he died. It was on a Saturday night in May 1973, and about fifteen people were at the club, including Booker. Blackie came in around 1:15 a.m., walked over to a booth where two White people were eating, and sat down with them. Booker stopped what he was doing, went to the booth, and told Blackie to leave. He knew Blackie; almost everyone from the neighborhood knew him. He was dirt poor, often drunk, and rarely had even a few dollars to his name.

When Booker asked him to leave, Blackie stood up, but he didn't go. Instead, he walked toward the back of the restaurant. Booker followed him, and the two began to argue. Finally, Blackie made his way to the front door, but instead of leaving, he turned around and continued to argue with Booker, who took out his gun, held it by the barrel, and hit Blackie in the mouth with it.

Then Booker shoved Blackie out onto McLaurin Street, following him to make sure he really did leave. When he was satisfied that the encounter with Blackie was finally over, Booker went back inside to check on one of his tables. He acted as though nothing out of the ordinary had happened, because nothing out of the ordinary had happened. The whole thing took less than a few minutes and was over almost before it had begun.

That same night, an eighteen-year-old girl named Irene married her high school sweetheart. The two of them made their way down McLaurin, stopping at each of the clubs to share their good news with the locals. By the time they arrived at Booker's Place, the ruckus between Booker and Blackie was already over. The young couple went inside, found a few friends, and told them they'd just gotten married. It was getting late and the couple didn't want to stay for too long, so just a few minutes after they arrived, Irene and her new husband were heading for the door.

As she made her way through the tables, Irene looked out onto McLaurin, which was illuminated by the light pouring out of Booker's Place. In that light, she saw people hanging out on the sidewalk and in the street. Then the scene began to change. Just before Irene reached the door, she noticed the people in the light were starting to run. McLaurin was a rough street, so she just figured a fight was breaking out. Then her eyes narrowed in on something. Booker's station wagon was parked on the street, and by the rear bumper, standing next to the curb, was Blackie, and in his hands was a gun.

It would later be revealed that what Blackie was holding in his hands that night was a sawed-off shotgun with #00 buckshot shells. When someone saws off the end of a shotgun, it's either to make it easier to conceal or to make it more deadly, because a sawed-off shotgun has a wider spray. From a short distance, one shot can leave a large hole in a thick door. The #00 shells are large and were designed to hold eight or nine pellets each, but that night they were holding many more. Someone had refilled the cartridges with pellets designed for much smaller shells. Depending on their size, the cartridges could have been holding anywhere from fifty to well over a hundred small metal pellets. The gun and its ammunition had both received adjustments that made them more efficient at destruction. Blackie only fired one shot that night, but one shot was all it took.

What happened next happened incredibly fast. Facing the barrel of a gun, Irene turned and threw her back against the wall next to the door. Before she could gather her thoughts, a loud blast exploded into Booker's Place. Without registering pain, she felt shotgun pellets quickly sink into her flesh, then her body slid to the floor.

When the shot was fired, Booker was standing in front of his register, giving change to one of his waitresses. Just as she turned to walk away, someone screamed, "Watch out!" The waitress was hit with pellets in her forehead and her arm. She started to run, but then heard someone else yell, "Don't run. Get down on the floor." So she threw her body to the concrete floor, and while she was falling, she saw Booker grab his right side, come from behind the counter, and run out the front door.

With that one shot, Blackie had blown open the door and wounded four people. Afterward, he turned and ran up McLaurin Street toward the tracks. Booker climbed over the people on the floor, the broken glass crunching under his feet, and made his way out to the street. Holding his side with one hand and his gun with the other, he chased Blackie, firing shot after shot at him. After running to the end of the block, Booker's body gave out and he fell to the ground.

Back in the club, there was confusion.

Someone said, "Booker's been shot. Somebody should call his wife or the police or something."

The stunned patrons slowly began standing up and heading toward the broken door past Irene, who was still sitting with her back against the wall. Her husband came over and knelt down in front of her.

"I'm shot," Irene told him.

"No, you're not," he said as he pulled her up.

"Yes, I am."

"No, you're not," he said again, but helped her to lie down in one of the booths anyway.

Booker made his way back to his restaurant. Maybe he crawled or maybe he was able to walk, but by the time his customers were coming out into the street, Booker was lying on McLaurin with blood pouring from his side.

A young officer named Jimmy Tindall got the call over the radio about someone being shot at Booker's Place. He knew Booker and he knew his café, so he and his partner headed over. As he made his way down McLaurin, he saw a crowd of people standing out on the street. Someone may have helped Booker up, because by the time Tindall pulled his patrol car up, Booker was standing. His white coat was soaked with blood. Booker looked at Officer Tindall and said, "I'm hurt bad." Tindall helped Booker into the back of the squad car and rushed him to Greenwood Leflore Hospital. After dropping him off, Tindall and his partner returned to McLaurin to interview the witnesses.

Bo Williams, Booker's nephew, had been working at the club earlier that evening. His apartment wasn't far from Booker's Place, and he was just getting ready for bed when he heard sirens. He looked out the window and saw a crowd gathered in front of the club. He put his shirt back on and headed out. By the time Bo arrived, Booker was already gone, but the customers told him what had taken place.

There was a large puddle of blood on the ground in front of the restaurant and plenty of blood and glass on the floor inside. Not knowing what else to do, Bo began to clean. He picked up broken glass and used white towels to soak up the blood. He figured the place would need to be clean for business the next day. Booker was larger than life; it hadn't occurred to Bo that he might never return.

As he worked, the noise that had summoned him there was dying down. The officers who'd come back to collect statements from

Booker's customers had released them. Stunned and confused, the people in the crowd slowly made their way back to their homes.

Eventually, everything was quiet. Later, still in the early morning hours, the pay phone inside the restaurant rang, and Bo answered it. The woman on the other end of the line was one of Booker's waitresses. She was on vacation in Chicago and had called to speak with Booker. Bo told her that Booker wasn't there, leaving out the reason why.

A few moments later, another phone rang; this one was in Chicago inside Margurite Butler's house. It was the waitress. She told Margurite she had a funny feeling. "You call Booker's Place, because something's wrong there. I called and Honey's nephew, Bo, was there, but Bo doesn't work this time of night."

Margurite hung up and immediately called Booker's Place. Bo answered the phone again, but this time he told the whole story. Margurite called her mother and broke the news to her.

Years later, Margurite would struggle to find the words to describe her mother's countenance during those days. "I just thought my mother would not make it. I really did. I just thought she would not make it, because, you know, at the same time she was dealing with all that stuff with Erby."

Erby, Booker's half brother, had been living in Mississippi and working for a moving company when the owner, a man named Archibald, fired him earlier that year. Two days before Booker was shot, Erby returned to the moving company. He went inside while one of his cousins waited in the car. Inside, Erby brutally murdered Archibald, his sister, and his adult daughter. When he returned to the car, Erby told his cousin that he "beat them because they wouldn't die." It was later determined that after shooting his three victims, Erby Butler Jr. had used his bare hands to beat Archibald and his sister to death.

Word of his violence quickly made its way back to the neighborhood in Chicago where Rosie was still living. Reporters and neighbors were constantly calling Rosie's home to ask her questions or to harass her. Within hours of receiving the call about Booker being shot, Rosie left her house. On the lawn, someone had placed a sign with the word "murderer" written on it. Rosie caught a flight to Mississippi, where she had two sons in trouble. Rosie was in danger of losing Booker again. Along with that fear, she also had to carry the horror of knowing that a child she'd born had taken three lives for no reason at all.

AT THE HOSPITAL, IT was discovered that numerous pellets had moved through Booker's arm and into his side. He had several small holes in his arm and the right side of his chest, but the majority of the shotgun pellets had gone into his abdomen, where they penetrated his stomach, small intestine, and liver. He also had huge, gaping holes in his large intestine and was in shock from having lost so much blood.

Vera and Rosie rarely left his side. "I'm gonna be alright," Booker told them over and over again from where he lay in his hospital bed.

Even though he was on the run from the FBI, Erby stopped by the hospital, but Vera refused to let him see Booker. Andy Pinkston also came by to visit his old friend, and one of the last people to see Booker alive was Andy's father, Jess Pinkston. As Jess walked down the hospital hallway toward the room, he could smell the infection rotting inside his friend's body. Just as he had with everyone else, Booker assured Jess that he was going to be alright, but Jess could tell that Booker was near the end.

After Jess left, Vera was in the waiting room collecting her thoughts when the doctor came over and asked for the family of Booker Wright to gather. She walked over to him. The doctor looked down at her and said, "He's gone."

Vera was stunned. "How can he be dead?" she thought. "I just saw him."

The story of his death spread through Greenwood like wildfire, because, Black or White, almost everybody knew Booker. Honey and Gloria were broken up, and Rosie Turner had lost her firstborn son for a second time.

The one thing people took solace in was that he had three days in the hospital, during which time he got the chance to see the people who mattered to him one last time. Booker shared his final days with the family he loved. Everyone, that is, except my mother.

Greenwood

The film crew left after eight days in Greenwood. I rented a car and stayed a couple more days to do additional interviews and to spend some time with my cousin Rena and a few other family members. In the end, I spent a lot of time in my hotel room, thinking. Alone and exhausted, I found myself going around and around with thoughts about my great-grandmother, Rosie Turner.

The amount of pain she experienced in her life struck me as unquantifiable. Just thinking about what Rosie must have been experiencing in the days before and after Booker was shot left me speechless. An aching scream welled up inside me, rattling my very bones, but I couldn't get it out. Rosie ran away from home to avoid rape when she was eleven or twelve at the oldest. Then she became pregnant and was a single mother at thirteen, only to have her child taken from her through a form of manipulation too complicated for the young mother to understand, let alone undo.

Decades later, another child of hers killed three people out of spite, and within days of that horror, the child she wasn't able to raise was lying in a hospital bed fighting for his life. I pictured Rosie sitting with him until the end, inhaling the foul stench of his infection.

That was too much pain for one life.

I felt such love and such sorrow for my great-grandmother. I wanted to find a way to carry her burden with her, to walk with her, to let her know that, after decades of living in silence, someone saw her, saw her pain, her perseverance, her triumph, and her solitude. I was going to stand with my great-grandmother in that place of burden and tell her that when the world saw her body as an object for work or sexuality, I saw a little girl. When the world saw her as the mother of a murderer, I saw a mother with broken dreams whose child had lost his way. Each day, I woke up in my hotel room with an intention to write burning inside me. I wanted to write my way through Rosie's story, using her voice in the hopes that somehow, all these years later, I could lighten her load, lessen her sorrows. But her story was too painful for me to meditate on for long periods of time. In the end, I didn't have the courage to do it.

In the years before I saw Booker's video, when I was just beginning to learn about Black life in the South, I was sharing some of my findings with a friend. When I described Black boys not being allowed to attend a full year of school and the regular violation of Black female bodies, I called the situation a tragedy. She quickly suggested that I be more careful with my words, because for many people "tragedy" might be too strong a description.

During those lonely summer days in Greenwood, when the intensity of the sun's rays was never strong enough to brighten the spirit of the day, I found myself thinking a lot about what my friend said. As I drove through those stagnant, silent streets and did research at the local library and visited with my aunts, uncles, and cousins, my friend's words kept coming back to me. After all I'd seen, I agreed with her. Somewhere there is always a more heartbreaking story.

But this wasn't a story from a history book or something I read in a headline and then forgot by lunch. For me, at least, Greenwood's story was personal.

While I understood that the system my ancestors lived through was not uniquely designed to harm only them and that, like countless others, they were caught up in the growing pains of a nation as it wrestled with its own fractured beliefs about race and difference, that knowledge was of little comfort to me, because we each get only one life. For Booker and Rosie, their lives weren't necessarily about major political and social movements. They had their own hopes and dreams, just like everyone else—hopes and dreams they were forced to pursue as the world stood on the sidelines throwing social and economic obstacles in their paths again and again, and then ridiculing them for not achieving more, for not going farther.

Those last few days in Greenwood, I was filled with a sense of sadness, but also a sense of wonder about who Booker and Rosie, and even my parents, might have been, the lives they could have enjoyed if they'd only lived in a world where they were seen as people, in a world that recognized their basic right to human dignity.

Finally, the day arrived when I needed to leave. As I was driving out of town, I remembered how Greenwood had once seemed so small to me. It didn't have a Sephora or even a Target. For as long as I could remember, I'd always viewed the town as small and simple, like a child's puzzle that I could hold in my hands, turning it over and around to examine from any angle I chose. Before that summer, I really thought I understood the deep complexities of this place because I'd done some research. It was a foregone conclusion to me that integration was completed long ago and that what pained the town now was nothing but racism and resentment.

I finally saw what had been right in front of my face the entire time: Greenwood didn't truly integrate. Laws were side-stepped, new schools opened, and people moved north or out of town altogether to escape change. This idea seemed so obvious now that the town was disappearing in my rearview mirror. Greenwood wasn't simple at all. The town had a way of casting details in a new light, revealing new dimensions to explore.

Hours before Medgar Evers was murdered, President Kennedy spoke about the discrimination, violence, and the all-but-insurmountable economic barriers facing Blacks. The president said, "Legislation cannot solve this problem alone. It must be solved in the homes of every American in every community across our country." When I first read that sentence, it seemed like beautiful rhetoric, a way to get people to be a little more engaged. I hadn't yet grasped just how critical the individual citizen is when it comes to any sweeping change.

Greenwood taught me that a new law often just serves to highlight the moment in history when someone with power decided a system was wrong. But the dates I'd memorized in school—the ones I was told were the markers of monumental victories in the Black struggle—those dates didn't necessarily indicate the end of anything.

Creating new laws was only the beginning. Civil rights legislation couldn't keep one group from devaluing another; it couldn't stop them from maintaining distance and nurturing ideas that only served to deepen divisions. No law is complex enough to address the myriad, nuanced ways in which a group of people can be systematically held back, degraded, and quietly denied the right to a life of respect, safety, prosperity, and peace.

The Greenwood I was leaving that day was like an excavated city, half-destroyed by a human disaster, its remains serving as the archaeological evidence of what happens when integration is piecemeal at best, when people change laws without changing themselves. Half of Greenwood was as beautiful as a living dream; the other half was as warped and twisted as the vilest corners of the human heart.

As I turned onto the road that would lead me out of town, I expected myself to be overcome with sadness about the reality of the place I was from, but I wasn't. If nothing else could be said, I now knew my place in the grand story, and my children would know theirs.

Thinking of my two sons made my throat tighten. When I'd first learned about Booker, it was during a time in my life when I was pretty convinced that I'd come from nothing, that I'd come from people who didn't care about family at all. Raising my own kids had often felt like trying to write a symphony after just a few music lessons.

I'd had no idea that I came through a tradition of overcomers. I'd had no idea of the trauma, the pain, and the horrors they'd survived.

Eventually, I was on a road that reminded me of the night my aunt had driven my sister and me from the airport into Greenwood. It was a lonely road flanked by trees so tall they seemed to skim the sky. I pulled the car over, climbed out, and sat on the hood.

Wind was rustling through the leaves, and I knew I was not alone. As I sat there, looking up into the trees, searching them with my eyes, I knew there was something alive in Greenwood, an inherent paradox, a sorrowful spirit that had haunted me and called me home. Greenwood is where I'm from, both figuratively and literally. I will always wear its mark.

After a few more minutes, I climbed back into my car and started driving. I felt small next to those trees, but not afraid like I had when I was younger. This time I felt saved.

To me, those trees were generations of aged mothers and fathers watching over me, their legacy. The trees were so close together. All I could see up ahead, and all I could see in my rearview mirror, was a wall of green. It felt as though the dense trees were momentarily parting to allow me to pass before quickly coming back together again.

I thought of the fields, the ones hidden behind the trees. I imagined men, women, and children dressed in rags, stooped over and dripping with sweat from the relentless heat, all the while singing the blues. Strangely, for the first time, that image wasn't distressing. It comforted me, and I knew then what I had never known before.

The song of the slave is my soul's lullaby.

And then I heard myself say, "There *is* magic here."

Part Nine
Inheritance

*Did I learn of roses and aircraft and snowfall
because my mother's dreams had traveled her
body with their images intact and electric and
full of messages from the outside world?*

Pat Conroy
The Lords of Discipline

Booker's Song

I have four film clips of Booker, three of which have no sound. The soundless clips are all from the Lusco family's collection of home videos. Two of them appear to have been taken around the same time, possibly in the 1950s when Booker was in his late twenties or early thirties.

In one, he's hanging out in the kitchen with some other men who are all White. Everyone, including Booker, is passing a cup around and taking sips from it. Their reactions are humorous. Either the drink is strong and sour or just disgusting. Whoever has the camera is capturing their scrunched-up faces after each sip. They're all laughing. Booker spits his out in the sink. The video feels like a bunch of coworkers letting loose after work.

The other video from about that same time period is one of Booker and Andy Pinkston. Andy is in Booker's arms. The little boy is too shy to look up at the camera, until Booker tickles him and gets him to laugh and look into the lens. The trust that flows between Andy and Booker in those few moments is almost palpable. Booker is comforting Andy with his body and coaxing him gently, giving the child a kind of affection Booker himself may have only ever received in the earliest years of his life from Rosie.

In the last film clip, Booker is dancing at what appears to be a family Christmas gathering, recorded not long before Booker's appearance in Frank's film, in the early 1960s, when the citizens of Greenwood—both Black and White—were being forced to choose sides. There's something awkward about the footage. People appear to be dancing, celebrating, but Booker isn't joining in. When he does join, he seems reluctant, as if he doesn't really want to. The setting of the film clip is relaxed, but something in Booker's face belies discomfort. It's subtle, but it's definitely there. He is unsettled.

I have two digital audio recorders filled with conversations I've had about Booker, in addition to all the interviews Raymond and his crew captured on film. Plus, I can't even begin to quantify all the phone conversations and unplanned moments I've had in which people shared their memories of my grandfather with me.

From what I can tell, aside from what he said in Frank's film, most of which was about his customers, Booker never uttered a single unkind word about the Lusco family.

I don't know why. Maybe because they were there, even if it was only about physical proximity, when Booker was a boy, all alone, struggling to make it. They were there when he fell in love, became a father, got divorced, and then fell in love again. They were there when he opened Booker's Place, a restaurant of his own. For twenty-five years, the Lusco family, and at least a few of their regular customers, were the only constants in his life.

Booker understood something that I hadn't even begun to consider until I met Noll Davis, and didn't fully grasp until sometime later. Empathy is powerful. When Booker appeared in Frank's documentary, he set alight a fire of compassion in the souls of complete strangers throughout the nation. He didn't speak about voting rights or access to public spaces, as important as those issues were—instead he won them over with his vulnerability. He stood in front of a camera and revealed the deepest parts of himself as if he believed that if people could really see him, really understand what it felt like to be

Black in his world, that it would arouse in them not just sorrow but indignation and a commitment to action as well.

More than anything, I wanted to be just like him.

In the years that followed my summer in the Delta, I returned to Greenwood again and again. I was delighted with what I'd learned about Booker, but what I saw in him so amazed me that I continued to long for more. More memories, more stories, more pieces of him from the people, both Black and White, who were blessed enough to have known him.

On one of those trips, I spent a long, lazy afternoon with a woman whose name I won't mention. She'd grown up in Greenwood and moved away, only to return later in her life. Her house was filled with her mother's paintings. Every wall in the living room and hall had paintings hung from the ceiling on down. More paintings lined the floor, leaning up against the wall. Others, which weren't in frames, were stacked on tables.

She'd known Booker when she was as child. She'd been friends with some of the Lusco girls and would often play in the restaurant before it opened in the afternoons when school had let out. She told me about how Booker played with the children and helped to take care of them. I smiled and tucked away a pretend memory of me at five years of age playing with Booker.

Toward the end of our time together, we were saying our goodbyes and I was walking behind her as she led me to her front door when I heard her say, "You must miss him very much."

I was surprised. We'd been together for hours, and somehow I'd failed to mention that I had never met Booker. I told her he died before I was born. She immediately spun around and exclaimed, "Oh, no!"

For a beat longer than was comfortable, she just stared at me. Then she said, "My mother was not a woman of touch. She rarely hugged me. What I remember about Booker is that he would hug us and he would play with us."

I wasn't sure if it was what she'd said or how she'd said it, but I felt a rush of emotion as I held her gaze, which, for a moment, was flooded with grief.

She lived on an incredibly quiet tree-lined street just west of the lovely oaks that still line Grand Boulevard in North Greenwood. As I drove off, the only sound I heard was the crunching of dried leaves that had fallen on the ground. Like in my meeting with Noll Davis, she'd tripped up and said a few things she probably didn't mean to. While trying to convince me that Greenwood was no longer segregated, she explained how several Black families had moved into her neighborhood. "My friends ask me why I don't move over to the other side of Grand to get away from them, but they're good—"

She stopped herself and then said, "People don't come in good or bad." I wondered if she was going to say that her neighbors were "good niggas," as some of Booker's customers said about him so many years ago. She tensed up, as if she feared I might call her out on what she'd almost said. But I didn't.

I was trying to be like Booker. I was struggling to look straight on, without a filter, at a woman who'd missed the deep suffering that had taken place right in front of her. As she tried to convince me that everything in Greenwood had changed, I did something that she and so many others had refused to do for people like me, for Rosie, or for Booker. I chose to see her—her flaws, her prejudice, and her humanity—whether or not she chose to see me. My choice had nothing to do with her and everything to do with the kind of person I was choosing to be.

I was still wrestling with—and may always wrestle with—my feelings toward Whites who did next to nothing to help Blacks, who continue to look back on their own biographies through a filter of good intentions. I'd just finished reading Sara Criss's memoirs of the civil rights movement. At one point she described "Negro crowds gathering in front of White-owned stores in their section of town and taunting the owners." When describing the Blacks who were determined to integrate the Lefore Theater and the Whites who didn't want it integrated at all, Sara referred to them as two "groups who were trying to stir up trouble," making life difficult for the "decent, respectable citizens" of Greenwood.

Sara wrote her memoirs in the 1990s, and historian Charles M. Payne published *I've Got the Light of Freedom* in 1995. While Payne was looking back and seeing activists, Sara still saw taunting and people stirring up trouble. It's as if she was stuck in the emotions she felt when she was driving down Grand Boulevard on April 1, 1963—lamenting the loss of the town she loved so dearly and hoping against hope that things could just go back to being the way they were before.

With the hindsight of decades, she still missed that, at its core, the civil rights movement wasn't about going to the movies or sitting in the front of a bus. For many, it was about having the ability, the right, the dignity to go or to sit anywhere that anyone else could. She spent her entire life living among people of color but still somehow had managed to miss their basic humanity. Sara loved her family, wanted to protect it, and had dreams for her children. Like many others in her community, she seemed blind to the simple fact that Blacks had the same dreams.

While Sara raised her own children on a modest budget, many of her contemporaries were enjoying lives of comfort, seasoned with extras like bridge and garden clubs, mentions in the society pages, live-in maids and childcare providers, lavish parties, country club memberships, vacation homes, and much, much more. The Southern way of life was an expensive way of life. Maintaining its accoutrements required a class of people who would work without complaint under unfair labor practices and squalid living conditions.

It's true that many Blacks were silent about the harsh working conditions, the lack of investment in educating their children, and the general absence of respect and dignity they received from society.

But their silence did not equal consent.

As Southern Whites were building economic security for their own families, there must have been moments in which something from deep inside themselves cried out, reverberating like a never-ending echo, originating in a shared sense of humanity. It was this very thing, this sense of commonality—as seen in human longing, the capacity for hope, the slow-healing nature of wounds inflicted by humiliation, the natural inclination to flinch at pain and retreat from violence, the persistent nature of shame, the sense of healing that comes from free-flowing laughter, the colossal feelings of impotence felt when one cannot protect their own children, and so much more—it was this unchanging undercurrent of human life that Booker so deftly connected to in strangers far and wide. My grandfather spoke to something alive in each of us that, like the green foliage that blanketed his town, always, always bends toward the light.

I wasn't sure if it was a daily act or something that occurred here and there over a lifetime, but I was becoming more and more convinced that at some point, Whites were faced with a choice. They had to choose to either act upon or ignore the basic and obvious fact that no one would be forever content with the life forced on Blacks by the South's economic structure and unpunished racial crimes.

After I returned home, I began sharing my experiences with people, and there were two responses I encountered again and again. The first was a discussion about whether or not looking back was worthwhile. People would ask, "What good does it do to resurrect the past?" "Why not just celebrate how much the world has changed since Booker was growing up in the Mississippi Delta?"

The world *has* changed.

Decades ago, even while being made rich by Black labor, Senator

James Eastland alluded to a yet-to-come season in human events when it would be "necessary to abolish the Negro race." It's no wonder that many viewed Eastland as the perfect representation of racial hatred. But he was also a practiced expert in the exploitation of Black workers. In 1961, Eastland spent "$566,000 to produce his cotton for a profit of $324,000 (equal to $2,130,000 in 2006). This represents profit of 57%." While traveling throughout the nation and making speeches about imagined deficiencies in the basic nature of Blacks, it was Black men, women, and children who were building his empire. Working on his farm for "30 cents an hour," or "$3.00 for a 10-hour day, $18.00 for a six-day, 60-hour week."

In spite of this gross history of injustice, it's been said that even Senator Eastland had a change of heart after the civil rights movement. The vile rhetoric he spewed against Blacks slowly eroded as he aged. Many argued that Eastland's shift was made to keep himself alive politically, but others close to him believe his softening was sincere.

The spark that set the civil rights movement aflame has undergone a change of its own—a change to the story. Carolyn Bryant, the woman whose words led to her husband brutalizing and then murdering fourteen-year-old Emmett Till in 1954, recanted her courtroom testimony six decades after the fact. Her admission that she'd lied on the stand cast even further doubt on the notion that Till did anything at all on that fateful day in her store. Bryant had managed to essentially avoid publicity in the years after the trial. Nevertheless, she chose to revisit the story. I found myself wondering why. She was free from it, free from responsibility, free from public disgrace.

Maybe Carolyn Bryant's freedom belied an internal punishment of memory.

Just as some things changed, others were exactly the same.

In the summer of 2012, a reporter for the Greenwood *Commonwealth* interviewed Judge Gray Evans, who once again spoke of his recollections of what happened to my grandfather at the hands of a police officer, someone who was supposed to protect and serve. Evans said that on the night in question, Curtis Underwood "was on a motorcycle" and that "he stopped and just beat the hell out of Booker. For no reason. There were no words spoken. Nothing. And he was not prosecuted for it."

Evans also shed some light on why he didn't do something himself about the violence perpetrated against my grandfather all those years ago. The retired judge explained that he was instructed by both the chief of police and the city judge "to let the matter drop."

The officer, Curtis Underwood, was still alive and resided in a town about forty-five minutes outside Greenwood. The reporter reached out to him, and about the Judge's claim that he'd beaten my grandfather, Underwood said, "I never touched him. He should have been. He was drunk as could be. It was a heck of a confrontation, but he was not touched." Maybe to make his position abundantly clear, Underwood went on to explain to the reporter that Booker "was not a bit more pistol-whipped by me than you were pistol-whipped by me."

And so it goes. If some are marked by nostalgia, others shame, and others regret, maybe some continue to be inflamed by the fires of change that came along and swept Greenwood up, dreams and all.

THE OTHER RESPONSE I received again and again when I returned home from Greenwood and began sharing the experience with people was a critical assessment of White Southerners. While shaking their heads and making "tsk" sounds to highlight their disapproval, I found people who were eager to make declarative statements about the basic nature of White Southerners.

They were convinced that, had they been the ones living in Mississippi, Alabama, Tennessee, Florida, or any of the other states where tangible and intangible crimes against Blacks flourished, they would have taken up the cause. They believed, without a doubt, that they would have done the right thing. From their vantage point, it was a given that Southern Whites were despicable and their actions unfathomable.

I couldn't keep myself from wondering how this blanket assessment was any different from Eastland's proclamations about Blacks all those decades ago.

Sometimes if I was having this conversation with someone at a play date, art class, or other homeschooling activity, I'd look over to where our kids were playing together and I'd wonder if they really would have taken their blond-haired, blue-eyed children across the tracks to live in the rundown shacks in Black neighborhoods, where they'd attend ill-equipped schools with poorly trained teachers and outdated materials. Would they use their children as an experiment to find out if the dishonest propaganda was really true, that Blacks were oversexed and intellectually inferior?

They assume that I hate Southern Whites, and that I enjoy disparaging them, but I don't. I'd spent my entire life lamenting the emptiness I felt because I wasn't close to my family. In White Southerners I saw lovers of family running scared, threatened by false ideas, haunted by the atrocities their ancestors committed, who were spending their energy standing in resistance to change, all in an effort to preserve a way of life that died long ago and that was always perverted with injustice. The meeting I had that afternoon with the woman who didn't realize I'd never met Booker was not a singular event. The way the two of us shared a deeply emotional moment even though we hardly knew each other was something I experienced over and over again with White Southerners.

When I met Whites who'd known Booker, their faces would light up at the memory of my grandfather singing the menu. I believed, because I could feel it, that some of them had true affection for him. It was a complicated kind of affection to be sure, one that had to be marred with shame and regret as the shifting world around them made it impossible to continue denying the infectious strain of cruelty and inhumanity in the town they cherished and adored.

In spite of the emotional history that will always hang between me and the White citizens of Greenwood, the honest truth is that I can't help but love anyone who loved Booker Wright. Their affection for him—their sweet, unchanging, delightful affection for him—wins me over every time.

Remembering

B y 2012 I was thinking seriously about writing a book, and I
wanted to look more closely at the work Raymond and I had
done together in Greenwood, so he arranged for me to have access to all the interviews we'd filmed. One afternoon, I was sifting
through some files when I came across an interview we'd done with
my mother. We'd shot it in a restaurant the day after my meeting
with Noll Davis.

Whenever I was in Greenwood, I struggled to place my mother
there. Even though my father hadn't lived in Greenwood in four
decades, he was clearly comfortable in the Delta. He had a persona,
a way of relating to his hometown that he could slip on, and it fit
just like a glove.

My mother, on the other hand, seemed stifled by the Delta, as if
she'd never been anyplace so small, so dusty, or so poor. Mississippi
seemed to assault her senses. I often caught her smiling politely at
people as if to avoid hurting the feelings of the desperate souls who
actually had to live there.

As I watched the clip, I remembered the moment she walked
into the restaurant looking like she'd just stepped out of a magazine. Her hair was shiny and thick, her eyes barely peeking out from
beneath a layer of black bangs. Her high, well-defined cheekbones

held the perfect amount of blush, as though carefully placed there by an expert makeup artist. She moved gracefully in her high heels and seemed to shift the weight of every room she entered with an irresistible gravity. My mother was sixty-one years old, and she was simply stunning. At one point, when she was out of earshot, a member of the crew—who was twenty years younger than she—asked me if she was single.

Raymond and I sat down on one side of a table facing my mom and my aunt Vera. The two of them wore coordinating outfits of dark blue. The table was set up to look like we were eating lunch. Delta-style tamales, indecipherable from soggy cigars, lay ignored on oval-shaped, beige-spotted plates before us. Napkins, water glasses, coffee mugs, and a randomly placed bottle of orange soda crowded the tabletop.

The crew was silent, ghostlike. Nevertheless, like everyone else we'd interviewed before them, my mother and aunt were painfully aware of the large camera pointed toward their faces and the microphone wires that snaked beneath their clothes. With Raymond's disarming demeanor, they both eventually relaxed, and we all descended into a moment. My mom and Vera shared stories about their father that I'd never heard before. They laughed and cried, and for a sliver of time, we felt like family.

Raymond wanted to learn what Booker shared with them in regard to his views on civil rights. My mother explained that her father shielded them from what was happening in their town. They spent most of their time in a community that Whites never entered; therefore, they had little experience with being made to feel ashamed because of the color of their skin.

"When we were with him," Vera said, "he was always so happy, no matter what was going on. He always had that smile. Always. He was famous for that smile. When we were younger, we went to the elementary school that was actually right down the street from the café, McLaurin Elementary School."

"Right down the street. McLaurin Elementary," my mom joined in.

"And when we would get out of school, sometimes in the afternoon we would go down there," Vera went on. "So, he would always tell us, you know, to make sure when we cross the street that we're careful. So we cross the street . . . when we would get halfway down that walk, we could see Daddy standing in front of the café. He would stand there and we'd just be walking, and then when we get almost there, he would hold his arms like this"—she spread her arms out as wide as she could—"and then Kat and I would just run and jump in his arms, and he'd just grab both of us and hold us together, and then he'd—"

"Twirl us around," my mother said, leaning her head back and smiling.

"Twirl us around," Vera continued, "and he did that all the time. Whenever we came down that walk, we couldn't wait, because we knew he was going to have open arms."

I rewound the clip and watched it over and over again. I'd never before heard my mother speak of her father with such affection.

ONE AFTERNOON WHILE VISITING Greenwood, I decided to stop by the house where my mother was raised. I entered Baptist Town and drove past one of the other suspected burial sites for Robert Johnson, and past the large building of McKinney Chapel Baptist Church, built in the late 1800s and after which the neighborhood was nicknamed. The houses and buildings in Baptist Town were among some of the most run-down in Greenwood.

I slowed my car down as kids rode bikes and played chase on the road in front of me. The day wore a heavy silence, but the smiling children and the ever-growing bushes, trees, and vines that crept up walls, shaded porches, and cradled the lives of the citizens of Baptist Town were like a crown of defiance in an image of deep poverty. As the last child passed my car, I made a right turn onto McConnell.

There were only two, maybe three housing plots on the street before it dead-ended. Her house was supposed to be the last one on the left. When I pulled up to it, I gasped and heard myself say, "They're tearing it down." It wasn't until I was standing right there, in the place where a house should be, that I remembered my mother telling me during our preproduction conversations that the house she'd grown up in was condemned by the city and that she and all her siblings were pulling together the money to pay for it to be demolished.

The house was now a large mound of debris. Wood pieces that were once part of the walls, the floor, or the porch had been ripped or shredded into varying shapes and sizes and then tossed onto the ground. Mixed in with the scattered pieces of my mother's childhood home were leaves and chunks of branches from recently chopped-down trees. All of this was covered with hunks of wet paper, fabric, and other detritus. That expanse of disorganized destruction was all that remained of the house my mother grew up in.

Most of what I knew of my mother's childhood she'd revealed in unexpected moments of emotional honesty, not unlike what Booker did on the news, followed by a disappearance in plain sight—those moments when her body was still in the room but it seemed as though her soul had been carted off.

When I was young, the little my mother shared about her past affected her in a way that frightened me. She rarely offered up any details of her life before California, and I didn't ask, in part because what she did share left me speechless. Her life before motherhood struck me as something fractured, like a bone splintered with cracks so deep it barely held together. When I did have questions, I normally sought out her cousins and siblings to fill in the gaps in the story.

My great-grandfather, a man named Lonnie Cooley, had built the house himself. More of a carnival funhouse than well-designed living quarters, the floor sloped down in certain places and up in others, the walls were uneven, and the rooms sat at awkward angles.

After divorcing Booker, my grandma Doris moved back into the house with her parents and went on to have four more kids. Doris worked during the day and liked to go out at night, so my mother and her siblings were raised primarily by their grandparents.

I gathered that my great-grandparents weren't delighted about having to rear their daughter's children. My mother told me once that she was seven when her grandmother started calling her "whore."

Whippings, sudden outbursts of violence, and humiliating tasks—like cleaning up after my great-grandmother when her bowels failed and she'd walked through the house, leaving her waste on the floor—were not uncommon in my mother's childhood.

She and her siblings woke every morning, hours before school, to tend to the garden, which served as their primary food source. They lived on tomatoes, collard greens, potatoes, and anything else the ground would gift them with. There wasn't a lot of money for the purchase of toys, but my mother, her siblings, and her cousins would stuff soda pop bottles with thread or old fabric to make dolls for themselves. The dolls always had blonde hair.

My mother's siblings described her as a having a natural determination, like she was born to stare down whatever circumstances threatened her with. Vera said that when they were younger and she went with my mom to the department store in Greenwood, the saleswoman would follow them around. It made Vera nervous, but it made my mother angry. She would turn to the woman and say, "Why are you following us? You're not following those people over there."

In my twenties, I'd imagined how she might have responded if she were in my shoes, going into the department store again and again and being looked over while White customers were helped.

At the time, I imagined her pointing it out, even making a scene. In retrospect, the response I imaged she might have felt right to me. Calling them out at the risk of being labeled requires boldness.

For years, I thought she made too many things about race, but she was right all along. I'd convinced myself that being ignored in department stores or singled out at work were situations that were unrelated to race because I wasn't strong enough to face the truth. Like Booker, my mother was ready for the fight wherever, whenever it cropped up.

She was from Greenwood. She was a survivor. Her father protected her as much as he could, but there were times when she still had to make her way in a town that resented her because of her caramel-colored skin.

In that world of racism and inequality, the thing that illuminated her life, flooding her sepia-tinted days with Technicolor, was her father, Booker—the man who would stop his work to stand out on the sidewalk in front of his café, day after day, just so that she could run into his arms on the way home from school. The man who couldn't tell her enough how much he loved her. And then, he was gone.

The night Booker was shot, my mother was living in Indiana. She hadn't yet met my father, and she was trying to salvage a relationship with her current boyfriend, the father of her first child, my older sister. Before leaving, she went to Booker's Place to say good-bye to her father. The two of them had one of those life-changing arguments. My mother was finally confronting him with her own wounds from growing up with divorced parents, only being with her father during the summers. Watching him build a life apart from her.

It was a fight she'd never forget. By the end, they'd both calmed down and said good-bye before she moved to Indiana. But she always thought she'd see him again.

When he was lying in his hospital bed, Vera and Rosie both asked Booker repeatedly if they could call my mom, to tell her to return to Greenwood. Even as his life was sliding out of him, Booker was persuasive, commanding, and he swore to them that he'd be better by the time she got back to town. It was a waste of time and money for her to come all the way back to Mississippi with her young child in tow.

He made them both promise not to call my mother. He was convinced he'd recover and that he'd be able to tell her about it himself. Why should she worry?

When they finally called my mother, it was to deliver the news that her father was dead.

She came back to Greenwood, but before she even had time to truly mourn, she won what can only be described as the "marriage lottery" for a little Black girl from Baptist Town. A professional football player moved her to a land of abundance, placed the keys of a Cadillac in her hand, and filled her purse with cash.

My mother was broken and made new in the blink of an eye.

She gathered up as many of her shattered bits as she could and then began the lifelong ritual of the walking wounded, which for her meant donning a California costume of high heels, expensive handbags, and flashy smiles. But otherwise, she was outwardly silent, hiding the hymn of mourning and memories that lingered in her soul.

She was a survivor whose loved ones expected her—needed her—to settle into an existence of bright, happy tomorrows. To placate us, she did not speak about what came before, because there was no place to lay those stories in our new world. There can be no complaining in the land of milk and honey.

Maybe she didn't know that I was drowning because she was drowning, too.

I'd always thought of my mother as strong. For as long as I could remember, the mere sound of my crying was intolerable to her. I'd presumed that she viewed my weakness as a virus she might catch if she didn't eradicate it. But I'd been incredibly, desperately wrong.

While she was raising me, my mother was barely holding on, carting around her own sorrows, too weighed down to carry mine as well.

It was while standing in front of the torn-down home of my mother's youth that I suddenly remembered something. The entire scene began to play in my head. My mother is sitting in a chair at a casual family gathering. It's one of the few times she's talking about her past. She tells us that when she was a young girl, she lived in a house located next to a body of water. Sometimes when the water was rising, its sound would get louder, and as she fell asleep, she would often wonder if the waters would overtake the wall, flooding her home. Even the memory of this bothered her so much that, right there in her chair, she closed her eyes and rocked back and forth, and her shoulders shook as an almost imperceptible shudder went through her.

As the scene faded from my mind, I looked around for the river. I realized suddenly that there wasn't a wall next to where her family home used to be, and the closest river was miles away. Where a wall should have been, based on her description, was a deep, dark collection of untended, untamed growth.

Had I somehow misremembered what she'd said?

Beneath my feet, surrounding me, stretching out as far as I could see, were weeds, grass, and vines intertwined with the abandoned planks and debris. It occurred to me that the lush, vibrant vegetation was reclaiming something. Snaking its way across the property, moving slower than the eye can see, the earth was consuming the stories and the memories of that place, making them a part of the woods.

I looked to the spot where I knew a bedroom had once been. There was a mess of green life and debris on the ground, and beyond it, a thick gathering of trees. It was in that space, just in front of the trees, that I was finally able to see my mother as she may have been in Greenwood.

She's a little girl, and she's trying to fall asleep. Her eyes are closed, and her pigtails, a rich, deep shade of black, rest against a white pillow. Under a thin blanket, her limbs bump up against her sister, who's lying next to her. She inhales deeply and descends into a space where reality ebbs away and dreams can bend the mind. She hears something that makes her face twitch and her lips squeeze together. It's a violent sound, one that beats and echoes, a pulsing ache of humanity that rises from the river, races through the fields, and moves into the depths of her. That roar will haunt her, but she will not know she is haunted.

In the still and quiet darkness, my mother hears the unmistakable sound of a river.

The Booker Wright
Literacy Project

Yvette Johnson has created a foundation to support literacy efforts in the Delta and beyond. The Booker Wright Literacy Project works to identify ways to increase access to effective literacy initiatives for children and adults with dyslexia and other reading disorders.

For more information, please visit the following website: yvettecreates.com.

Thoughts on Sadness

This book deals with a time when I believed life was no longer worth living. In ways much less direct, this book also explores the lives we forge (or settle for) when unnamed traumas are lurking in our past.

I'm not an expert on how to get through the darkness. What I do know is that, even in the darkest of times, there are moments of unexplained light. Like a lot of other people, I usually have to fight just to feel life's joyful light shining on me. But there are also times when the light shows up completely on its own. In other words, there are times when I don't have to fight, and it just gets easier. Remembering this has helped me to hold on more times than I can count.

I've also learned a few practical lessons. Get help when you need it, even if you don't want it. If you're daydreaming about driving your car into a brick wall, then please, tell someone. Scream from the rooftops if you have to—not literally, of course; that location might be too tempting. Call a suicide hotline. Tell your primary care physician. Find a therapist.

However, you don't have to wait until you're in crisis to find a therapist. Just like in other relationships, I've noticed that I don't click with every therapist I see for treatment. When I'm interviewing therapists I look for someone who I enjoy spending time with, who has some good ideas about how to improve my coping skills, who gets me, and who is interested in helping me live a life that aligns with my values, not theirs. When you find a therapist that works for you, I'd encourage you to stay connected to him or her so that if you do hit the wall, you've got a safe place to go.

In the meantime, consider this: I've gone through multiple periods in my life when suicide seemed like the most logical choice. I'm typing this while my oldest son is building a backyard furnace, my youngest is playing chase with his bearded dragon, and my lifelong dream of being a published writer is about to come true.

Life can turn around in an instant. Major change, the kind of change that our minds aren't sophisticated or faithful enough to conjure up, is not only possible but also likely, if we can just hang on and wait for morning to come.

Acknowledgments

What amazed me most over the ten years of working on this project, and what continues to bring me joy, is the response people offer to Booker's two-and-a-half-minute monologue. When my grandfather opened up, he was giving all of us a blueprint for how to move forward, reminding each and every one of us that no matter how deep our divisions, we share something: a sense of humanity that cannot be undone by hate, legislation, or anything else. In a world where movements flare up and then pass away, it's the flame of commonality we all share that lasts forever.

Thank you, Booker Wright, for gifting me with this beautiful story that has changed my life in ways I am still uncovering. A video of Booker's monologue can be found at yvettecreates.com. His expression of heartache stands the test of time.

During the ten years that it took to bring this book from dream to publication, there were three people who sacrificed the most. Milton, thank you for being such a good sport about all the travel I've done. More than once I picked up and took off with very little notice, but you were always there to make sure our boys' lives continued as smoothly as possible.

Bishop and Dexter, there are no words. My entire life is made fresh and new every day because of the joy you bring. Thank you for being born.

And this might be the hardest note of gratitude. Wherever you are, Bob Ricker, thank you for seeing me when no one else did.

And now, to the building of this story. What follows is a sampling of the many people whom I owe deep thanks.

John T. Edge was the first person to tell me about Booker's story, but he himself heard it from others. For more than a decade John T. held onto it, studied it, even cherished it, and then handed it over to me. Thank you for your stewardship of this great work.

A spunky, fast-talking college professor named Dr. Sherry Rankins-Robertson lent me her belief in this story each time mine faltered. In the four years between when I heard about Booker's news appearance and when I actually had the chance to see it for myself, she was there. Dr. Rankins-Robertson introduced me to an expert in the rhetoric of the movement, Dr. Keith Miller; an expert in family history writing, Dr. Duane Roen (who is known for saying "only write on the days that you eat") and; lastly, she introduced me to an expert in exploring what it feels like to be Black today, Dr. Neal Lester. Thank you all.

In 2011 I was swept up in a tsunami of sorts when I went from being a stay-at-home mom to a film producer who did live television interviews and traveled the country giving talks about Booker Wright. This was only possible because of Raymond De Felitta. Raymond is a special kind of filmmaker. In life and on the screen, he is always interested in who people are behind their masks.

In addition to bringing my grandfather's story to the masses through film, Raymond offered me advice that ended up being quite profound. He told me that 1) a bad book that's finished is always better than a good idea for a book that never gets finished, and 2) he shared that when he was a little boy he'd hear his father banging away at a typewriter for hours on end. Many times when I wanted to give up on this project I pictured Raymond's dad, Frank, in his small, windowless office, staying the course until the day's work was done. Thank you, Raymond, for giving me the tools to continue when doing so seemed utterly futile.

Frank De Felitta, who welcomed me into his home and celebrated my mere existence at one of his famous grand, decadent, yet somehow lazy afternoon lunches. Frank was a writer and a filmmaker, so he made a film that told a story. We may not always be able to turn our lives upside down to become activists. Look at Frank's example: *Stay where you are, make change there.*

Moirtii Ghosh, thank you for all of your work in helping to capture Booker's world in *Booker's Place: A Mississippi Story.*

Being ahead of their time seems to be something NBC does well. In 1966 they told a story about the South that few wanted to hear, and just after the new millennium began, a producer named Tim Beacham discovered Booker's film clip and began pitching it to them as a story to be revisited. Because of his persistence, millions of people were able to learn about Booker while watching an episode of *Dateline* in the summer of 2012.

Now, to the even harder stuff. Writing.

Just after Christmas Day 2011, I got a call from an agent in response to my horribly written proposal. If anyone has ever taken a chance on this book, it was Scott Hoffman. What is this book, anyway? A memoir? A biography? Historical nonfiction? He didn't care if it didn't fit nicely into a box; he cared that it was good.

When the lack of being able to easily categorize this book made many editors turn the other way, Scott threatened to open his own house and publish it himself if that's what it took. Thankfully, he connected me to Malaika Adero, who saw what I was trying to do with this story. She moved on before I was finished but left me in the capable hands of Todd Hunter, who worked behind the scenes to keep this book alive while I struggled with draft after draft.

In 2015 I hit a wall. I'd given the writing of this book everything I had, and it still felt like a kind of Frankenstein. There wasn't a through line. The story was all over the place, and I declared, in Shakespearean fashion, that I could never again fall in love with this book. I decided to hire an independent editor to restructure it, tell me what to do, and get me over the finish line.

Enter Stuart Horwitz, who gave me the sweetest gift of all. He told me I didn't need him. To be clear, he still cashed the checks I sent, but he also reminded me that at my core I am a writer. He was happy to dig in and restructure the story, but he was convinced I could do it on my own. Thank you for helping me to finish this book, Stuart. But even more, thank you for treating me like a writer.

For sharing their memories of Booker, Rosie, and the town of Greenwood with me, I am indebted to Vera Douglass, Leroy Jones, Katherine Wright, Margurite Butler, Bo Williams, John Pachter, Anita Batman, Allan Hammons, Bill Ware, Allen Wood, Jess Pinkston, Mary Carol Miller, Eddie Miller, Benton Jordan, Silas McGee, Honey Wright, Noll Davis, Hiram Eastland, Rena Jones, Cassandra Jones, and Senator David Jordan. Emily O'Bryant, thank you for taking me on a memory tour of Greenwood. Amy Evans, your writing about Lusco's Restaurant was an invaluable resource. Andy and Karen Pinkston were kind enough to open up the Lusco family vault of videotaped memories so we could have a few more glimpses of Booker.

Nicki Newburger and Kathryn Green unearthed critical information time and time again in their work researching this story. Also, a note of thanks to Chris Epolite, Jess Winget, Sarah Collins, Jason Baumann, Adeline Low, Alison Moser, Erin Loosli, Linda

Wolf, and Darcy DiCosmo for taking care of the things that mattered most while I did this important work.

For reading early drafts of this book: Julie Bailey (who read five versions of this book in total). Suzanne Collette and Jenna Free, who both read it when it was almost twice as long as it is now. Allen Wood, your reading and reaction to this book warmed my heart. Thank you for seeing what I was trying to do and for pointing out where I could do better.

And for making sure that I did not walk the writer's path alone: Jenny Milchman, Windy Lynn Harris, Jodi Picoult, and Susan Pohlman. Hedgebrook Writer's Residence came along and provided me with the time and space I needed to remember that writing is about much more than words.

And Jeffrey Berglund for opening my eyes to all that is possible when people manage to write down their souls.

For carrying this project over the finish line: Lisa Nicholas and Sonja Singleton, the most patient woman in all of publishing.

This book would most likely not be in your hands right now if not for the people I affectionately refer to as the Dream Team: Robert Raben, Donald Gatlin, and Oliver Wells. Thank you for your guidance and insight, and for all the ways each of you is helping to make this world a better place.

Notes

In writing and researching this story I had the opportunity to interview, on-camera and off, family members, business leaders, activists, community leaders, and lots and lots of everyday folks.

Their voices fill multiple audio-recording devices, along with hours and hours of video recordings. What follows is a description of source material used in the making of this book.

Information about Lusco's history came from interviews with John T. Edge, Karen Pinkston, and an oral history article (although at 129 pages, it might really be a book) written by Amy C. Evans from an interview she did in 2003 with Karen Pinkston. Amy's article can be downloaded from the Southern Foodways Alliance at the following link: southernfoodways.org/interview/karen-pinkston/.

Information about life on the Black side of Greenwood was supplied by many interviewees, including my father, Leroy Jones, John Pachter, and several others.

Most of Rosie Turner's story was shared with me by Honey Wright and later by Rosie's daughter, Margurite Butler. The details about Booker's childhood came from both Honey and Margurite, but also from Katherine Jones, Vera Douglass, and Marie Tibit.

Preface

I was first introduced to the story of the 1927 Flood when I was reading about weather disasters with my kids. When I wanted to learn more about the river, the source that seemed to be the most quoted and the most respected was a book called *Rising Tide: The Great Mississippi Flood of 1927 and How It Changed America* by John Barry (1st edition), published by Simon and Schuster in 1998. I cannot recommend this book enough.

It's so much more than a book about a flood. Barry captures the stories of real people, including their quirks, hopes, insecurities, and failings in a way that makes his more-than-five-hundred-page book almost impossible to put down. I relied on it heavily in my effort to understand why the Mississippi was unique, a river among rivers. Barry's work also provided me with invaluable insight into the minds of the people who spent their lives trying to tame something that was always more of a willful being than a natural waterway.

Many of the quotes in the Preface are extracted from *Rising Tide*, pages 97–98.

In 1994, the Oxford University Press published a paperback edition of a book by James C. Cobb, *The Most Southern Place on Earth: The Mississippi Delta and the Roots of Regional Identity*. The book is a treasure trove of first-person accounts of lives lived in the Delta. Cobb's book provides a rich and often troubling window into Black life in the Delta, from its early plantation days into the late twentieth century. It describes the hardships Blacks faced on the young plantations and how they were required to work constantly. The quote about slave masters raping their female slaves and then raping their daughters is from *The Most Southern Place on Earth*.

James Eastland's proclamation about his right to kill Blacks can be found in the Harper Perennial 2013 reissue edition of *Let the Trumpet Sing: A Life of Martin Luther King, Jr.* by Stephen P. Oates. There are several other sources in which people recall receiving one of the aforementioned flyers. A few have misquoted Oates and claimed that Eastland actually said those words, but it would appear that he arranged to have them distributed during his speech.

Where He Was King

In the summer of 2007 I interviewed my father, Leroy Jones, over the phone. During that phone call he took me back to Booker's Place and shared how Booker handled himself inside his restaurant.

The quote from the Ku Klux Klan can be found at a variety of sources on the Internet. It's been quoted in multiple books, including *The Ku Klux Klan in Mississippi: A History* by Michael Newton, published in 2010 by McFarland Publishing. I received copies of the hate sheets from the University of Mississippi at Oxford's library archives.

Other sources for this chapter include Charles Payne's *I've Got the Light of Freedom: The Organizing Tradition and the Mississippi Freedom Struggle*, published by the University of California Press in 1995. Payne's book was critical in helping me gain an understanding of the steps made by individual people that created a nationwide movement and changed federal laws. The majority of the descriptions in this chapter about punishments inflicted on Blacks by the White Citizens' Council come from Payne's book, specifically pages 38, 41, 46, and 158.

Another helpful source that illuminated the pressure experienced by Blacks in Greenwood was *The Race Beat: The Press, The Civil Rights Struggle, and the Awakening of a Nation*. This entire book serves as a fascinating record and powerful reminder of the critical role the American press filled during the civil rights movement. Details in this chapter include information from page 313. This book was written by Gene Roberts and Hank Klibanoff, and published in 2007 by Vintage Books.

John Dittmer's book *Local People: The Struggle for Civil Rights in Mississippi* also detailed the harrowing experiences of Blacks in the Delta during the civil rights movement. Stories for this chapter came from page 46. Dittmer's book was published in 1995 by the University of Illinois Press.

A truly excellent book that details the way the civil rights movement swept through the nation is Taylor Branch's *Parting the Waters: America in the King Years 1954–63*. Page 713 details how regularly delivered food from the federal government was blocked in order to punish Blacks for trying to assert their rights.

Activists who were part of organizations like SNCC, CORE, COFO, and SCLC had to find ways to communicate without having their long-distance calls routed through operators who might not connect the calls to their requested destination. Civil rights workers came up with a system of communication in which calls could be placed to a specific number in cities like Greenwood or Atlanta. The phones were answered around the clock, and then the information provided was typed up and turned into a WATS report. This ensured that if someone was in danger or being harassed, they could get word to someone.

A WATS report filed on July 21, 1964, includes the account of an eyewitness who saw police officers throwing bricks through the windows of three cafés on McLaurin the previous evening. One of those cafés was Booker's Place. The report can be found here: crmvet.org/docs/wats/wats64-0721_cofo.pdf.

Get Off This Place

Details about the overall impact of the 1927 Mississippi River Flood come from the editors of the Encyclopedia Britannica article "The Mississippi River Flood," which can be found at the following website: britannica.com/event/Mississippi-River-flood-of-1927. Other quotes from this chapter come from *Rising Tide*, specifically pages 156, 183, 313, and 319.

A Catalyst

I read the excerpt about my mother's uncle, Charlie Cooley, in a book called *Weary Feet, Rested Souls: A Guided History of the Civil Rights Movement*, written by Townsend Davis and published by W. W. Norton & Company in 1999.

A Magical Town

I never had the opportunity to meet Sara Miller, but I challenge anyone not to feel deep affection for her after reading her collected memoirs, which were published by her daughter Mary Carol Miller on the following website: daughterofthedelta.com.

In 2013 West Washington Books published Volume 1 of *Greenwood: Mississippi Memories*. This treasure of photographs and memories was collected by Mary Carol Miller, Allan Hammons, and

Donny Whitehead. Volume 2 and Volume 3 were both published the following year, in 2014. The photographs in these three books, along with their thoughtful introductions and insightful photo notations, were critical in helping me tell the story of Greenwood's early years.

Other sources for this chapter include an article about Mary Carol Miller on the website Today in Mississippi. The article, "Penchant for Preservation," was written by Debbie Stringer and can be found here: todayinmississippi.com/index.php/featured_article /article/3734.

Details about US Flood Policy in the early 1800s come from an article called "Bioregional Approach to Southern History: The Yazoo-Mississippi Delta," published on January 28, 2010, by Mikko Saikku with the University of Helsinki. The article can be found in the archives of SouthernSpaces.org.

Information about stores and businesses that opened during Greenwood's early days can be found both in *Greenwood: Mississippi Memories* and the website aboutgreenwoodms.com, which was created by Donny Whitehead.

The story about the origin of Hambone's Meditations can be found both in *Greenwood: Mississippi Memories* and in an article by Franklin Harris published in 2015. The article was written for the Jim Crow Museum of Racist Memorabilia and can be found on the Ferris State University website at the following web address: ferris .edu/HTMLS/news/jimcrow/question/dec15/index.htm.

A Testing Ground for Democracy

Mary Carol Miller's website Daughter of the Delta was again a wonderful resource for this chapter. Detailed recollections about Emmett Till's murder came from *Voice of Freedom: An Oral History of the Civil Rights Movement from the 1950s through the 1980s* by

Henry Hampton and Steve Faycr. *Voices of Freedom* was published by Bantam Books in 1990. Another helpful source was an article on PBS's website related to the show *The American Experience*. The article, "People and Events: Mamie Till Bradley (1921–2003)," can be found at the following website: pbs.org/wgbh/amex/till /peopleevents/p_parents.html.

Town on Fire

Howard Zinn's description of the Greenwood SNCC office came from a book by Martin Duberman called *Howard Zinn: A Life on the Left*, which was published by the New Press in 2012. This chapter also relied on some of the posts from Daughter of the Delta and Dittmer's *Local People*. Also helpful was an article in the *Boston Globe* written by Eric Moskowitz called "They Heard the Call of Freedom: A Summer That Haunts."

Information about treatment of Blacks by police officers came from Silas McGee, Cobb's *The Most Southern Place on Earth*, Willie Bailey, and Johnnie Walls.

A Moralist

The newspaper articles quoted in this chapter are as follows:

Trenton, New Jersey, *Trentonian*
Sharon, Pennsylvania, *Herald*, Rick Du Brow, May 2, 1966, *D.23,181*
Fort Wayne, Indiana, *News-Sentinel*, April 30, 1966 *D. 76,639*
What's On? TV Radio, Ben Gross, A New Day is Dawning in Mississippi (New York Daily News)

Newsday, On Television, Barbara Delatiner, April 6, 1966

Lafayette, Indiana, *Journal and Courier,* April 30, 1966, D. 42,569

Seattle, Washington, *Times,* May 2, 1966, CJ Skreen Magic
    Missing in Broadcasting

More citations can be found at www.yvettecreates.com.

A History Lesson

To learn more about the horrific murder of Malcolm Wright, visit the Northeastern School of Law website: nuweb9.neu.edu/civilrights/malcolm-wright/.

Information about the treatment of Black female bodies came from *The African-American Odyssey: Volume Two Since 1863* by Darlene Clark Hine, William C. Hine, and Stanley Harrold. The second edition was published by Pearson Education in 2003.

Payne's *I've Got the Light of Freedom* was instrumental to what I learned in this chapter.

A Murder Story

The majority of the content in this chapter was taken from the court transcripts of the Lloyd Cork murder trial.

Booker's Song

Information about Senator James Eastland's personal finances are from "The Struggle for Voting Rights in Mississippi—The Early Years," which is part of the website Civil Rights Movement Veterans (www.crmvet.org). This website includes a plethora of firsthand accounts of movement activists. The article used as a resource for this chapter can be found at the following link: http://www.crmvet .org/info/voter_ms.pdf.

The Blood of Emmett Till by Timothy Tyson, published by Simon and Schuster in 2017, was the source for Carolyn Bryant's ground-breaking revelation.